GUIDE TO THE MEMORIALS

OF CRICKETERS

For Elizabeth, Anna and Helen

First published in Great Britain by
Association of Cricket Statisticians and Historians
Cardiff CF11 9XR
© ACS, 2017

British Library Catalogueing-in-Publication Data
A catalogue record for this book is available from the British Library.

ISBN: 978-1-908165-83-1
Typeset and printed by Imprint Services, Northallerton

GUIDE TO THE MEMORIALS

OF CRICKETERS

----

compiled by Michael Ronayne

(above) Unlike others featured in this book, Charles Sheldrick was not a famous cricket person, but he was given a splendid cricket design on his gravestone at Sawston, Cambridgeshire.

THE AUTHOR AND CRICKET

Ever since being enthralled by the 1961 Old Trafford Test match Michael Ronayne seems to have spent most of his life practising, playing, watching, researching and thinking about cricket. He has had the pleasure of playing in Holland, Finland, Czech Republic, Italy and Goa as well as all over Norfolk, mostly with the Earlham Village cricket club. He played 354 games with EVCC and once took 28 wickets in a season for 238 runs, the second best in the club history.

The headstone of Harry Bagshaw at Eyam is inscribed "For when the one great scorer comes to write against your name, he writes not that you won or lost but how you played the game" This epitomises Mike's attitude to cricket. He had a great sense of fair-play. His team–mates and friends described him as a true gentleman, kind and courteous who had great love of the game and the friendship it engendered. He played with style and grace and as in life, applied the straightest bat. His extensive knowledge of cricket was said to be more than the rest of them put together! He was a fine cricketer with particularly good bowling skills but also taught others about the spirit of cricket.

The Library at Lord's Cricket Ground holds copies of Michael's earlier publications, notably Test Cricket Tours No 3 Australia. No 4 South Africa, No 5 West Indies, No 6 India, No 7 Pakistan, No 8 New Zealand - all published between 1984 and 1987. Also, "Selecting the English Team 1946-1988" published in 1987 and "The Pakistan Eaglets" published in 1989.

A member of the Association of Cricket Statisticians from shortly after its foundation, Michael was also an active member of the Norfolk Cricket Society, The Cricket Society and Cricket Memorabilia Society, whilst his website http://test-cricket-tours.co.uk/ gives an uncommon account of detail about every Test cricket tour made between 1877 and the 2015 World cup.

Born in 1950, Michael taught in London and Norfolk schools for thirty years before moving to the back of the classroom to support and assess trainee teachers. He lived in Norwich with his wife Liz and two daughters. Sadly, Michael passed away in October 2016, just after completing the manuscript for this book. It is therefore being published by the ACS in tribute of his outstanding research on behalf of the Association for many years. Our thanks to his family for their help in ensuring that Michael's meticulous efforts can be shared with others.

Andrew Hignell

(Hon. Secretary of the ACS)

Footnote - Thanks also to Chris Overson and John Winnifrith for their kind assistance with proof-reading.

CRICKETERS COMMEMORATED

Starting my collection of cricketers' memorials in the 1980s, publishing it on a now-defunct website in the late '90s, and updating my records from time to time, has been hard work because I had hoped to include "everyone who was anyone" in top cricket in England & Wales - players, captains, journalists, administrators, selectors, umpires - but this was over-optimistic. Memorials for a number of them have proved elusive: Albert Relf, for example, or Arthur Carr or Cyril Washbrook, as well as many others. Doubtless, for some of them, the source of information I need is out there, in an obvious place where I happen not to have looked, and I may even now (post-printing) be shaking my head at how I missed it.

Once or twice the search has been long and followed many blind alleys but it was pleasing to find at last a grave site for the likes of Hendren, Mason, Surridge and MacKinnon; or eventually accepting that many important cricket people (such as Cardus, Gover and Crawford) did not have a grave or personal memorial - except sometimes a written entry in a Book of Remembrance. Occasionally luck played its part in tracking down a location, but mostly it was the cemeteries, crematoria and funeral directors who kindly answered my enquires and enabled me to fill in the picture. Others who helped are listed in the Acknowledgements. As one said, "You do set yourself some challenges, don't you."

As the years pass, the number of people interred with a headstone decreases. Simultaneously, the proportion cremated without any memorial increases, their ashes being scattered in a favourite place, often known only to the family. Yet I have included cases where there is no known gravestone or plaque in order to provide as much information as is known. Other ways are usually found to commemorate the leading players, especially on the very grounds where their cricketing fame was won, by naming rooms, stands, gates and seating after them.

The passing of time inevitably brings the sad loss of some of these memorials. Graves like Faulkner's have already become dilapidated, and they will all decay in time. The Sutcliffe Gates at Headingley are disused and those of White, Tate and Leyland have been removed. With the redevelopment of Old Trafford went the sole memorials to Cyril Washbrook and Neville Cardus, and the same happened on other grounds. Thankfully, the headstones on a number of graves have been restored including, "W.G.", Bligh, Daft, Greenwood, Trott, Wisden, and others.

With each entry in the guide I have given a brief flavour of the person's importance while trying to keep the statistics light. There is no intention of providing full biographical and career details which may be found on *CricketArchive*. The emphasis, and my own interest, is on the memorials.

I hoped to demonstrate why a memorial was set in a particular location, which may often be unconnected to the place of death. Dark red is used to highlight the memorial location or the person's final resting place.

I have included very few cricket personalities who died less than ten years ago, and none from abroad unless there is a strong connection with England, as in cases like Constantine, Midwinter, CLR James and Worrell.

Key : f-c = first-class, nr = near, CWC Young Cricketer = Cricket Writers' Club Young Cricketer of the Year, CCC = county cricket club, * = not out, FOWNC = Friends of West Norwood Cemetery *Sat Nav* = nearest postcode to the memorial, WW = World War 1 or 2; 'pair' (of spectacles) = score 0 in both innings; "double" = when an all-rounder scores 1,000 runs and takes 100 wickets in an English season.

The dark red colour indicate the location of memorials such as a plaque or grave and the final resting place where ashes were dispersed.

☐ Bobby ABEL

Blue plaque placed in 2005 at Southwark Park, Rotherhithe, where he learned his cricket as a boy. Was a consistent opening bat for Surrey for twenty seasons, and represented England 13 times in Test matches. Small and moustachioed, crowd called him "The Guv'nor." Scored in excess of 33,000 f-c runs, with 74 centuries, twelve being struck in the 1900 season alone. Highest 357* in 1899. On retirement appointed coach at Dulwich College but, owing to poor health, not retained. Died on 10 December 1936 at home in Handforth Road, Stockwell, and after funeral at St Martin's church, Kennington, buried at Nunhead Cemetery, London.

Grave (reference 136/ 22802) has a fine, clear headstone lying beyond the sealed catacombs. Turn right and grave is on left-hand side in trees.

Southwark Park Café Gallery (plaque) *Sat Nav* SE16 2EH   Nunhead Cemetery *Sat Nav* SE15 3LP

Biography: *"Bobby Abel: Professional Batsman"* by David Kynaston (Secker & Warburg, 1982).

☐ Charles ABSOLOM

The first player in f-c cricket to be given out obstructing the field (against Surrey,

in June 1868). Known as "Navvy", made tour of Australia and played in one Test (1878-79). Travelled the world and became ship's purser on the 'Muriel', but died in hospital on 30 July 1889, after accident at Port-of-Spain docks, when crane unloading sugarcane fell on him. He was buried in Laperouse Cemetery, Phillip Street, Woodbridge, Port-of-Spain, Trinidad. No memorial known in England.

• It would be great to find out whether Absolom's grave has a headstone but it is rather impractical to do so at this distance from Trinidad. Apparently, the burial records have suffered from damp and graves from neglect, while the cemetery has become frequented by vagrants and drug dealers!

☐ C.W. [Charles] ALCOCK

For 35 years, was Secretary of Surrey. Organiser of 1880 match between England and Australia at The Oval, later recognised as first Test in England. Editor of 'Cricket' magazine. Also, vice-president and hon. secretary of Football Association. Died at home in Arundel Road, Brighton, on 26 February 1907. Body conveyed by train to London for interment at South Metropolitan (now called West Norwood) Cemetery. Buried in area '86', a short distance north of cemetery's southern boundary road. Grave at plot 14689 lies a metre north of Jupp (not the cricketer). Buried with wife Elizabeth who died in 1936, aged 96. Base of grave only remained; its cross restored and rededicated on 28 July 1999 by Friends of Norwood Cemetery, with assistance from The Oval and the Football Association (F.A) [see newsletter 36 at http://www.fownc.org/newsletters]

West Norwood Cemetery   *Sat Nav* SE27 9JU

Biography : *"The Father of Modern Sport: The Life and Times of Charles W. Alcock"* by Keith Booth (Parrs Wood Press, 2002)

□ [Sir George] 'Gubby' ALLEN

His uncle played cricket for Australia; he was born in Sydney in 1902. Fast bowler. As a City stockbroker, available to play for Middlesex only as amateur. Appointed England captain in 1936. Chairman of MCC cricket committee and chairman of England selection committee in 'fifties. Became MCC treasurer and president: no-one since Pelham Warner (his alleged real father) held more power over English cricket. CBE 1962, knighthood 1986. Died 29 November 1989 after demanding to be taken from nursing care to his St John's Wood home which backed on to Lord's Ground, so he could die in view of the pavilion. Ashes interred in the Allen family grave at Brookwood Cemetery: plot 41, St Stephen's Kensington section, to right of central memorial. In 1989 'Q' Stand at Lord's Ground was renamed in his memory as the Allen Stand.

Brookwood Cemetery *Sat Nav* GU24 0BL Lord's Cricket Ground *Sat Nav* NW8 8QN

Biography : *"Gubby Allen: Man of Cricket"* by E W Swanton (Hutchinson, 1985)

□ Ted ALLETSON

Nottinghamshire batsman. His name famous for a 1911 match against Sussex at Hove. Scored 189 runs in 90 minutes to turn the match; included 34 runs in one over from Killick. In retirement a pit deputy. Died at son's home in Worksop on 5 July 1963, and funeral at City Road Crematorium, Sheffield, on 16 July. Cremated remains scattered on 16 August 1963 on strewing area in section 9 of City Road Cemetery. No memorial there. Plaque and the bat used in record match placed in 'The Good Innings' public house in Worksop, when opened in 1975. In 2003 the bat sold at auction to private collector for £15,000, and now no memorabilia in pub.

The Innings, Worksop   *Sat Nav*   S 81 0RS

□ Bill ALLEY

Australian batsman for N.S.W. Unlucky not to be selected for 1946 Test tour of NZ after scoring 3 centuries in the season, but Hamence got his place. Lancashire League cricket for Colne. Joined Somerset 1957-68. Last man to score 3,000 f-c runs in English season (in 1961); achieved the 'double' in following season at age of 43. F-c umpire who stood in ten Test matches In retirement, lived at Staplegrove, Taunton. Died in Musgrave Park Hospital, on 26 November 2004. His funeral at St James's church followed by cremation at Taunton Deane. Ashes interred in Gardens of Rest but with no memorial.

Biography: *"My Incredible Innings"* autobiography (Pelham, 1969); *"Standing the Test of Time"* autobiography (Manchester, 1999).

□ Rex ALSTON

While a master at Bedford School, played cricket for Bedfordshire. Commentator on BBC radio's outside broadcasts, especially cricket but also rugby, athletics, tennis. After

1961 was correspondent for *Daily Telegraph*. Lived at Cranleigh, Surrey. Aged 93 when he died on 8 September 1994, nine years after his obituary was mistakenly published in *The Times*. Headstone in churchyard of St Peter & St Paul, Ewhurst.

St Peter & Paul church, Ewhurst *Sat Nav* **GU6 7PX**

Biography: *"Taking the Air"* (Stanley Paul, 1951), *"Watching Cricket"* (1962) autobiographies.

□ *Harry ALTHAM*

School master at Winchester School and 1st XI coach. In holidays amateur with Hampshire. Articles in '*The Cricketer*' magazine became acclaimed book *"A History of Cricket"*, second edition written with E.W. Swanton. Joined M.C.C. committee in 1941, appointed treasurer in 1950. Chairman of selectors in 1954 and M.C.C. president in 1959. CBE 1957. Died on 11 March 1965 in Yorkshire where on speaking engagement at cricket dinner; collapsed with heart attack at Sheffield home of his host. Funeral at Winchester College chapel on 16 March. In 1970 ceiling of the Langton Chapel in Winchester Cathedral restored and a stone laid in his memory at screen of chapel. In 1971 gates unveiled into New Field, Winchester, with wall plaque to commemorate Altham. In May 1971 M.C.C. president unveiled tablet in honour of Altham's work in Memorial Gallery at Lord's Cricket Ground, made from part of Thomas Lord's old gravestone. His brainchild, the M.C.C. Indoor School, originally named the Altham Rooms.

Altham Gate, New Field, Winchester *Sat Nav* **SO23 9PN**   Winchester Cathedral *Sat Nav*   **SO23 9LS**
Lord's Cricket Ground *Sat Nav* **NW8 8QN**

□ *Les AMES*

Wicket-keeper/ batsman for Kent and England. 47 Test appearances for England 1929-39. Three times (1928, 1929, 1932) achieved wicket-keepers' double of 1,000 runs and 100 dismissals in f-c season. Keeping to Tich Freeman, he stumped 64 batsmen in 1932 season. Scorer of over 37,000 first-class runs, including 100 hundreds, with 3,000 runs in 1933 season alone. Finished playing 1951 after leading a Commonwealth tour of India. Test selector for eight seasons and M.C.C. tour manager three times. Secretary of Kent, guiding county to 1970 championship. Served as president of Kent C.C.C. too. CBE 1973. Presented honorary degree of MA by University of Kent 1985. Died 27 February 1990, in Kent & Canterbury Hospital. Ashes scattered in the silver birch area at Barham Crematorium on 8 March. The Iron Stand at St Lawrence (now Spitfire Ground), Canterbury, renamed The Leslie Ames Stand in 1973 Behind ground is the Ames-Levett Indoor School.

The Spitfire Ground, St Lawrence, Canterbury *Sat Nav* **CT1 3NZ**

Biography : *"Close of Play"* autobiography (Stanley Paul, 1953); *"Les Ames"* by Alan Hill (Christopher Helm, 1990)

□ *Bill ANDREWS*

Opening bowler for Somerset, subsequently league player and coach at Somerset CCC

and Millfield School. Sacked four times by the county, twice as player and twice as coach, and always taken on again. Introduced himself with 'Shake the hand that bowled Bradman!' Died at Worlebury (Weston-super-Mare), Somerset, on 9 January 1989. Part of his ashes scattered by Brian Rose on pitch at Taunton county ground and part on Clarence Park at Weston. Plaque on wall of memorial garden beside the Colin Atkinson pavilion at Taunton County Ground.

Taunton County Ground *Sat Nav* TA1 1JT

Biography : *"The Hand that Bowled Bradman"* autobiography, with David Foot (MacDonald, 1973)

• In his biography, amidst the ups and downs of Andrews' career, he comes across as a struggling professional trying to make a living from the game at a time when amateurs were often unfairly favoured. I was a little disappointed to find that he has no grave and his ashes were dispersed - admittedly in locations very dear to him. But there was a memorial after all, and it was pleasing to see that his name can be found at the Taunton County Ground. **Colin Atkinson** (1931-91) was not a player of the top rank at f-c level but was honoured by the county naming the pavilion after him for his years of service as captain, chairman and club president, and indeed for getting the new pavilion built at all. He combined all this with his duties as the Headmaster at Millfield School.

Edgbaston Cricket Ground *Sat Nav* B5 7QU Lodge Hill Cemetery, Selly Oak, Birmingham *Sat Nav* B29 5AA

• Col W Swynfen Jervis died on 3 April 1920 at Southsea, Hampshire, and was buried in Highland Road Cemetery, Portsmouth.

☐ *William ANSELL*

Birmingham school teacher who guided formal creation of present Warwickshire C.C.C. Became joint-Secretary with Col W.S. Jervis, and was driving force urging county to develop a ground at Edgbaston in preference to Leamington Spa. The William Ansell Stand opened on western side of Edgbaston ground in 1967, but replaced in 2011 by West Stand. Last lived on Bristol Road and died 21 October 1919. He was interred in Lodge Hill Cemetery in section A3, grave 50.

☐ *Arthur APPLEBY*

Left-handed fast bowler for Lancashire and in 1880s best amateur bowler in country. Missed overseas tours through heading the family corn-milling business, as well as being county councillor and magistrate. Played in Lancashire League and local matches up until his death, which came on 22 October 1902 at his home in Enfield, nr Accrington. Buried at All Saint's church, Clayton-le-Moors.

All Saint's church, Clayton-le-Moors *SatNav* BB5 5HT

Bill Andrews commemorated in the memorial garden below the Atkinson pavilion at Taunton County Ground.

The Harry Altham Gates and engraved stone at New Field, Winchester.

☐ John ARLOTT

Plaque on birthplace, Old Cemetery Cottage, Chapel Hill, Basingstoke. Writer and B.B.C. radio broadcaster on cricket from 1946. Journalist, becoming cricket correspondent on The Guardian in 1968. Made final ball-by-ball commentaries in Centenary Test match and Gillette Cup final at Lord's in 1980, before retiring to live on Alderney in Channel Isles. Died of respiratory disease on 14 December 1991 and buried in St Anne's churchyard, Alderney. Headstone engraved with "So clear you see these timeless things that, like a bird, the vision sings." Blue plaque arranged by the Cricket Society unveiled at his former home, The Old Sun, at Alresford, Hampshire, in 2009.

Birthplace in Basingstoke *Sat Nav* RG21 5TD The Old Sun, Alresford *Sat Nav* SO24 9BU St Anne's church, Alderney *SatNav* GY9 3XJ.

Biography: *"Basingstoke Boy: The Autobiography"* by John Arlott (Willow Books Harper Collins, 1990); *"Arlott on Cricket: His Writings on the Game"* edited by David Rayvern-Allen (London, 1984); *"John Arlott: A Memoir"* by Timothy Arlott (Andre Deutsch Ltd 1994) *"Arlott, the Authorised Biography"* by David Rayvern Allen (Harper Collins, 1995)

☐ Tom ARMITAGE

Right-handed batsman and lob bowler for Yorkshire, taken to Australia by Lillywhite in 1876-77. Played for England in the first Test Match. In 1886 emigrated to United States to coach and play cricket; then car worker. Died at daughter's home in Pullman, Cook County, Chicago, from stomach cancer on 21 September 1922. Interred in Mount Greenwood Cemetery, Chicago, where a marker placed at grave site by his great grandson-in-law in 1986.

• Further information and photo at www.findagrave

☐ Ted ARNOLD

Born in Devon and opted to join Worcestershire in 1895 as all-rounder before county entered championship. Fast-medium bowler and right-handed batsman. Achieved 'double' for four consecutive years. Important part of Ashes-winning 1903-04 team in Australia, dismissed Trumper with first ball in Test cricket. Invited on 1907-08 tour but supposedly forgot to reply in time, and offer was then withdrawn. Left county in 1913 and pursued interests in the turf. Died at home of daughter, The Fountain Inn in Worcester, 25 October 1942. Funeral held at Astwood Cemetery, Worcester, but illness or wartime duties prevented many former colleagues from attending. The grave, no 30631, is marked by a rectangle of kerbs, lies beside the path and behind Westwood, but no headstone nor any engraving apparent.

Astwood Cemetery *Sat Nav* WR3 8HA

☐ Bill ASHDOWN

Opening batsman with Kent 1920 to 1937 but made debut in 1914 at age of 15 and played a final match in 1947, so becoming only man to appear in English f-c cricket before WW1 and after WW2. Also noted for scoring two triple centuries in county cricket yet never chosen for England. F-c and Test umpire. Leicestershire coach until 1961, then coach at Rugby School. Died in St Luke's Hospital, Rugby, on 15 September 1979 and cremation at Canley Crematorium in Coventry. His memorial is an entry in the Book of Remembrance: "Gone are the happy years we spent together but love and memories live forever."

☐ F.S. ASHLEY-COOPER

Leading statistician and authority on the game's past, for thirty years responsible for births & deaths and records section in Wisden. Avid collector, possessed some 4,000 pamphlets and biographies, of which he wrote more than 100 himself. Sold his collection to Sir Julien Cahn and in time it passed to M.C.C. Secretary of Notts. C.C.C. 1920, but resigned for ill-health. Died on 31 January 1932 at home, Oak Cottage, Milford, Surrey, at age of 54. Cremation took place on 4 February at St John's Crematorium, Woking. No memorial. His ashes scattered on Garden of Remembrance.

Biography: *"F S Ashley-Cooper: A Biographical Sketch And Bibliography"* Peter Wynne-Thomas (ACS, 2003)

☐ [Sir] Hubert ASHTON

Batsman at Trinity College, Cambridge, 1919-22 where awarded his blue and scored century at Lord's. Selected for Gentlemen v Players but ignored for Test team in 1921 when England called on 30 players, although most promising batsman in country. In 1922 went to Burma with oil company and lost to cricket. Knighthood 1959 (for political service as M.P. for Chelmsford). President of M.C.C. in 1960. Died 17 June 1979 in Harold Wood Hospital, Brentwood, from heart attack. Funeral held at St Peter's church, South Weald, Essex, on 21 June. Sir Hubert's grave and headstone, next to that of brother, Gilbert, lies in cemetery extension on opposite side of road to St Peter's church. Wooden memorial plaque to him inside church.

St Peter's church at South Weald *Sat Nav* CM14 5QJ

☐ Ewart ASTILL

Made county debut for Leicestershire 1906 and a regular 1907-13 as off-spin bowler. Served in machine-gun corps in WW1, then scorned League offers and rejoined county. 'Second career' in late 1920s when an ever-improving batsman. Chosen for 9 Test appearances on M.C.C. tours of South Africa and West Indies after 40th birthday. Leicestershire's first regular professional captain. Retired 1939. Also county billiards champion. In WW2 captain in national defence force, the Home Guard. Coach at Tonbridge School until asthma enforced retirement. Died in a Leicester nursing home on 10 February 1948. Funeral held at Victoria Road church, followed by interment at Welford Road Cemetery, Leicester. Astill is buried in his parents' grave, plot B of consecrated section, grave 1055, next to the path.

Welford Road Cemetery Visitor Centre *Sat Nav* LE2 6BB

Biography : *"W.E.Astill: All-rounder Debonair"* by Antony Littlewood (ACS Lives in Cricket publications, 2014)

☐ 'Dick' ATTEWELL

Began career at 16 with Nottingham Commercial Club. Took his chance in Notts. 'schism' of 1886. Restrictive medium-paced bowler for Notts. and in ten Test matches for England on his three Australian tours. Shrewsbury School coach until 1913. After illness of six months, died at Long Eaton home on 11 June 1927, one day short of 66th birthday. Buried in West Park Cemetery, Long Eaton. The cemetery is in Lime Grove. Through cemetery gates, pass chapel and head for far left plot. Grave number is C229 and has inscription on kerbing but no headstone

West Park Cemetery, Long Eaton *Sat Nav* NG10 4LF

'Dick' Attewell's grave in West Park Cemetery, Long Eaton.

The graves of Alec and Eric Bedser in All Saints, Woodham, Woking.

☐ Harry BAGSHAW

Left-handed batsman with Derbyshire and member of M.C.C. groundstaff. Died in Crowden, Cheshire, 31 January 1927. Buried in Eyam churchyard, Derbyshire, in umpire's coat with cricket ball in hand. To find his grave: follow the right-hand perimeter wall down to far churchyard.

Headstone, which has an upraised umpire's finger, is inscribed 'For when the one great scorer comes to write against your name, he writes not that you won or lost but how you played the game'.

Eyam churchyard   *Sat Nav*   S32 5QH

• His must be one of the most heavily-visited of all gravestones with a cricketing connection, though Bagshaw was far from being a leading first-class player. The grave site is part of the tourist trail for hundreds of visitors who come to see the plague village of Eyam. In the churchyard is a prominent sign, pointing to Cricketer's Grave.

☐ Fred BAKEWELL

Opening batsman and expert short-leg fielder for Northants between 1928 and 1936. Only six Tests and never against Australia despite average of 45. Scored 241* v Derbyshire at Chesterfield immediately before arm injury sustained in car crash which ended career. Died at Seymour Road home in Westbourne, Bournemouth, on 23 January 1983. Cremation at Bournemouth Crematorium (North Cemetery) and ashes scattered on number 2 rosebed. Entry in Book of Remembrance as a permanent memorial.

☐ Dick BARLOW

Obdurate opening bat for Lancashire 1871-91, known as 'The Stonewaller' for defensive innings. Also, skilful slow-medium left-arm bowler and useful fielder. Represented England in 17 Test matches and toured Australia three times with English 'Test teams' in 1880. At his home installed a stained-glass window depicting cricket, now kept at Old Trafford Ground. 'R.G.', as locally known, died after long illness on 31 July 1919 at residence 'Ivyholme' in Woodland Grove, Blackpool, Lancashire, where lived with his daughter and son-in-law. Funeral held on 4 August and buried in Layton Cemetery, Blackpool, just inside entrance to cemetery. When his wife died, Barlow had erected monument over grave including his own name, leaving space for his date of death. Memorial has carving of bat and three stumps, with the leg stump down, and "bowled at last". A terracotta bat and stumps motif originally placed above doorway of his home Alderlea is now on house 'Rose Lea' in Woodland Grove, Blackpool

Layton Cemetery *Sat Nav*   FY3 7BD   Woodland Grove *Sat Nav*   FY3 9HD

Biography : *"Forty Seasons Of First-Class Cricket"* autobiography (John Heywood Ltd, 1908); *"The Story of a Cricket Stained-Glass Window"* by Keith Hayhurst (Lancashire CCC Foundation, 2016)

• The information about the terracotta design above Barlow's home Alderlea comes from www. amounderness. co.uk but the contemporary newspaper reported that Barlow died at his home which was named as 'Ivyholme'. Now Alderlea is renamed 'Rose Lea' it has become a bit confusing! In the redevelopment of the Old Trafford pavilion, Barlow's stained-glass window has been set in the back wall to allow natural light to pass through it.

Edgbaston Cricket Ground *Sat Nav* **B5 7QU**

Biography : *"Sydney Barnes: The greatest bowler of all time"* by Wilfred S White (Hudson 1935); *"Master Bowler"* by Leslie Duckworth (Hutchinson 1967, Sportsmans Book Club, 1968); *"S.F.Barnes: His Life And Times"* by Andrew Searle (Empire, 1997)

• His name has no connection with the small Stanley Barnes Stand, constructed at Edgbaston in 1989. Stanley Barnes was a Birmingham neurologist who served a short term of office as Warwickshire CCC's president in the 1950s.

☐ *Sydney BARNES*

Arguably, the greatest bowler to play cricket. Played for his birth town, Smethwick's first XI, at age of 15 and in handful of matches for Warwickshire before joining Rishton club in Lancashire League. MacLaren took him to Australia in 1901-02 when not nationally known and he snapped up 19 wickets in two Tests before knee injury. On return joined Lancashire C.C.C. until financial disagreement, whereupon returned to Leagues. Therefore short first-class career and only 27 Tests in which he nevertheless took 189 wickets at record strike rate of 7 wickets per Test. In all cricket said to have taken 6,229 wickets. Elected honorary member of M.C.C. On 80th birthday bowled a lively opening over in testimonial match at Stafford. Worked for Staffordshire County Council as writer of copperplate on legal documents until hip injury, and died on 26 December 1967 at son's home in Chadsmoor, Staffs. Funeral held at St Luke's church, Cannock, on New Year's Day and body cremated at Bushbury, Wolverhampton. The urn of ashes was offered to M.C.C. at Lord's but was eventually laid to rest under pillar of the wicket gate at Edgbaston Ground, Birmingham, and plaque unveiled on 11 June 1974, indicating where he entered ground for first county match in 1894.

☐ *William BARNES*

Leading professional from early days of Test cricket: right-handed batsman and fast-medium bowler, appeared in 21 Tests in 1880s and three times went to Australia with English sides. Started as young amateur before joining Notts. as professional in 1875; played regularly from then until disagreements with committee 1894. In retirement coached at Lord's and finally publican of Angel Inn at Mansfield Woodhouse, where died on 24 March 1899, after illness of three weeks. Following service at St Michael's, interred at Mansfield Woodhouse Cemetery, On A60 road, Leeming Lane. Walk up path approx. 60 metres. Gravestone is 10 metres in, on left-hand side.

Mansfield Woodhouse Cemetery *Sat Nav* **NG19 7BB**

☐ *Ted BARRATT*

Round-arm spin bowler, much admired by W G Grace. Born in Stockton-on-Tees but employed by Surrey. Took all ten wickets in innings for the Players v Australians 1878. Landlord of the Duchy Arms pub, near The Oval, where died from consumption on 27 February 1891, aged 46. Buried at West Norwood Cemetery. Sign once on The Cricketers pub in Stockton, now redeveloped as shops, had borne his likeness.

West Norwood Cemetery *Sat Nav* SE27 9JU

☐ *Ken BARRINGTON*

Reliable batsman for Surrey and England. Assistant groundsman at Reading C.C. when spotted by Surrey. With the county from 1953. Named as C.W.C. Young Cricketer of Year 1955. Played in 82 Test matches for England; scored over 6,800 Test runs with 20 centuries, first to score hundreds on all six English Test grounds (as there were then). Nicknamed 'The Colonel'. Often under-rated leg-break bowler. Through 1960s senior professional and adviser to England captains. Made 13 overseas tours, as player or manager. Test selector. While assistant manager/coach of England's team in West Indies, died from heart attack in Barbados hotel on 14 March 1981. Body flown home and funeral held near Surrey home on 23 March at Randalls Park Crematorium, Leatherhead. No memorial, ashes scattered in the glade. Memorial service at Southwark Cathedral, attended by nine past England captains and address given by one of them, David Sheppard, Bishop of Liverpool. On 6 May 1981 new pavilion in Caversham named in Barrington's memory with plaque unveiled by wife Ann. Courage Old England cricket match at The Oval on 19 September 1982 initiated fund for Ken Barrington Indoor Cricket Centre, and in 1983 Surrey began public appeal for centre at Oval's Vauxhall End which produced £1¼ million. Centre opened by Queen in 1991.

The Kia Oval, Kennington *Sat Nav* SE11 5SS

Biographies: *"Running Into Hundreds"* autobiography (Stanley Paul, 1963); *"Playing It Straight"* autobiography with Phil Pilley (Stanley Paul, 1968); *"Ken Barrington: A Tribute"* by Brian Scovell (Harrap, 1982); *"England Expects"* by Mark Peel (Kingswood Press, 1992)

• On calling at Randalls Park Crematorium office the reception staff did not need to look up records but could tell me at once about what happened to Barrington's ashes, so often do people enquire about him. There is some hope that one day a memorial will be placed to him. More than thirty years after his tragic early death the passage of time barely softens the widespread feeling of loss. Geoff Wellsteed's excellent "Inside the Boundary" records Barrington's various connections with Reading, as well as expressing his own admiration for him.

☐ *Denzil BATCHELOR*

Born in Calcutta, 1906, son of a Bombay High Court judge. General sports journalist and leading cricket writer and broadcaster. When leaving to go to the Gillette Cup final at Lord's on 6 September 1969, taken ill and died of heart attack. Buried in Gunnersbury Avenue Cemetery, West London. To find grave, walk past Katyn war memorial, turn left then first right. Batchelor's grave is on corner plot, a flat grey slab. In his name Wombwell Cricket Lovers Society made an annual award for services to cricket.

Gunnersbury Cemetery *Sat Nav* W3 8LE

☐ *Willie BATES*

Huddersfield-based professional with Yorkshire from 1877. Important all-rounder for England in early days of Test cricket: right-handed spin bowler and batsman. Made 15 Test appearances, all abroad. On fifth tour of Australia struck in the face by a ball at net practice and eye damaged, so sent home. Co-ordination affected and cricket career ended. While attending funeral of a fellow cricketer from local club, caught a cold and died of pneumonia at home, Spa Bottom, in Lepton, Yorkshire, on 8 January 1900. Buried three days later at Kirkheaton Cemetery, near Huddersfield. To find his memorial walk uphill from parish church, turn right down Lane Side into Cemetery Lane. Climb main path from cemetery gates and Bates's grave is near top on right-hand side. Main slab has capsized and headstone, which has shield design on flanks, is tipping forward.

Lane Side Cemetery, Kirkheaton *Sat Nav* HD5 0EP

□ *George BEAN*

Long-time member of Lord's groundstaff. After handful of matches for Notts in 1885, represented Sussex 1886-98. Batsman, described by *The Times* as "brilliant rather than sound." Played 3 Tests on Lord Sheffield's Australian tour 1891-92 at peak of career. At time of death was coach at Haileybury School. Died of pneumonia 16 March 1923 at Warsop, Notts. Funeral on 19 March; coffin borne by nephews to churchyard in Sutton-in-Ashfield, where (like Morley, Barnes, Briggs, Wass and others) he had been born in village.

St Mary Magdalene church, Sutton-in-Ashfield *Sat Nav* NG17 2EB

□ *Lord Frederick BEAUCLERK*

Son of Duke of St Albans and a descendant of Charles II. One of cricket's earliest aristocratic players, said to be a brilliant batsman. Bowled slow underarms, precise in pitch and length. Played for wagers in single-wicket and odds matches at Lord's Ground in Dorset Square. Also, autocratic establishment figure in game's hierarchy. Second M.C.C. president (1826). Died in Grosvenor Street, London, on 22 April 1850. Has memorial tablet, erected by widow, near altar in St Mary's parish church at Winchfield, Hampshire, where he inherited an estate. The 17th century Winchfield Inn was formerly named The Beauclerk Arms.

St Mary's church, Winchfield *Sat Nav* RG27 8DB

•. Beauclerk hired Thomas Howard to represent him in a famous single-wicket match in 1810, playing against George Osbaldeston and his professional William Lambert for a purse of fifty guineas. Howard was buried in nearby St Mary's, Elvetham, but there is no memorial.

opened in May 2012 by Ken Schofield CBE. Two roads named Bedser Close in his honour, one in Kennington and one in Woking.

Horsell, Woking   *Sat Nav*   GU21 4HQ.   All Saints church, Woodham   *Sat Nav*   GU21 5SH   Bedser Bridge *Sat Nav* GU21 4AA

Biographies : *"Our Cricket Story"* autobiography with Eric Bedser (Evans Brothers 1951); *"Following On"* autobiography with Eric Bedser (Evans Brothers, 1954); *"Twin Ambitions"* autobiography with Eric Bedser (Stanley Paul, 1986); *"The Bedsers"* by Alan Hill (Mainstream Publishing, 2001).

☐ [Sir] Alec BEDSER

Medium-fast bowler. Another Redingensian, like May and Barrington, who was recruited by Surrey: left school at 14 to become solicitor's clerk before joining the RAF in 1939, when he played twice for county but then had to wait seven wartime years before resuming for Surrey. England's principal opening bowler 1946-1953. Held record for most Test wickets (236) until 1963. Retired from first-class cricket 1960 and proprietor of office stationery firm. Appointed England selector 1962-85 and chairman for a record thirteen years. England tour manager in Australia. Knighted in 1997. The Marylebone Club hosted a 90th birthday lunch in 2009. Lived in Carlton Road, Horsell, Surrey, and died in Nuffield Hospital, Woking, on 4 April 2010. Funeral held at All Saints Church in Woodham on 20 April. On eastern side of church is a Garden of Remembrance with two identical beds as memorials to Alec and his twin Eric. Woking Council commissioned statues of the Bedser twins, Alec bowling and Eric batting, to be positioned on each end of a new pedestrian bridge opened over Basingstoke Canal in Woking in 2013. The Bedser Trail, a 1.2 km circular path around Horsell Common

☐ George BELDAM

Patient and watchful batsman with Middlesex who also appeared for London County and The Gentlemen. Pioneer and leading exponent of cricket photography in 'Great Batsmen, their Methods at a Glance'. Produced plates for golf and tennis, too. Also invented a non-skid tyre approved by the R.A.C. Died at Frensham Vale, near Farnham, Hants., on 23 November 1937 and buried in Surrey's Brookwood Necropolis. Beldam's grave (plot 17, number 200644) lies on St George's Avenue. His headstone is a small boulder, bounded by random York stone walling.

Brookwood Cemetery   *Sat Nav*   GU24 0BL

Biography   *"Third Man In: Lost World of a Camera Artist"* George Alastair Beldam Collection (1995).

☐ William BELDHAM

From Wrecclesham, near Farnham, Surrey, joined Hambledon team in 1785 and by age of 25 reckoned the best bat in England. "Silver Billy" (so called because of fair hair) lived through greatest changes the game has seen: pitched deliveries, straight bats, defence, lbw, and mastered them all. Just pre-dated round-arm bowling, last appearance of 45 year-long career being in 1821. Became farmer then publican at Tilford, where died aged 96. Buried in a long, narrow plot at extreme western end of St Andrew's churchyard, Farnham. Three others of his family lie in same plot but, because headstones are of local stone which weathers badly, none of Beldham graves can now be identified. Parish archives give date of death as 23 February 1862, conflicting with date given in Wisden. Once, pub sign on 'The Cricketers' at Wrecclesham portrayed Beldham; the pub at no.1 The Street went out of business and is now an Indian restaurant. At least, his portrait is prominently displayed in Long Room at Lord's.

St Andrew's parish church, Farnham *Sat Nav* GU9 7PW

□ George BENNETT

Medium-paced bowler and batsman with Kent for twenty years. Member of Stephenson's 1861-62 side to Australia. Later coach at Eton College and in winter bricklayer on Darnley's Cobham Hall estate. Died in Shorne Ridgeway, near Gravesend, Kent, on 16 August 1886 and buried in Shorne churchyard. Many years after burial, his grave was located where undertaker had carved a 'B' on fence opposite, and a fund commenced for his tombstone.

St Peter and St Paul's church, Shorne *Sat Nav* DA12 3EB

• Numbered 126, the stone now lies flat on the bank in section C of the graveyard (this information from the Kent Archaeological Society website).

□ Morice BIRD

As Harrow schoolboy made two centuries in Eton v Harrow match at Lord's 1907 and invited to play for Lancashire. In 1909 joined Surrey and captain from 1911, aged 23. Made two tours of South Africa with M.C.C. for ten Test appearances. After WW1 returned to Harrow School as coach before appointed cricket instructor at The Oval. Died at Broadstone, Dorset, 9 December 1933 and buried in Broadstone Cemetery. Grave 269 in section B. Follow cemetery drive just past first bend: grave is on RHS, five spaces in and 14 grave spaces from eastern hedge.

Broadstone Cemetery *Sat Nav* BH18 8AF

□ Hon Ivo BLIGH

Fine sports player at Eton and Cambridge University. Scored so well in first full season with Kent, only narrowly beaten by G.F.Grace to place in Oval Test XI of 1880. Ill-health prevented him playing in 1882 and on doctor's orders hardly played after 1883, yet nevertheless took 1882-83 team to Australia to win back 'The Ashes'. Married Florence Morphy, at whose house in Rupertswood a bail was burnt to create The Ashes. Urn containing the Ashes bequeathed to M.C.C. on his death, to be kept permanently in Memorial Gallery at Lord's. Succeeded

☐ Colin BLYTHE

Kent debut 1899, having learned on nursery field at Tonbridge's Angel Ground. Represented England only two years later on MacLaren's 1901-02 tour of Australia. Appeared in 19 Test matches. Career record of more than 2,500 wickets which cost only 17 runs each. Brilliance as a left-arm spinner diminished by anxieties over worsening epileptic seizures. Sometimes omitted on medical advice from England XI. Prior to leaving with first troops sent to France in 1914, appointed Eton coach and retired from first-class cricket. Sergeant in Royal Engineers. Was killed with six comrades by shellburst in mud at Passchendaele on 8 November 1917 and buried in mass grave behind the lines. Kent erected obelisk at St Lawrence Ground to players who fell in War, including Kenneth Hutchings, but was generally known as The Blythe Memorial. His war grave in Belgium is in Oxford Road Cemetery : plot one, row L, grave 2. Cemetery is two miles north of Ieper on road to Wieltje, Belgium. In parish church of St Peter & St Paul, Tonbridge, Kent, where he lived, is a further memorial to him at eastern end of south aisle. Blue plaque placed outside his former home, 29 Goldsmid Road, Tonbridge, and nearby road given name Colin Blythe Road.

brother as Earl of Darnley in 1896 and lived at Cobham Hall. Was M.C.C president 1900. Died of heart failure at Puckle Hill House, Cobham, nr Gravesend, Kent, on 10 April 1927 and buried in Cobham parish churchyard. Unlike most of Darnleys, who are buried in family plot on church's eastern exterior wall, his tombstone stands next to wall 20 metres west of churchyard path. In chancel stained-glass window installed in memory of Bligh and Countess.

St Mary Magdalene church, Cobham *Sat Nav* DA12 3BZ

Biography : *"St. Ivo & The Ashes, A Correct, True & Particular History Of The Hon. Ivo Bligh's Crusade In Australia"* by R D. Beeston and M C B Massie (1883; Kessinger 2009) *"Ivo Bligh"* by Peter Wynne-Thomas and Peter Griffiths (Famous Cricketers Series, ACS 2002); *"Cricket's Burning Passion: Ivo Bligh and the Story of the Ashes"* by Scyld Berry and Rupert Peploe (Methuen, 2008)

• I took my photograph of his grave in 1984 and the engraving looks readable yet it had deteriorated enough for The Cricket Society to need to restore the headstone in 2011.

Goldsmid Road, Tonbridge *Sat Nav* TN9 2BT
Tonbridge parish church *Sat Nav* TN9 1HD

Biography : *"Colin Blythe: Lament for a Legend"* by Christopher Scroble (SportsBooks, 2005)

☐ Jack BOARD

Played for Frenchay cricket club in Bristol. Advised to take up wicket-keeping by W G Grace, he proved athletic and reliable for Gloucestershire 1891-1914. Also a sound batsman but competition from Lilley and Storer restricted international opportunities to six Tests, despite making 3 overseas tours. Cricket coach in Manchester and overseas. Travelling home from South African coaching engagement, died of heart attack on board the 'Kenilworth Castle', 15 April 1924. The ship's log missing but it was understood that he had a burial at sea. Plaque at his former home 22 Manor Road, Bishopston, Bristol.

Manor Road, Bishopston *Sat Nav* **BS7 8PY**

• The shipping company now responsible for the Castle Line records told me in 1980s that the ship's log for the Kenilworth Castle voyage was missing - so it is really a matter of conjecture whether Board was buried at sea. Looking through Bristol newspapers of 1924, did not provide any clarification or confirmation.

☐ Arthur BOOTH

Left-arm spinner, given Yorkshire trial 1931. League and minor county cricket with Northumberland. In 1946 'Little Arthur' unexpectedly topped national averages with 111 wickets at 11.62, helping Yorkshire to championship; but then retired to Bradford Leagues. Became school coach at Manchester and scout for Warwickshire. Lived at Littleborough. Died in Birch Hill Hospital, Rochdale, Lancashire, on 17 August 1974. Buried in grave O72 at Dearnley Burial Ground, sometimes known as Littleborough Cemetery.

Dearnley Cemetery *Sat Nav* **OL15 8NJ**

☐ Major BOOTH

From Pudsey, was batsman with famous St Lawrence club. A first team regular with Yorkshire from 1910. All-rounder (bowling fast-medium) selected for tour of South Africa 1913-14, playing in two Test matches.

At peak of cricket career when enlisted in Army. As Lieutenant, died in Battle of the Somme, near La Cigny, France, on 1 July 1916. Aged 29. Roy Kilner had fortune to injure his wrist and so missed same battle. Booth buried in Serre Road Military Cemetery No 1 outside village of Puisieux, Pas de Calais, France, on road to Maillet. Grave number is I.P.14. In September 1920 a service at St Lawrence church, Pudsey, where he worshipped. Wall tablet unveiled in his memory.

St Lawrence church, Pudsey *Sat Nav* **LS28 7BD**

Biography : *"Tragic White Roses"* by Mick Pope (Adelphi Press, 1995)

☐ Bernard BOSANQUET

Ordinary fast-medium bowler when changed to leg-breaks and by means of experiments with billiard ball, discovered art of googly bowling. Practised hard in nets and immediately effective when tried in a match. Hero of 1903-04 Test series in Australia and in 1904 enjoyed best season but then, as bowling declined, became solely a batsman. Died in Ewhurst, Surrey, on 12 October 1936 and buried in family tomb in Enfield's Lavender Gardens Cemetery. Son Reginald was newsreader who died in 1984. The cemetery is in Cedar Road, opposite Gibson Hill station. Grave is just north of chapel on grassed island at junction of several paths.

Lavender Gardens Cemetery, Cedar Road *Sat Nav* **EN2 0TN**

□ Bill BOWES

Tall (6' 4"), bespectacled, fast-medium bowler on M.C.C. groundstaff. With Verity was Yorkshire's leading bowler in 'thirties. Finest county figures were 16-35 in match at Kettering in 1935. Played 15 Test matches, with 6-33 v West Indies at Old Trafford his best for England. In WW2 gunnery officer in North Africa: captured at Tobruk and spent 3 years in Italian prison camp. Retired from playing in 1947 with benefit return of £8000, then a Yorkshire record. Journalist on *Yorkshire Post*, reporting county cricket. Suffered heart attack at his Menston home, died at Otley General Hospital on 4 September 1987. Funeral at Rawdon Crematorium a week later. Ashes strewn on Daffodil Hill within Rawdon but no memorial. In 2013 City of Bradford council named mews development on former site of Menston club on Farnley Road in his honour.

Bill Bowes Court, Menston *Sat Nav*   LS29 6GF

Biography: *"Express Deliveries"*   autobiography (Stanley Paul, 1949)

□ Thomas BOX

Right-handed bat and greatest wicket-keeper of his time. Turned out for Surrey and Hampshire as guest but played mainly for Sussex between 1826 and 1856, "... filling, well nigh to perfection, a post which, if insufficiently represented, must make the best eleven worthless." [C.F. Trower *Sussex Cricket, Past & Present"]* Died suddenly at Prince's Ground in London on 12 July 1876; supposed to have dropped down dead while working the telegraph. Buried in Brompton Cemetery in a grave long since covered over.

□ [Walter] 'Bill' BRADLEY

Success in club cricket as fast bowler for Mote Park, Maidstone, led to offer to play for Kent as amateur. Also played for London County and six times for Gentlemen v Players. Though reputed to be one of worst number 11 batsmen, scored 23 on first of his two Test appearances v Australia in 1899, his best season as a bowler. More notably took wicket with his first ball. Died at Earlsfield, Wimbledon, 19 June 1944 and buried in family plot at Elmers End (now Beckenham) Cemetery - approx a cricket pitch distant from WG Grace's grave but reached only through a tangle of vegetation.

Beckenham Cemetery *Sat Nav*   BR3 4TD

□ Len BRAUND

Fine all-rounder: leg-break bowler, right-handed batsman and outstanding slip fielder. From 3 unsuccessful seasons with Surrey and 3 more with London County while qualifying, to Somerset in 1901 for 3 particularly brilliant summers: 1901, '02, '03 in which his all-round figures were 426 wickets taken and 4,444 runs scored. Won England place, selected for three Australian tour parties. Indispensable member of England's Test side in 23 matches in early 1900s. Retired from county cricket after WW1. F-c umpire 16 seasons and coach. Despite both legs needing amputation in 1940s, a frequent enthusiastic spectator at cricket. Hon membership of M.C.C. 1949. Died at Putney 23 December 1955 and funeral at London's Golders Green Crematorium, where his ashes strewn on the main lawn. His memorial was an entry in Book of Remembrance on permanent display in the Chapel.

Golders Green Crematorium   *Sat Nav*   NW11 7NL

☐ Walter BREARLEY

Bustling, energetic fast bowler with Lancashire. Short career, did not represent county until aged 26. Holding a sincere belief in inferiority of all batsmen, was renowned for his energy and enthusiasm. Only 4 times invited to play for England and never for an overseas tour. Taken ill in his rooms in Euston Hotel, London, died in Middlesex Hospital on 30 January 1937. Funeral held on 2 February at St Martin's church, Bowness, Cumbria, where his wife's family hailed from, and buried in Bowness-on-Windermere Cemetery. He lies in grave of the Bownass family on a plot to right of cemetery gates. His name is inscribed only on kerbing.

Bowness-on-Windermere Cemetery *Sat Nav* LA23 3HB

☐ Johnny BRIGGS

Born in Nottinghamshire, but his parents moved to Widnes. Joined Seaforth club at end of 1877 season and at age 16 called on by Lancashire. Not only useful batsman, making ten centuries including one in a Test, but without peer as slow left-arm bowler after specialising in this style from 1885 onward. Made six tours of Australia with English sides and one to South Africa, appearing in a total of 33 Test matches. First man to 100 wickets in Tests. Took 15 wickets for 28 runs in match v South Africa at Cape Town in 1888-89. For over 100 years (until 1999) only he had scored a century and taken a hat-trick in Test cricket. Epilepsy ended career. Died at Cheadle Royal Asylum, Manchester, on 11 January 1902, aged 40. Funeral at Stretford Cemetery, Manchester, on 15 January, attended by more than 3,000 people. Mourners included his Lancashire colleagues and music hall comedian George Robey. Buried with wife Alice (died 1914). Gravestone surmounted with obelisk with crossed bats, stumps, ball and a fallen Lancashire rose.

Stretford Cemetery *Sat Nav* M32 8HX

Biography : *"The Life of John Briggs"* by Herbert Turner (1902, reprinted by Red Rose Books, 2000); *"Johnny Remembered"* by Malcolm Lorimer (self-published Lancashire Heroes series, 2005)

☐ 'Jem' BROADBRIDGE

Born Duncton, West Sussex, 1795. Round-arm bowler for Sussex. Following in footsteps of John Willes, he and William Lillywhite swayed acceptance of 'round-arm' by 1835. Also "an extremely hard-hitter" [Haygarth] but "fox-headed" [Altham]. Died 12 February 1843, three years after giving up cricket. Duncton's The Swan Inn was purchased by John Wisden in 1867 and leased to Jem Dean; inn later re-named 'The Cricketers Inn', in honour of Dean and Jem Broadbridge.

Holy Trinity churchyard *Sat Nav* GU28 0JZ   The Cricketers Inn, Duncton *Sat Nav* GU28 0LB

☐ Bill BROCKWELL

Joined Surrey from Ham C.C. as professional 1886. All-rounder: fast-medium bowler and opening right-handed batsman, appearing in 7 Test matches and making two tours in 1890s. On retirement had little success seeking an occupation outside cricket. Died of pneumonia in infirmary in Richmond, Surrey, on 30 June 1935. Funeral held at Richmond Cemetery on 4 July and attended by J T Hearne. Brockwell has no memorial : body lies in grave 9653 in block 8 of cemetery, behind Anstey's grave, which is next to the path amid some trees.

• For such as Brockwell, who died destitute with no gravestone, might occur the thought 'When I am laid in earth, Remember me, but forget my fate.'

☐ Freddie BROWN

Born in Peru where his father was in business. All-rounder who bowled leg-breaks or medium-pace for Cambridge University and Surrey. First called up to play for England in 1931. Chosen for 'bodyline' tour of Australia though not in the Test matches. In WW2 won MBE in evacuation of Crete but captured at Tobruk and spent war in prison camp. Career revived after becoming Northants captain and took M.C.C. side to Australia in 1950-51 losing 4 Tests but winning one 'elusive victory'. England selector and chairman in 1953 when chosen to play his 22nd and last Test. Lord's asked him to manage two M.C.C. tours, to South Africa and Australia, and the Rest of the World XI 1970. President in 1971-72 and Chairman of the Cricket Council 1977. C.B.E. 1980. Died at his home in Ramsbury, nr Marlborough, Wiltshire on 24 July 1991, and buried on 30 July in western side of churchyard of Holy Cross church, Ramsbury.

Holy Cross church, Ramsbury *Sat Nav* SN8 2QH

Biography: *"Cricket Musketeer"* autobiography (Nicholas Kaye, 1954)

☐ George BROWN

Brilliant batsman and versatile, fearless sportsman, also able to keep wicket, which he did on Tests on South African tour of 1922-23. Died St Paul's Hospital, Winchester, Hampshire, on 3 December 1964. Funeral service, at which John Arlott made the address, held on 9 December at Parliament Street Methodist church, followed by cremation. Ashes scattered on 11 December on pitch of the old Southampton County Ground, as he had requested. No memorial known.

☐ Jack BROWN

A match played at his birthplace, Driffield (north of Hull), in 1969 to mark centenary of his birth. Batsman for Yorkshire from 1889 (aged only 19) to 1904. Twice played an innings of 300: but greatest innings was 140 in 95 minutes for England on 1894-95 tour of Australia – then fastest century in Test cricket - to win final game of series. Owned sports outfitting business at Halifax and Leeds. Health broke down in May 1904 and had to resign from Yorkshire. Died from heart attack in a Westminster nursing home on 4 November 1904, at age of 35. Funeral held at Lawnswood Cemetery, Leeds, where F S Jackson and Lord Hawke joined members of family at graveside.

Lawnswood Cemetery *Sat Nav* LS16 6AH

☐ David BUCHANAN

As a boy, attended Rugby School. Spin bowler who played for The Gentlemen, and took nine in an innings v the Players in 1868. Prominent in establishing Warwickshire

C.C.C. Captained county for four years after the club's formation and became treasurer. Died at Northfield House, Rugby, his home of 32 years, on 30 May 1900. Buried in Clifton Road Cemetery, Rugby (grave number 61 in section H). Walk up main cemetery path and grave is a plot across on right-hand side. Was decided to raise a subscription fund for a new pavilion as his memorial at Rugby C.C. ground in Webb Ellis Road. Nearby (off Bilton Road, the B4642), Buchanan Road and the park were named after him by a council decision in 1937.

Clifton Road Cemetery *Sat Nav* CV21 3QT   Rugby Cricket Club (pavilion) *Sat Nav* CV22 7AU

☐ *Claude BUCKENHAM*

Essex and England fast bowler. Used to say he gave up county cricket and went to league cricket in Forfarshire because of all the catches slip fielders missed off his bowling. Died at his son's home in Dundee on 23 February 1937. Buried in Balgay Cemetery, Dundee, Lair 113, Section KK. There is a large headstone.

Balgay Cemetery *Sat Nav* DD2 2UJ

☐ *Syd BULLER*

After one match keeping wicket for county of his birth Yorkshire in 1930, remained in 2nd XI until transferred to Worcestershire. Appointed coach and 2nd XI captain. Joined umpires list in 1951. Renowned as fair and fearless umpire, earning respect of all players in 33 Tests in which he stood, and awarded MBE in 1965. On 7 August 1970, officiating in Warwicks-Notts. match at Edgbaston, collapsed and died in pavilion during stoppage for rain. Funeral at St John's church, Worcester, followed by cremation at Astwood Cemetery where ashes were scattered on top lawns of Gardens of Remembrance. No plaque but entry in Book of Remembrance. Only other memorial is a seat dedicated to Buller and his wife at New Road Ground, Worcester.

☐ *Harry BUTT*

Joined Sussex as young professional in 1890 as wicket-keeper and regularly appeared until WW1. Toured South Africa with Lord Hawke's XI in 1895-96 and played in three Tests. Career record of 1,228 victims put him second to David Hunter at the time, now tenth. Became a Test umpire. Retired to Hastings where he died on 21 December 1928 and buried in the Borough Cemetery, Hastings, Sussex. Grave, number N13 in Div F, Section A, has scroll and kerbs.

Hastings Borough Cemetery *Sat Nav* TN34 2AE

☐ *Julius CAESAR*

Batsman for Surrey. Went on the first cricket tour abroad in 1859 to North America, and in 1863-64 on the second tour of Australia. Coach at Charterhouse and cricket outfitter in Godalming. Died of heart disease on 5

David Buchanan grave, Rugby   (below) Percy Chapman in parent's grave at Wokingham.

hairdresser. Died 28 August 1919 after working in garden of daughter's house, where he lived at Reigate. Buried on 2 September in graveyard of St Mary's parish church, in Chart Lane, New Reigate. The grave is number B487. End of an era : Caffyn was last surviving member of first team sent to Australia in 1861-62 and last from Surrey XI that used to play full strength of England.

St Mary's church cemetery *Sat Nav* RH2 7RN

Biography: *"Seventy One Not Out"* autobiography (William Blackwood, 1899)

March 1878 at Railway Tavern. Buried in Nightingale Cemetery, Godalming. Grave is 100 metres downslope, to east of former chapel. Caesar died broke, and had no headstone until local authority drew up plans in 2000 for a memorial, dedicated in 2004. Godalming Cricket Club instituted a 'Caesar Shield' for colts cricket.

Nightingale Cemetery [entrance is in Deanery Road] *Sat Nav* GU7 2PG

Biography : *"Julius Caesar, The Ill-Fated Cricketer"* by Geoff Amey (Bodyline Books, 2000)

• See also in this cemetery the 'iceberg memorial' to the wireless operator who died in the 'Titanic'. Godalming Library's website has a page about famous locals and includes an image of Caesar's new headstone when it was renewed. I was struck by how quickly it had weathered since then.

☐ *William CAFFYN*

Chosen for England's pioneering tours as one of best batsmen in country. Went to North America 1859, Australia 1861 and 1863, when remained as coach to Melbourne club. Returned 1871 but lost place in Surrey team, left cricket and became barber and

☐ *[Sir] Julien CAHN*

Immensely rich businessman who had cricket ground laid out at West Bridgford for his own team of international cricketers to play there. The Sir Julien Cahn Pavilion commemorates his name at the ground (now called West Park). Sponsor of five tours overseas to cricketing outposts. Long-serving president and patron of Nottinghamshire C.C.C. Made a baronet in 1934 for his philanthropic work. Died of heart attack in library of his home, Stanford Hall, near Loughborough, on 26 September 1944 and cremated at Wilford Hill Cemetery, Nottingham. Ashes taken away to be scattered on private cricket field. Requested there be no entry in Book of Remembrance nor any memorial tablet. His library containing more or less every cricket book then published regrettably broken up and sold at auction, while Stanford Hall bought by Cooperative Society in 1945 to open as training college, now being redeveloped as a rehabilitation centre.

Stanford Hall *Sat Nav* LE12 5QW Sir Julien Cahn pavilion, West Bridgford *Sat Nav* NG2 7JE

Biography : *"The Eccentric Entrepreneur: Sir Julien Cahn: Businessman, Philanthropist, Magician and Cricket-Lover"* by Miranda Rijks (The History Press, 2011)

Freddie CALTHORPE

Made debut as batsman for Sussex v All-India in 1911 but subsequently appeared for Warwickshire, for ten years as captain. Led M.C.C. v West Indies on 1929-30 tour, first Test matches played in Caribbean, after which played only half a dozen more county matches. In declining health, dropped dead on golf course at Worplesdon Hill, Woking, on 19 November 1935. Funeral at Woking Crematorium attended by many figures from cricket's establishment. Ashes later buried at Brookwood Necropolis, Surrey. His headstone, a cross with kerbing, is in plot 28 on St. Chad's Avenue.

Brookwood Cemetery   *Sat Nav*   GU24 0BL

[Sir] Neville CARDUS

Eminent cricket writer, known for portraits of Lancashire heroes of his day. Once off-spin bowler in club cricket. School coach, as assistant to Ted Wainwright, at Shrewsbury School. Cricket correspondent and music critic of the *Manchester Guardian* and *Sunday Times*. Awarded CBE in 1964 and knighted in 1967. Died in his sleep at the Nuffield Hospital, London, on 28 February 1975 and cremated at Golders Green Crematorium. Ashes dispersed on Lawns of Remembrance with no personal memorial. On 3 July 1987 John Arlott officially opened the Sir Neville Cardus Press Gallery at Old Trafford.

Old Trafford Cricket Ground   *Sat Nav*   M16 0PX

Biographies : *"Autobiography"* by Neville Cardus (1947; republished Hamish Hamilton 1984); *"Second Innings: More Autobiography"* (Collins, 1950); *"Cricket All the Year"* autobiography (Collins, 1952); *"Close of Play"* autobiography (Collins, 1956); *"His Own Man: the Life of Neville Cardus"* by Christopher Brookes (Methuen, 1985); *"Neville Cardus Reflects"* edited by Bob Hilton (Lancashire C.C.C. 2012); *"Conversations with Cardus"* memoirs by Robin Daniels (Victor Gollancz, 1976)

• The new "Players and Media Centre" was a major part of the Old Trafford ground redevelopment in 2013 and is now named after the stockbrokers and investors, AJ Bell Trust, rather than Cardus.

Dudley CAREW

Cricket writer. School at Lancing College where Evelyn Waugh among fellow pupils. Wrote for *The Times* from 1920s onwards, reporting cricket matches for the paper, as well as football and book or film reviews. Cricket novels, like *England Over* (1927), *Son of Grief* (1936), and essays *To the Wicket* (1946). Retirement in 1963. Died on 22 March 1981 in Cuckfield Hospital, Sussex. Funeral at Surrey and Sussex Crematorium, Worth, nr Crawley.

Biography : *"The House is Gone: a Personal Retrospect"* (Hale, 1949), *"A Fragment of Friendship"* (Everest, 1974) both autobiographical.

Surrey and Sussex Crematorium, Crawley   *SatNav*   RH10 3NQ

Arthur CARR

Good enough to appear for Notts (v Gloucs 1910) while still at Sherborne School. Accepted county captaincy 1919, and in 1925 scored more than 2,000 runs; became England captain following year. Helped to devise 'bodyline' strategy ahead of 1932-33 Australian tour. Was sacked as Notts captain in 1934 over role in bodyline. In WW2 served until 1941 with 16th Lancers. Died on 7 February 1963; collapsed after shovelling snow outside his home, Clumber Cottage, West Witton, Yorkshire. Funeral at Darlington Crematorium.

Biography : *"Cricket with the Lid Off"* by Arthur Carr (Hutchinson, 1935)

- Arthur Carr's ashes were taken away from the crematorium by the funeral director who has long since ceased trading. Efforts to locate his grave, if he has one, were unsuccessful but I am very grateful to Richard Sanderson for trudging through local graveyards in his efforts to help me find one.

☐ Percy CHAPMAN

Debonair, young hero sought by public after repeated defeats by Australia. Personified dashing amateur cricketer: good-looking, tall, attacking batsman and magnificent fielder. Came from effortless success at each of Uppingham School, Cambridge University, minor county Berkshire and Kent into England Test team 1924, and captaincy at The Oval in 1926 to win back 'The Ashes' and retain them in 1928-29 series. Then career went into sad, slow decline. Kent captain till 1935 and sporadically 1936, then gave up for business reasons. Last match 1939. Died in Alton Hospital, Hampshire, 16 September 1961. Funeral at St John's Crematorium, Woking on 22 September and ashes interred in the grave of his father, Frank Chapman - number 1020 – and next to his mother Bertha in All Saints churchyard, Wokingham.

All Saints church, Wokingham *Sat Nav* RG40 1UE

Biography : *"Percy Chapman   a Biography"* by David Lemmon (Queen Anne Press, 1985)

- Chapman's parents were interred in the graveyard adjacent to Norreys Avenue beside the path approx 60 yards south of the storage hut, beneath a yew tree.

☐ Henry CHARLWOOD

Dashing, hard-hitting batsman, 'The Hope of Sussex', one of four brothers to play for county. Stalwart for Henfield club, north of Brighton. In 1872 became second man to be given out for hitting the ball twice. Made 1876-77 tour of Australia, appearing in the first two matches in Test history. In 1879 went to Scarborough to take on Bell Hotel at Blands Cliff. Collapsed while reading at bar on 6 June 1888. Funeral at Dean Road Cemetery, Scarborough, and buried in grave 26, row 14, section F. Grave is surmounted by 1.5 metre-high cross.

Dean Road Cemetery *Sat Nav*   YO12 7JH

☐ William CHATTERTON

Steady, graceful batsman for Derbyshire, and fine slip fielder. On Lord's groundstaff for 20 years and appeared for M.C.C. His single Test played on W.W. Read's 1891-92 visit to South Africa when easily top of tour batting averages. Derbyshire captain for three seasons. Later publican in Derby and coach at Cambridge, and asked to lay out cricket field at Sandringham. Died of consumption on 19 March 1913 at his father's home in Flowery Field, Hyde, within ten miles of birthplace. Funeral at Hyde Chapel attended by friend Frank Sugg, and buried at Gee Cross.

☐ Frank CHESTER

Promising young off-spinner and right-handed batsman with Worcestershire. Invalided at Salonika in 1917, where he lost arm below the elbow. Became first-class umpire, serving in 33 seasons to 1955 and standing in 48 Tests. Died suddenly at home in Bushey, Hertfordshire, on 8 April 1957 and buried in Bushey parish churchyard (located in High Street). Interred between two small yew trees approx ten metres south-west of church.

St James's church, Bushey   *Sat Nav*   WD23 1BD

Biography : *"How's That!"* by Frank Chester (Hutchinson, 1956)

☐ Stanley CHRISTOPHERSON

Reckoned a top amateur fast bowler in his day but only one Test appearance. With father and nine brothers, formed a family XI. Career with Kent cut short by arm injury so turned to business and finance, becoming wartime chairman of Midland Bank. Emulated Lord Hawke, only other president of M.C.C. to serve for more than one year, by holding position through War years until 1946. Died at Hospital of St Elizabeth & St John in St John's Wood, on 6 April 1949. Cremated at Golders Green Crematorium, London, and ashes dispersed on lawns two days later.

• He had a strong connection with Norfolk being High Sherriff and president of the county cricket club. He lived at Sheringham. It surprised me that he did not choose to have a grave in the town cemetery which overlooks the sea and his beloved Sheringham golf club where he was club captain and which still displays his photograph on the walls of the members' lounge.

☐ William CLARKE

Nottingham-born in 1798, Clarke was a slow underarm leg-break bowler, then medium-paced round-arm. Despite handicap of losing eye in early life, was the champion of bowlers. Reverted to underarm style when many who played it well had left the game. Was landlord of the Bell Inn at 18 Angel Row, Nottingham, where a plaque placed high on front wall in 2001. Through second marriage took on the Trent Bridge Inn in Nottingham and developed the field next door into a cricket ground. In 1846 "… abandoned this loss-making venture and went to London .. to create his privately run All-England Eleven" [from history. trentbridge.co.uk]. Died in Wandsworth, London, on 25 August 1856 and was buried in South Metropolitan (now West Norwood Cemetery) in grave 65/5078. Became an unmarked plot. When area was cleared 35 years ago as a Garden of Remembrance, planned that small plaque would record it was Clarke's grave. In the 2000s Nottinghamshire club administrator Alex Picker collected enough funding for a new headstone over his grave. In 1990 Sir Richard Hadlee renamed a stand at Trent Bridge Ground in honour of Clarke.

The Bell Inn, Angel Row, Nottingham   *Sat Nav*   NG1 6HL
Trent Bridge Ground *Sat Nav* NG2 6AG   West Norwood Cemetery *Sat Nav*   SE27 9JU

Biography : *"William Clarke: The Old General"* by Peter Wynne-Thomas (ACS Lives in Cricket publications, 2011)

• There is no evidence of the original memorial at Norwood but "…. in 1966 Peter Wynne-Thomas found what he was fairly sure were the railings that surrounded the grave." [this from Bob Flanagan's 1995 booklet on the West Norwood Cemetery's Sportsmen]. The new memorial to Clarke was erected in January 2005 by E.Gill and Sons of Newark, who provided it at cost price following donations from cricket fans across the country.

☐ Johnny CLAY

Fast bowler at Winchester School, turned to off-breaks. At his best in 1930s, winning Test cap in 1935. Glamorgan skipper between 1924-27 resigning for business reasons. Player and county treasurer in 1930s, ensured survival of club. Returned to county cricket after WW2, took 6-48 in vital match v Hampshire, helping

William Clarke's new headstone being put in place in West Norwood by fund-raiser Alex Picker in 2005.

(below) Colin Cowdrey's grave at Poling, near Arundel, Sussex.

COLIN
THE LORD COWDREY
OF TONBRIDGE
C.B.E
1932 ~ 2000
"...some journey, some life,
some coverdrive,
some friend."

Glamorgan to 1948 county title. Test selector for two seasons. Died at Cowbridge on 11 August 1973 and funeral held at St Hilary's church, Cowbridge on 14 August: buried in graveyard. A Johnny Clay steeplechase used to take place annually at Chepstow racecourse but is no longer run today.

St Hilary's church, Cowbridge   *Sat Nav*   CF71 7DP

☐ James COBBETT

A 'crack' batsman and round-arm spin bowler from Frimley, Surrey. Moved to London to join the M.C.C. groundstaff at Lord's. One of finest all-round players of his generation. Died of consumption at his Marylebone home, 31 March 1842, aged 38. Buried in Kensal Green Cemetery. An upright stone of red granite, with rails, marks his grave on South Avenue, and is inscribed: "This stone was erected by a few of his brother cricketers as a last tribute to the memory of one who lived respected and died regretted."

Kensal Green Cemetery, London   *Sat Nav*   W10 4RA

☐ A.E.J. [Albert] COLLINS

The scorer of once record high innings in all cricket, 628* for Clark House v North Town at Clifton College in 1899. Never appeared in first-class cricket. In WW1 served as Company Captain in Royal Engineers and died in First Battle of Ypres, Belgium, on 11 November 1914. The Army Graves Service was unable to find his body so commemorated by name on Panel 9 of Menin Gate Memorial at Ypres (now Ieper) in West Flanders. His bat was displayed in pavilion with scorecard and picture of him after his record innings. Plaque unveiled by Duke of Beaufort, now set in wall opposite

the Tribe Building, overlooking Collins' Field at Clifton College.

Clifton College (access by permission)   *Sat Nav*   BS8 3EZ
Menin Gate is in east of Ieper, Belgium, on road to Menen and Kortrijk.

Biography : *"A Season's Fame: How A E J Collins made cricket's highest individual score"* by Derek Winterbottom (Historical Association, 1991)

• Collins' record was overtaken in January 2016 when a 15 year-old in Mumbai, Pranav Dhanawade, scored 1009 not out – but with a much heftier bat.

☐ Denis COMPTON

Batsman and slow left-arm bowler from Hendon, joined M.C.C. groundstaff 1934. Youngest player ever to score 1000 runs in English season. Chosen for first of his 78 Tests for England 1937 and scored century in 1938 Ashes series, aged 19. Record holder for most f-c runs in an English season (3,816) and most centuries (18) in 1947. Football for Arsenal including 1950 Cup Final, though collision in 1938 caused left knee injury which later hampered mobility. Scored 100th hundred in 1952. Retired 1957 to become sports writer and commentator. CBE 1958. Lived at Little Manor, Burnham Beeches, Buckinghamshire. The two stands at Nursery End of Lord's Cricket Ground, named in honour of Denis Compton and Bill Edrich, officially opened by Compton on 27 May 1991. Shenley Cricket Centre, Herts, renamed the Denis Compton Oval. Annual 'Denis Compton Awards' launched

1996 to provide promising cricketers with wider experience by playing in South Africa. Compton's death came in hospital in Windsor, Berkshire, on 23 April 1997 (St George's Day) through septicaemia following a hip operation. Funeral in Fulmer church and ashes later scattered on pitch at Lord's. A Compton-Miller Medal inaugurated 2005 for best player of each Ashes series.

Shenley Cricket Centre, Radlett Lane *Sat Nav* WD7 9DW
Lord's Cricket Ground *Sat Nav* NW8 8QN

Biographies : "Playing for England" autobiography (1949); "In Sun and Shadow" autobiography (Stanley Paul, 1952) "End Of An Innings" autobiography (Oldbourne, 1958); "Denis Compton: A Cricketing Sketch" by E W Swanton (Sporting Handbooks, 1948); "Denis Compton - A Biography" by Ian Peebles (Macmillan, 1971); "Denis Compton: Cricketing Genius" by Peter West (Stanley Paul, 1989); "Denis Compton" by Frank Keating (Richard Walsh Books, 1996); "Denis Compton: The Untold Story" by Norman Giller (Andre Deutsch, 1997); "Denis Compton: The Life Of A Sporting Hero" aka "Denis Compton: The Authorised Biography" by Tim Heald (Aurum Press, 2006).

• Brother Leslie Compton also played cricket for Middlesex and football for Arsenal. Died in 1984 and ashes scattered in beds at Golders Green Crematorium where there is a plaque to him and his wife Diana.

bronchial condition but suffered fatal heart attack in a Hampstead hospital (London) on 1 July 1971. Body flown home and lay in state in Port of Spain's Cathedral of the Immaculate Conception. State funeral on Thursday 8 July. Cortege and gun carriage bearing casket passed through the city to cathedral and then to RC church at Arouca, 15 miles east of Port-of-Spain. Interred in Constantine family plot where his father, a poor cocoa farmer, and grandfather, a slave, also buried. Second West Indian, after Frank Worrell, to be given memorial service in Westminster Abbey. Commemorated with English Heritage blue plaque at former London home 101 Lexham Gardens; and another placed in 2011 at Lancashire home, 3 Meredith Street in Pendle where lived between 1930 and 1949 while playing for Nelson.

Lexham Gardens plaque, Kensington *Sat Nav* W8 6JN
Meredith Street, Pendle   *Sat Nav*   BB9 0BZ

Biographies : "Cricket in the Sun" autobiography (Stanley Paul, 1947); "Learie Constantine" by Gerald Howat (Allen & Unwin 1975); "A Look at Learie Constantine" by Undine Giuseppi (Nelson, 1974); "Learie Constantine" by Peter Mason (Caribbean Lives, Signal Books, 2008).

☐ [Sir] Learie CONSTANTINE

Born Diego Martin, Trinidad, 1902. Typified the exciting West Indian cricketer: hard-hitting batsman, spectacular fielder and fast bowler. On West Indies' tour of 1928 joined Giffen, Armstrong and other overseas players achieving 'double' in England. Signed for Nelson and played Lancashire League until 1939, paving way for other overseas professionals. War ended Test career after 18 appearances. MBE 1946. Embarked on legal and political career; Minister of Works and High Commissioner for Trinidad government; member of Race Relations Board; knighted 1962 and elevated to peerage 1969. Intending to retire to Caribbean in 1971 for worsening

☐ 'Sam' COOK

Named 'Cecil' but always known as 'Sam'. Accurate slow left-arm bowler for Gloucestershire who dismissed batsman with first ball in f-c cricket; and eventually took nearly 1,800 wickets. Capped for England once. Umpire in 1965 season, then 1971-86. Died in his birthplace, Tetbury, on 5 September 1996 and buried in far section of St Saviour's churchyard, Tetbury: section N, row 5, grave number 26. Well-kept headstone.

St Saviour's, New Church Street *Sat Nav* GL8 8DS

Biography: "Sam Cook" by Alan Gibson (Richard Walsh Books, 1992)

In loving
memory of
a dear wife
and mother
DAISY ANN
COOK
died 20th July
1988
...d 67 years

Also
in memory of
a dear father
CECIL (SAM)
COOK
died 5th Sept
1996
aged 75 years

☐ Bill COPSON

Derbyshire fast bowler, one of many to
emerge from mining industry. Bowling
prowess hardly noticed until 18 when G
R Jackson put him into county side, and
he took Sandham's wicket with first ball.
Toured Australia 1936-37 but his three Tests
not until after WW2. Took 8-11 v Warwicks
1937, including five wickets in six balls.
Retired 1949, having taken nearly 1,100
wickets. County coach, league professional,
first-class umpire. Suddenly taken ill at
work at Clay Cross Foundry, and died on
13 September 1971. Funeral at Brimington
Crematorium, Chesterfield. Tree planted
by side of driveway entrance to the
crematorium, and dedicated to memory of
Copson and his wife.

Brimington Crematorium *SatNav* S43 1AU

Biography: *"More than Miner Interest"* by Kit Bartlett
(ACS Lives in Cricket publications, 2008)

☐ [Lord] Colin COWDREY

Teenage prodigy at golf and squash as well
as cricket. Aged 13, was youngest schoolboy
to play at Lord's. Blue plaque placed in
2013 on Ferox Hall in Tonbridge High
Street, where he was a boarder at Tonbridge
School in 1940s. First appearance for Kent
1950. Stylish and graceful stroke-player on
the field, courteous and kind off it. Cricket
Writers' Club picked him as its Young
Cricketer of the Year in 1953. On Australian
tour 1954-55 maiden hundred at Sydney
(103 out of 191) not only brought England
recovery from collapse but demonstrated
potential. Played in 114 Test matches, a
quarter of them as captain, but never secure
in the position owing to perception he
lacked either steel or dynamism. Toured
Australia with M.C.C. six times, lastly
called up as a reinforcement against Lillee
and Thomson in 1974-75. Kent captain from
1957, led county to the Gillette Cup in 1967
and championship in 1970. In 1976 retired
from f-c cricket with nearly 43,000 runs to
his name and over 600 catches: famously
asked himself how he could justify a quarter
of a century of his life spent standing at slip.
President of M.C.C. 1986, chairman of I.C.C.
1989-93, introducing the code of conduct
and match referees, and overseeing South
Africa's reintegration to Test cricket. CBE
1972, knighted in 1992 and peerage 1997.
Died of a heart attack at his Angmering
Park home on 4 December 2000, having
suffered a stroke earlier that year. Buried
beside church gate of St Nicholas, Poling,
near Arundel, Sussex. Epitaph, written by
John Woodcock : "...some journey, some
life, some cover drive, some friend." At
memorial service in Westminster Abbey
on 30 March 2001, tribute given by former
Prime Minister John Major. His old car
number plate MCC 307 is in Arundel Castle
cricket pavilion.

Tonbridge School *Sat Nav* TN9 1JX Church of St
Nicholas, Poling *Sat Nav* BN18 9PT Arundel Castle
ground *SatNav* BN18 9LH

Biography : *"Time for Reflection"* autobiography (Frederick Muller, 1962); *"The Incomparable Game"* autobiograpy (Hodder & Stoughton, 1970); *"MCC - the Autobiography of a Cricketer"* (Hodder & Stoughton 1976); *"The Last Roman - A Biography of Colin Cowdrey"* by Mark Peel (Andre Deutsch, 1999);

☐ George COX senior

Solid professional for Sussex from 1895 to 1928. Right-handed bat, sound in defence, and left-arm slow, occasionally medium-paced bowler. In county matches took more wickets than anyone except Tate, including, at age of 50, 100 in a season. County coach. Marker in memorial garden in n.w. corner of *Hove County Ground*. Devoted man of Sussex, lived all his life at Warnham. Died suddenly at daughter's house in Dorking 24 March 1949 and buried in Warnham parish churchyard. Son George also gave long service to Sussex.

St Margaret's church, Warnham   *Sat Nav*   RH12 3QW
Sussex County Ground, Hove   *Sat Nav*   BN3 3AN

☐ Albert CRAIG

"The Surrey Poet". Was born in Huddersfield and briefly a post office clerk, but came south and used to sell his verses among the crowds at The Oval, aided by a witty sales pitch such as "Can I sell a few to you gentlemen before I go among the public?" Died at Southwark on 8 July 1909. Funeral at Stockwell and buried in common grave in square 88 of Nunhead Cemetery. Later removed to private grave (29646 in square 16) but has no memorial.

Nunhead Cemetery   *Sat Nav*   SE15 3LP **Biography :** *"Captain of the Crowd: Albert Craig, Cricket and Football Rhymester"* by Tony Laughton (Boundary Books, 2008)

☐ Jack CRAWFORD

Born in Coulsdon, Surrey, where father was chaplain to psychiatric hospital (then called Cane Hill asylum, and since demolished in 2010). While a Repton schoolboy, joined Surrey 1904 to bowl lively off-cutters and took 44 wickets in 5 weeks. Leading public school cricketer of his time. Picked for M.C.C. South African tour of 1905-06 at age of 19. Next year achieved 'the double', but Test and county careers closed in 1909 following disagreements with Surrey committee. Emigrated to South Australia, playing for state until First World War. Came home at end of WW1, briefly rejoined Surrey. Manager with Elders & Fyffes. Career record conceals true potential, as does selection for only 12 Tests. Died at Ewell Hospital on 2 May 1963. After funeral at Ewell's St Mary's church, cremation at South London Crematorium, Streatham. Ashes scattered in the lavender garden at plot CK/35 but no memorial apart from his entry in Book of Remembrance.

Biography: *"The Practical Cricketer"* autobiographical (Health & Strength, Ltd, 1909); *"Trip to Kangaroo Land"* autobiography (Cricket Offices, 1909); *"A Flick of the Fingers – The Chequered Life and Career of Jack Crawford"* by Michael Burns (Pitch Publishing, 2015); *"Rebel with a Cause"* by Keith and Jennifer Booth (Chequered Flag, 2016)

• He was another major cricketer whose last resting place I could not find but really wanted to include. I had gained the impression that Crawford did something badly wrong and went to South Australia in disgrace but the recent biography by Michael Burns showed his disagreement with Surrey was relatively trivial. The publication of that book also seemed promising to help locate his grave but, as I turned to the last pages, alas it was not mentioned, Eventually a newspaper death notice enabled me to 'track Crawford down'. There turned out to be no memorial beyond an entry in the Book of Remembrance but it brought a lengthy search to a close.

Richard DAFT

Born into a large family of cricketers, which formed an occasional XI. Stylish back-foot player, able to score heavily on rough pitches of day. In 1870s only W.G. Grace was his superior, and Shrewsbury modelled himself on Daft. Succeeded George Parr as captain of All-England XI. Died from heart disease at his Radcliffe-on-Trent, Notts., home on 18 July 1900 and funeral held at Radcliffe Cemetery. Daft's grave is approx. 50 metres further along main path than Parr's on right-hand side, near gardeners' green hut. Cross had fallen but his name on pedestal. Grave renovated and rededicated in 2008.

Radcliffe Cemetery   *Sat Nav*   NG12 2FB

Biography : *"Kings of Cricket: Reminiscences and Anecdotes"* by Richard Daft   (pub J. W. Arrowsmith/ Simpkin, Marshall, Hamilton, Kent & Co, 1893); *"Richard Daft: On a Pedestal"* by Neil Jenkinson (ACS Lives in Cricket publications, 2008)

John DANIELL

In the eleven at Clifton School (contemporary of C.L. Townsend), and Cambridge blue 1899-1901. Either dogged or hard-hitting batsman as required, and magnificent field. Somerset debut 1898 and last match 1927; captaincy after Sammy Woods 1908-12, missing several seasons in India, and 1919-26. Officer in France in WW1. Known as 'The Prophet', England selector. Also, England rugby forward and captain. Died at Holway Farm House, Somerset, on 24 January 1963, and cremated at Canford in Bristol. His ashes returned (posted back to his family) - unknown whether any memorial was ever made.

James 'Jemmy' DEAN

Fast round-arm bowler and wicket-keeper known as "The Sussex Ploughboy". Played for county and M.C.C. for more than 25 seasons. Also, Clarke's All-England XI. Landlord of inn at Duncton and died on premises on Christmas Day 1881. Buried in parish churchyard of his birth village, Duncton near Petworth, Sussex. His likeness was depicted on inn sign outside The Cricketers at Duncton, but now shows W G Grace.

The Cricketers Inn, Duncton   *Sat Nav*   GU28 0LB

George DENNETT

Slow left-arm spinner. At the time the highest wicket-taker in f-c cricket never to play for England; Gloucestershire withdrew him from M.C.C. side to South Africa in 1905 fearing the strain might impair his performance next season. Coach at Cheltenham College 1926-34 until ill-health meant Alec Kennedy brought in to succeed him. Died 15 September 1937 at his home on Old Bath Road, Cheltenham. Funeral in the College chapel. Interred in Canford Cemetery, at Westbury-on-Trym, where he had played for the local cricket club whenever available.

Canford Cemetery   *Sat Nav*   BS9 3PQ

David DENTON

Made more runs for Yorkshire than anyone else except Sutcliffe: more than 33,000 with sixty centuries. Despite brilliance of batting and magnificent fielding, given only eleven matches for England. Ill-health brought career to close in 1921, also thwarted offers to

score for Yorkshire or coach at Haileybury. Later able to serve as first-class umpire. Died on 16 February 1950 at home in Denby Dale Road, Thornes, and, following service at Grove Methodist church, interred in Thornes parish churchyard. St James's church stands on A636 road, south of Wakefield. Denton's grave lies 40 metres due south of church and has black headstone with gold lettering.

St James's parish churchyard   *Sat Nav*   WF2 8DN

☐ *Hugh de SELINCOURT*

Literary and drama critic, noteworthy as writer of dozens of village cricket stories, esp *"The Cricket Match"* (1924). Journalist John Parker wrote a sequel to it 50 years later, called *"The Village Cricket Match"* (1977). Fanatical club cricketer with Storrington C.C. Died at home, 'The Sand Pit', Thakeham, nr Horsham, Sussex, on 20 January 1951. Ashes collected from Brighton (Woodvale) Crematorium, by funeral directors. Memorial is his entry made in North Chapel volume of Woodvale's Book of Remembrance.

• His cremated remains were taken away from Woodvale by the funeral directors who were based at that time in Storrington. But what happened to them is not known. Looking at the monumental inscriptions for both Storrington and Thakeham, de Selincourt's name does not appear.

☐ *Teddy DIVER*

School teacher at Wimbledon College, called up for Surrey and appeared for The Gentlemen as batsman. Became professional with Surrey when his school closed, but after one season returned to teaching in his home town of Cambridge. Eight years with Warwickshire C.C.C. which he captained before going to South Wales in 1901. Groundsman and professional at Newport C.C. Steel worker in Swansea [information from ACS Journal 28]. Died alone in poverty at his lodgings at Pontardawe, Glamorgan, 27 December 1924 and buried nearby at Alltwen Chapel. Gravestone paid for by contributions from his former clubs.

Alltwen chapel   *Sat Nav*   SA8 3BP

☐ *John DIXON*

Amateur batsman from Grantham, played with Notts from 1882. County captain 1889 to '99. Topped 1000 runs in 1897, including score of 268* which beat Shrewsbury's record. Test selector 1905, in which season

The Dixon Gates © John Sutton 2009 (image cropped) licensed under Creative Commons license Attribution-ShareAlike 2.0

played last match. Chairman of wholesale clothing company in Grantham. Died in Nottingham on 8 June 1931. Buried in The Rock Cemetery in Nottingham "… where a memorial stands, which also marks the grave of his wife, who died as recently as July 1975." [from history.trentbridge. co.uk] At Trent Bridge Ground the Dixon Gates, designed by local architect Harry Goodall, with plaque on piers. Formally dedicated on 2 May 1933, when Dixon's widow and daughters were the first to walk through them.

Church (The Rock) Cemetery *Sat Nav* NG1 4HT Trent Bridge Ground, Bridgford Road *Sat Nav* NG2 6AG

☐ *Basil D'OLIVEIRA*

From Cape Town. Denied opportunities by apartheid-era South Africa's government and their racial classification as 'coloured'. Arrived in Britain as Middleton C.C.'s professional in 1960. In 1991 sheltered housing in Middleton named as D'Oliveira Court. His widow Naomi unveiled a plaque at the cricket club in May 2012. Joined Worcestershire staff in 1964 and capped by England in 1966. Despite scoring 158 in final Test at The Oval 1968, omitted from M.C.C.'s 1968-69 tour party, which precipitated South Africa's eventual exclusion from international cricket. 44 Test appearances and 5 hundreds. The main stand at New Road Cricket Ground named after him in 2003. CBE 2005. Died in Worcester on 18 November 2011. Fund-raising to site a bronze statue by sculptor John McKenna at Worcester county ground started in 2012.

Middleton Cricket Club, Towncroft Ave *Sat Nav* M24 5DA D'Oliveira Court, Wood Street *Sat Nav* M24 5QU New Road Cricket Ground, Worcester *Sat Nav* WR2 4QQ

Biography : *"D'Oliveira -: An Autobiography"* (Collins, 1968); *"Time to Declare"* autobiography (J.M.Dent, 1980); *"Basil D'Oliveira: Cricket and Conspiracy, the Untold Story"* by Peter Oborne (Little Brown, 2005).

☐ *[Horace Edgar]* '*Tom*' DOLLERY

Learned his cricket at Reading School which has a plaque to him in Big School hall. Came to Warwickshire 1934 as attacking batsman from Berkshire and made 1000 runs a season throughout career. Forte was shrewd and skillful captaincy. First professional in 20th century county cricket to be regular skipper and led Warwicks to top, becoming champions in 1951. Four Test caps. Retired 1955. Test selector 1957-58. Died 20 January 1987 in Queen Elizabeth Hospital. Funeral at Lodge Hill Crematorium on 28 January and ashes taken away by family. Tom Dollery Suite at Edgbaston Cricket Ground officially opened by his widow Jeanne.

Edgbaston Cricket Ground *Sat Nav* B5 7QU Reading School (visit by appointment only) *Sat Nav* RG1 5LW

Biography *"Professional Captain"* (Stanley Paul, 1952).

☐ *J.W.H.T.* [*Johnny*] DOUGLAS

First-class career began with three ducks, perhaps why given to defence, hence 'Johnny Won't Hit Today'. Also, a fast-medium swing bowler, became captain of M.C.C. on three overseas tours. Tough and sometimes quick-tempered skipper was highly successful pre-WW1, but after War lost all five Tests in Australia 1920-21 then two more in 1921 before deposed for Tennyson. Yet his best county performance came in that year against Derbyshire, taking 9-47 and scoring unbeaten 210; too tired to bowl until end of second innings when captured two more wickets at no cost. Retired from county cricket 1928. Amateur soccer player and an Olympic middleweight boxing champion in 1908. Timber business in Theydon Bois, Essex. After six-week business trip in Scandinavia, embarked for Hull on 19 December 1930 on ship 'Oberon'; collided with another vessel in Kattegat.

Went down in three minutes; Douglas and his father lost. Memorial services at Leyton on 28 December and two days later at St Michael's, Cornhill. At his old school, Felsted, the memorial to Douglas took form of the 'New' Pavilion, opened in June 1933.

Felsted School (not public access)   *Sat Nav*   CM6 3LL

Biography : *"Johnny Won't Hit Today"* by David Lemmon (George Allen & Unwin, 1983)

☐ *Andrew DUCAT*

Like many contemporaries, played both cricket (for Surrey) and football (an FA Cup winner, and Fulham manager) professionally. One Test appearance in 1921. Became a sports reporter, also cricket coach at Eton College. Lived at Enton Green, nr Witley. Having been in a traffic accident earlier that morning, played for Surrey Home Guard v Sussex at Lord's on 23 July 1942, but collapsed with heart attack at the crease. Said to have already expired by the time he was brought to pavilion but taken to Paddington Hospital to be pronounced dead. Funeral at Golders Green Crematorium and ashes dispersed on the main lawn. His entry in the book of remembrance - "At Rest 1942. International cricketer and footballer. Loved and greatly missed by all" - may be viewed in the Chapel.

Golders Green Crematorium   *Sat Nav*   NW11 7NL

☐ *George DUCKWORTH*

Keen, competitive wicket-keeper. While Warrington-born, he came from second XI cricket with Warwickshire to play for Lancashire. Debut 1923, chosen following year for England. 24 Tests in all. On three M.C.C. tours of Australia and one of South Africa. Weak batting lost him his place to Ames. In 1938 to minor counties matches. Active retirement after WW2 as organiser of Commonwealth tours of India 1949-50, '50-51 and '53-54 ; baggage master and scorer on M.C.C. tours 1954-5, '56-7 and '58-9; county scorer; radio summariser. Died in Warrington General Hospital on 6 January 1966 and funeral held next day at Warrington parish church, followed by cremation at Walton Lea Crematorium. Ashes interred in Garden of Remembrance the day after cremation. In Birchwood, Warrington, is the Oakwood Gate double roundabout, a long traffic island that was named George Duckworth Island, though nicknamed locally as "dog-bone roundabout"

George Duckworth Island   *SatNav*   WA3 6AN

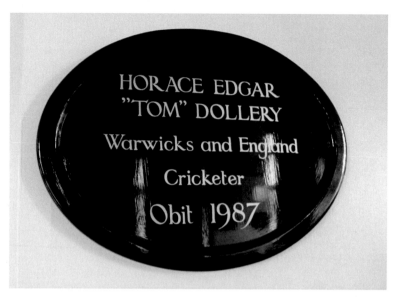

Tom Dollery plaque (Image © 2015 Frances Greaney, Reading School)

Oakwood Gate roundabout at Birchwood, Warrington, named as 'George Duckworth Island'
Image © 2007 Mike Harris - licensed under Creative Commons License.

☐ Bill EDRICH

One of four brothers from Norfolk family who played f-c cricket. Represented Norfolk aged 16 and subsequently signed for Middlesex as opening batsman. 1000 runs by end of May 1938 and Test debut v Australia, but only 88 runs in first 8 Tests before double-century (219) in the Timeless Test at Durban. Wartime bomber pilot, awarded DFC. In golden summer of 1947 scored 3,539 f-c runs, mostly in partnership with Denis Compton. 39 Test match appearances for England, averaging exactly 40. On retirement in 1958 into business. Returned to Norfolk and minor counties cricket 1965-71. Died on 24 April 1986, shortly after 70th birthday after falling down the stairs at home in Whitehill Court, Chesham, Buckinghamshire. Funeral service at St Mary's parish church, Chesham, in May. Ashes later collected to be scattered by his widow on the square at Lord's Cricket Ground. The Compton and Edrich Stands at Lord's opened by Denis Compton and cousin John Edrich in 1991.

Lord's Cricket Ground   *Sat Nav*   NW8 8QN

Biographies : *"Cricket Heritage"* autobiography (Stanley Paul 1948); *"Cricketing Days"* autobiography (Stanley Paul, 1950); *"Round the Wicket"* autobiography (Frederick Muller, 1959); *"The Cricketing Family Edrich"* by Ralph Barker (Pelham, 1976); *"Bill Edrich: A Biography"* by Alan Hill (Andre Deutsch, 1994)

☐ Tom EMMETT

Left-hander, bowling round-arm at brisk pace. Enjoyed long career as professional cricketer with clubs, touring sides, leagues and schools. From modest beginnings (turned up at first match with his kit wrapped in old newspaper) selected for George Parr's XI and for county. Made four pioneering tours with English teams and appeared in first Test match 1877. On retiring from Yorkshire, aged 46, appointed coach at Rugby School and county coach for Leicestershire. Died in poverty at home in Leicester. Cause of death: apoplectic fit (stroke) on 29 June 1904. Buried in Welford Road Cemetery, Leicester, in grave O 2946.

Welford Road Cemetery and Visitor Centre   *Sat Nav*   LE2 6BB

☐ Godfrey EVANS

Outstanding wicket-keeper. Won 91 Test caps, keeping his England place with few interruptions between 1946 and 1959. Always caught the eye with remarkable reflexes and agility, especially lightning-fast leg-side takes standing up to the stumps. Ebullient in the field, trying to energise his side. Stalwart of Kent, from joining groundstaff aged 16 and debut in 1939 to his retirement from f-c cricket in 1959 after being dropped by England "in the interests of team-building". Brief comeback in Canterbury week 1967. Dismissed 1,066 victims in all f-c cricket. CBE awarded 1960. Ever cheerful, became landlord of the Jolly Drover, West Sussex. For 20 years cricket advisor to bookmaker Ladbrokes. Died in Northampton General Hospital on 3 May 1999. His ashes scattered on the square at St Lawrence ground, Canterbury. One of twelve Kent cricketers named to be honoured in the Legends' Walkway at the ground. In Tonbridge a road, Godfrey Evans Close, was named in his memory; nearby roads similarly named after other Kent worthies, Blythe and Woolley.

Godfrey Evans Close, Tonbridge   *Sat Nav*   TN10 4JW
The Spitfire Ground, St Lawrence, Canterbury   *Sat Nav* CT1 3NZ

Biography : *"Behind the Stumps"* autobiography (Hodder & Stoughton, 1951); *"The Gloves are Off"* autobiography (Hodder & Stoughton, 1960); *"Godfrey Evans: A Biography"* by Christopher Sandford (Simon & Schuster, 1990)

☐ Arthur FAGG

Trial for Kent at age of 16. Opening batsman of high promise yet ill-health limited Test opportunities to only 5 appearances: early return from Australian tour 1936-37. In 1938 unique feat of two double centuries in match. Unfit for front-line War duty, so fire service and agricultural department, and coach at Cheltenham College. 58 centuries scored in career. After retiring in 1957 set up family greengrocer and florist at Southborough, run by son. F-c umpire from 1959-76 and Test umpire 1967-75. Lived at "Maridon" in London Road where Southborough Society affixed a plaque. Died in Tunbridge Wells 13 September 1977. After his funeral at Kent & Sussex Crematorium on 16 Sept ashes disposed of by burial in the Lawns of Remembrance.

Maridon, Southborough [private residence]   *Sat Nav* TN4 0 UJ

☐ Michael FALCON

Born Horstead House, Norfolk, 1888. Grand Old Man of Norfolk cricket, represented county from 1906 to 1946, and captain from 1912. All the attributes of great fast bowler but declined several offers to play f-c county cricket owing to career as barrister, businessman and MP. Occasional matches for The Gentlemen. Died suddenly at home in The Close, Norwich, on 27 February

1976. Funeral service at Norwich Cathedral, followed by cremation at Horsham St Faiths Crematorium. In his memory two benches placed at Norfolk's new ground, Manor Park in Horsford, north of Norwich.

Horstead House (private, but gardens open February) *Sat Nav* NR12 7AU   Manor Park, Horsford *Sat Nav* NR10 3AQ

Biography: *"Michael Falcon, Norfolk's Gentleman Cricketer"* by Stephen Musk (ACS Lives in Cricket publications, 2010)

☐ Frederick FANE

Born in Ireland, but schooled in England. Opening batsman with Essex and captain 1904-06. Made two Test tours with M.C.C. (and 3 other winter tours), appearing in 14 Test matches, including reluctantly captain when AO Jones unwell. Schoolmaster at Chigwell. In WW1 awarded Military Cross. Died 27 November 1960 after month's illness at home, 'Priors', in Brentford. Funeral at Kelvedon Hatch parish church and buried in churchyard.

St Nicholas church, Kelvedon Hatch *Sat Nav* CM14 5TJ

☐ Kenneth FARNES

Fast bowler with Essex in 1930s. Played as amateur, being schoolmaster at Worksop College. 15 Test appearances, taking 60 wickets. Killed on 20 October 1941, piloting plane of RAF Training Unit at Chipping Warden, near Banbury (not in Canada as was reported at the time; his unit returned from Canada six weeks before accident). Buried with full military honours within Brookwood Necropolis, Surrey, on 27 October when Percy Chapman among mourners. Farnes lies in grave 11 / plot 21a of RAF section of Brookwood Memorial, on left of central lawn, in front of second plot. Headstone records "He died as he lived, playing the game".

Biography : *"Tours and Tests"* autobiography
(Lutterworth Press, 1940); *"Ken Farnes: Diary of an Essex
Master"* by David Thurlow (Parrs Wood Press, 2000).

• His old club, Gidea Park, erected a modern scoreboard
to his memory at Gallows Corner ground in 1950. It burnt
down in 1973 but plaque was saved for display in the club
Long Room.

☐ *Aubrey FAULKNER*

Key figure in early South African cricket,
a great all-rounder, batting right-handed
and bowling leg-breaks. 25 international
appearances. Made three Test tours, firstly
to England as one of googly quartet in 1907,
again in 1912. In 1910-11 scored 545 runs and
took 29 wickets in Test series in Australia.
Served as Major in British Army in WW1,
winning DSO. Opened world's first indoor
cricket school in Walham Green, south-west
London. After long illness underwent two
successful operations but depressed by his
condition. Found dead on 10 September
1930, having gassed himself at cricket
school in Farm Lane, Fulham. After inquest,
buried in North Sheen Cemetery, Surrey, in
grave MC 275.

North Sheen Cemetery   *Sat Nav*   TW9 4LL

Biography : *"Aubrey Faulkner"* by Brian Bassano (ACS
Famous Cricketers series, 2001)

• Locating Aubrey Faulkner's grave in the 1980s, I found it
in a dilapidated condition and I thought the South African
Cricket Board might wish to know and consider getting
it repaired.   An enthusiastic reply from Ali Bacher asked
me to obtain a quotation for the grave's renovation but
in the end the Board felt it was unable to afford to see
the renovation through, and the grave is now in very poor
condition [for image, see www.findagrave]

☐ *Nicholas FELIX*

Instead of Wanostrocht, his real surname,
used 'Felix' to avoid association with his
father's school in Camberwell, Surrey.
Amateur batsman with Kent, best left-
hander of day, in career between 1830 (first
f-c match for M.C.C.) and 1852. Played
also for Clarke's All-England XI. In 1845
his "Felix On The Bat" published, one
of cricket's earliest instruction manuals;
he drew all plates himself. Thought to
have invented batting gloves, he certainly
invented early bowling machine, the
'catapulta'. Died at Wimborne, Dorset, on 3
September 1876 at home in 1 (now 23) Julian
Villas and buried in section 7 of Wimborne
Cemetery. Go up steep drive but, before it
divides towards two chapels, grave is five
spaces in from drive on LHS.

Wimborne Cemetery   *Sat Nav*   BH21 1FX

Biography : *"Felix on the Bat - a memoir of Nicholas Felix"*
by Gerald Brodribb (Eyre & Spottiswoode, 1962)

☐ *Percy FENDER*

Fine cricketer at St Paul's and for Public
Schools XI. Wisden C of Y 1915 at age of
23. Hard-hitting batsman, scored hundred
in 35 minutes against Northamptonshire in
1920 to break Jessop's record: remains the
fastest 100 in f-c cricket (apart from when
bowlers deliberately gift runs). Leg-spinner,
six times completed the 'double'. Shrewd
captain of Surrey 1921-31 when Jardine
replaced him, but never for England after
crossing Lord Harris. Newspaper journalist
and author of four England tour books.
After retirement concentrated on wine
trade. In late 1970s lost eyesight and lived
with daughter. Died on 15 June 1985 in an
Exeter nursing home. Buried in Higher
Cemetery, Exeter, Devon: plot reference

HL, grave number 123. Grave is on eastern side of cemetery, beside a broad circle in the tarmac path beneath a copper beech.

Higher Cemetery, Pinhoe Road   *Sat Nav*   EX1 2PX

Biography : *"P G H Fender, A Biography"* by Richard Streeton (Faber & Faber 1981)

previously always in best of health. Funeral on 19 November, paid for by friends who had just arranged a coaching post for him, held in Church of England Cemetery, now known as West Street Cemetery, Durban. Grave rediscovered in 1985 and wreath laid by Kim Hughes, captain of visiting Australian 'rebel' team.

Biography : *"Something Uncommon in the Flight : the Life of J J Ferris"* by Max Bonnell (Roger Page Cricket Books, Yallambie, Victoria, 2013)

☐ Bill FERGUSON

Australian-born 'Fergie' was scorer and baggageman to touring teams for over fifty years. First invited 1905 to assist Australians on England tour and afterwards reckoned he travelled 600,000 miles and scored in 208 Test matches. Awarded BEM in 1952 New Year Honours. Asked out of retirement by West Indians for 1957 tour but obliged by illness to give up halfway through. Died at home in Bath on 23 September 1957, days after release from Manor Hospital. Funeral at Locksbrook Cemetery, Lower Weston, Bath. 'Fergie' was buried in Walcot section, in family grave, Non 2nd Pink FJ 1007. Grave has marble kerbs and a headstone.

Locksbrook Cemetery   *Sat Nav*   BA1 3DQ

Biography : *"Mr Cricket"* by Bill Ferguson & David Jack (Nicholas Kaye, 1957)

☐ Jack [or John] FERRIS

Australian left-arm medium-pace bowler, toured England with Australian sides in 1888 and 1890, taking 199 and 186 wickets. Remained in England to play for Gloucestershire but first toured South Africa with W.W.Read's team, so representing two countries at Test cricket. Served in Brabant's Horse in Boer War and died of enteric fever in Addington Hospital, Durban, on 17 November 1900. 32 years of age and

☐ Arthur FIELDER

When Bradley retired in 1903, gained place in Kent XI. With beautiful action and real pace, became premier fast bowler of day. With Blythe played large part in winning four championships for Kent. 172 wickets in 1906 his best, and took all ten wickets in innings for Players v Gentlemen at Lord's. Twice selected for M.C.C. tours of Australia. Six Tests. Always batted last but added 235 with Woolley for Kent's last wicket in 1909, a record for county cricket. Ran newsagents and sweet shop in Beckenham. Died 30 August 1949 in St Thomas's Hospital, London. His ashes buried in Plaxtol churchyard, nr Sevenoaks, Kent.

Plaxtol parish church   *Sat Nav*   TN15 0QB

☐ William FINDLAY

Accomplished administrator, associated with Lord's for more than 30 years. Appointed assistant to Lacey in 1919, succeeded him as M.C.C. Secretary in 1926, and tenure included during Bodyline controversy. Was himself fine wicket-keeper in Lancashire's championship side of 1904. M.C.C. president in 1952. Died at retirement home in Tenterden, Ashford, Kent, on 19

'Felix' (Nicholas Wanostrocht) Wimborne Cemetery.

(below) Percy Fender Higher Cemetery, Exeter.

□ R.A. [Robert] FITZGERALD

Educated at Harrow School and Cambridge University. Hard-hitting batsman for Middlesex 1864 and Bucks from 1869. Led amateur team to North America 1872, wrote "Wickets in the West". Member of northern circuit, called to the Bar 1860. Hon secretary of M.C.C. 1863, then permanently 1867-76. Oversaw general expansion and improvement of club and pavilion. On 28 October 1881, after years of ill-health which ended career, died at residence in Chorley Wood (as area then called), Herts. Funeral on 3 November in Christ Church burial ground, facing Chorley Wood Common and in view of his house. His scrapbooks showing earliest known cricket photographs, which were taken by him, held in M.C.C. Museum at Lord's.

Lord's Cricket Ground   *Sat Nav*   NW8 8QN

June 1953 and buried in churchyard of Milstead parish church, near Sittingbourne, Kent, former home of wife's family. Grave marker is overgrown but with reasonably clear lettering, lies on northern side of church, near to a seat and shelter, 20 metres from path.

St Mary & Holy Cross church, Milstead *Sat Nav*   ME9 0RX

• A weeping ash was planted in 1953 in new Coronation Garden at Lord's with a circular seat to Findlay's memory placed around it.

□ Jack FLAVELL

Fast-medium spearhead of Worcestershire bowling attack when county won two championship titles in 1964 and '65. Worked as postman in winter to build strength in his legs. Won four caps for England. Retired after injuries in 1967 to start new career as restaurant owner. Died at Barmouth on 25 February 2004. Plaque placed in memorial garden at Worcestershire's county ground, New Road.

New Road Cricket Ground, Worcester *Sat Nav*   WR2 4QQ

☐ Wilfred FLOWERS

Reliable all-rounder from early Nottinghamshire cricket. First engaged by Worksop C.C. aged only 16. Two early 'Test' tours to Australia and played 8 times for England. Benefit match in 1899 to mark 21 years' service as member of Lord's groundstaff ended after only 3 hours of play, and then testimonial rained off, too. Had retired 1896 to become umpire until eyesight deteriorated and returned to lace trade; still at work in 70th year when died in Nottingham on 1 November 1926 and buried in Red Hill Cemetery.

Red Hill Cemetery *Sat Nav* NG5 8LS

☐ Paul FOLEY

Hon secretary of Worcestershire C.C.C. He instituted a competition for second-class counties in 1890s; obtained the land to rent at Worcester that became New Road ground; brought in new players; supported the club financially; and guided county to f-c status. Inherited the Stoke Edith estate in Herefordshire on death of a great aunt in 1900. Died suddenly in Westminster, on a visit to London, on 21 January 1928. Funeral at Stoke Edith church, 7 miles east of Hereford.

St Mary's church, Stoke Edith *Sat Nav* HR1 4HG

☐ Frank FOSTER

Unrelated to the Worcestershire Fosters. "A gilded cricketer who rose quickly and splendidly" [The Independent]. Right-handed batsman and left-arm fast bowler for Warwickshire 1908-14. Skipper for four seasons. Played innings of 305* at Dudley in 1914. Made one M.C.C. tour of Australia, when formed great opening pairing with S.F.Barnes. Only 11 Test matches. Career ended by motorcycle accident during WW1. Died in a Northampton psychiatric hospital 3 May 1958. Body cremated and buried at Brandwood End Cemetery, Kings Heath, Birmingham, on 9 May. From main gate, pass offices to right-hand side of mortuary chapel. Plot A2, grave no 116.

Brandwood End Cemetery *Sat Nav* B14 6EQ   New Road Ground, Worcester *Sat Nav* WR2 4QQ

Biographies : *"Cricketing Memories"* autobiography (London Publishing, 1930); *"The Fields Were Sudden Bare"* by Robert Brooke (ACS Lives in Cricket publications, 2011)

☐ R.E. [Reginald Erskine] FOSTER

Brilliant batsman and best of all the Foster brothers but, as a busy stockbroker, unable to devote time to cricket. Only one full season for Worcestershire and eight Tests for England, turning down all other opportunities. 'Tip' made record 287 on Test debut against Australia on 1903-04 M.C.C. tour. Double international, only man to captain England at both football and cricket. Died at home in Ovington Gardens, Kensington, London, on 13 May 1914. Cause of death: diabetes. Funeral at Golders Green Crematorium, followed by interment of ashes at Great Malvern Cemetery. Grave, to south of chapel and offices, has large flat cross and is number 2246. Restoration of the family grave by Malvern Civic Society to mark centenary of his death. Plaque also unveiled on centenary at Worcestershire's New Road Ground. Bat with which record score was made in Sydney lay in glass case in Malvern College pavilion; presented to M.C.C. Museum at Lord's 1983. Also, a bench in memory of all the Foster brothers on Malvern College sports field.

Great Malvern Cemetery *Sat Nav* WR14 2AS

• Anthony Collis intended to put out a biography in 2015 as part of a book he was researching on the Foster family, but is not yet completed

☐ *Arnold FOTHERGILL*

Newcastle-born, left-arm, medium-paced bowler, joined M.C.C. groundstaff in 1882 from minor counties cricket, appearing also for Somerset. Made 1888-89 tour to South Africa and played 2 Tests. Left M.C.C. to take up position as coach and groundkeeper at Repton and on retirement returned north to live with married daughter. Died after a heavy fall in Oakland Street, Sunderland, on 1 August 1932 and interred in Bishopwearmouth Cemetery.

Bishopwearmouth Cemetery *Sat Nav* SR4 7SU

☐ *George FREEMAN*

Fast round-arm bowler with Yorkshire from 1865, succeeded Jackson as fastest of his time. Short career ended by calls of business. Died of Bright's disease at Sowerby, nr Thirsk, on 18 November 1895 and interred in Sowerby parish churchyard. Record no 401.

St Oswald's church, Sowerby *Sat Nav* YO7 1JG

☐ *[Alfred Percy] 'Tich FREEMAN*

Record-breaking leg-spin bowler for Kent in 1920s and 30s. Made Kent debut in 1914 but best years came after 1928 season in which he captured 304 wickets. Took 200 wickets in each of seven subsequent seasons and finished career with total of 3,776 wickets: second only to Wilfred Rhodes. Less successful in Test cricket and chosen only 12 times for England. Retired 1936. Died at home, 'Dunbolin', in Bearsted, Kent, on 28 January 1965. Funeral held at Vintner's Park Crematorium, Maidstone, Kent. Ashes scattered on plot 4 of Gardens of Remembrance. Only memorial was entry in Book of Remembrance until wall plaque recording his many achievements unveiled at Kent's St Lawrence Ground in Canterbury in following August, alongside Ames' and Woolley's.

The Spitfire Ground, St Lawrence, Canterbury *Sat Nav* CT1 3NZ

Biography : *"Tich Freeman and the Decline of the Leg-Break Bowler"* by David Lemmon (George Allen & Unwin 1982)

• Freeman was one of twelve – Ames, Blythe, Cowdrey, Evans, Freeman, Knott, Luckhurst, Mynn, Shepherd, Underwood, Woolley and Wright – nominated for the Legends Walkway at Canterbury. It was planned in 2011 as a central, ground-level entrance route into the new three-tiered public square.

☐ Bill FRINDALL

Cricket statistician and scorer for BBC radio's *Test Match Special* from 1966 until 2008. Contracted legionnaires' disease during charity cricketing tour of Dubai with Lord's Taverners. Died at Great Western Hospital, Swindon, on 30 January 2009. Buried in Urchfont cemetery, opposite Walnut Close, Urchfont (nr Devizes, Wiltshire).

Urchfont Cemetery   *Sat Nav*   SN10 4RT

Biography : *"Bearders - My Life in Cricket"* autobiography (Orion, 2006)

• I found this headstone on a successful morning hunting for memorials. I had had no luck obtaining online, book or newspaper information for memorials to Bill Frindall, Freddie Brown and George Mann, and the only option seemed to be the long-shot of going to the parish churches in the villages where they died, and hoping I might come across a headstone. Reports after his tragically early death indicated only that Frindall's funeral was at Urchfont parish church. In hope rather than expectation I went to look for his gravestone but burials no longer take place there. Fortunately, a bell-ringing practice was in progress so local people were in the church, and the

Vicar suggested I might try the village cemetery - which I hadn't known about before. The cemetery is small and it was easy to locate Frindall's headstone there. Driving on to Ramsbury (a delightful village but parking problem), I searched the church cemetery for no more than two minutes before spotting Brown's headstone. Finally, I drove to West Woodhay, where the church is in a beautiful setting. On the right-hand side of the path to the church, I immediately came across George Mann's grave. He is commemorated on the headstone of his wife who died a few years before.

☐ C.B. *[Charles Burgess]* FRY

An English Heritage plaque unveiled in 2005 by his grandson Charles, then M.C.C chairman, at his birthplace 144 St James's Road, Croydon. Possibly the greatest all-round sportsman, brilliant at all sports at Repton School and Oxford University 1892-95. Won cricket blue in all four years and also athletics and soccer blues. Represented England at soccer and played in Cup Final of 1902. Cricket for Sussex, London County and Hampshire, scoring nearly 31,000 runs,

having begun with a duck in 1892. Total of 94 centuries in his career including six in a row in 1901, followed by an innings of 70. Appeared 26 times in Test matches for England and captain in Triangular

Tournament of 1912. However, never available for overseas tours. Blue plaque placed on 8 Moreland Court, Finchley Road, Hendon (NW London), where he lived after 1950. Died of kidney failure at Hampstead, London, on 7 September 1956 and, following private cremation at Golders Green, ashes interred at Repton parish church, Derbyshire, with plaque lying flat. Grave rededicated in 2008 and new upright stone incorporating plaque inscribed "Cricketer, Scholar, Athlete, Author - The Ultimate All Rounder."

144 St James's Road, Croydon *Sat Nav* CR0 2UY
Moreland Court *Sat Nav* NW2 2TP St Wystan's church, Repton *Sat Nav* DE 65 6FH

Biographies : *"Giants of the Game"* by R H Lyttelton (Ward, Lock & Co, 1899); *"Life Worth Living: Some Phases of An Englishman"* autobiography (Eyre & Spottiswoode, 1939); *"C.B.Fry"* (Sporting Lives series) by Denzil Batchelor (Phoenix House, 1951); *"C B, the Life of Charles Burgess Fry"* by Clive Ellis (Dent, 1984); *"CB Fry, An English Hero"* by Ian Walton (Richard Cohen Books, 1999); *"King of Sport"* by Ian Wilton (Metro Books, 2002).

☐ *Frederick GALE*

Born Pewsey Vale, 1823. Prolific author under name 'The Old Buffer'. From his great store of reminiscences came *The Game of Cricket* (1888) on cricket's earliest history and "..a withering denunciation of the 'averages mania'.." [Gideon Haigh, 2006]. Westminster solicitor. Died at residence in Charterhouse on 24 April 1904 and, according to entry in register, buried four days later in family vault in old churchyard at Mitcham church.

St Peter and St Paul church, Mitcham *Sat Nav* CR4 4LD

☐ *George GEARY*

Right-arm fast-medium seamer, with great control and real nip off the pitch, first played for Leicestershire in 1912. Career almost ended in WW1 when leg injured by propeller. Shouldered main burden of weak county bowling side and in each of 11 seasons took 100 wickets. Also, superb catcher at slip. 14 Tests, nine of them against Australia, and two overseas tours for England. Latterly bowled off-cutters and retired 1938 with more than 2,000 wickets in f-c career, to become coach at Charterhouse School. Later coached at Rugby School, from where retired in 1969. Oil painting by L.V.T.Praeter unveiled in members room in pavilion at County Ground, Grace Road, Leicester, and The Geary Stand on east of ground named after him in 1979. Died in Leicester Hospital on 6 March 1981. Funeral at The Church of the Martyrs, followed by cremation at Gilroes Crematorium. His ashes laid beneath paving slabs in Gardens of Remembrance. Alas, there was no memorial or plaque.

County Ground, Grace Road *Sat Nav* LE2 8AD

☐ *[Sir] Paul GETTY*

American-born son of J P Getty, oil billionaire. Anglophile and philanthropist, gave to many British causes such as £50 million to National Gallery and paying for M.C.C.'s Mound Stand redevelopment at Lord's. In 1992 established his own cricket ground at Wormsley, a 3000-acre estate in Chilterns. Honorary knighthood 1986 before taking British citizenship, then knighted by The Queen 1998. Died of chest infection on 17 April 2003, in the London Clinic (where earlier acquaintance with fellow patient Gubby Allen had inspired interest in cricket). Buried on Wormsley estate and has memorial tablet inside Lewknor parish church, south Oxfordshire.

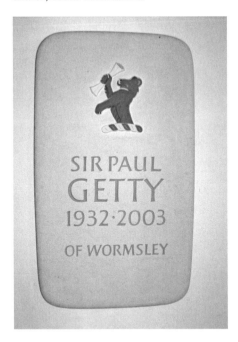

SIR PAUL
GETTY
1932·2003
OF WORMSLEY

Church of St Margaret, Lewknor *Sat Nav* OX9 5TH

• I learned from a source on funerary design that there were graves with cricketing motifs to be found at Sawston (Cambridgeshire), Wadsley (Sheffield) and Lewknor (Oxfordshire), though none of the grave occupants were famous players. While visiting the Chilterns to see Thomas Smith's grave at Lewknor I came across this memorial to Paul Getty inside the church.

☐ Alan GIBSON

Born 1923. Educated at Taunton School and Oxford (first in History). B.B.C. broadcaster including *Test Match Special* commentary and Round Britain Quiz. Cricket correspondent for *The Times*. His son and biographer described his copy as not so much a photograph in words of the day's play as a painting, usually impressionistic, sometimes distinctly abstract. After stroke,

spent four years in Rectory nursing home where he died on 10 April 1997. Funeral at Silver Street baptist church and at Taunton Deane Crematorium on 18 April. Ashes returned to the family and no known memorial.

Biography : *"A Mingled Yarn"* autobiography (Collins, 1976) ; *"Growing Up with Cricket"* autobiography (Geo Allen & Unwin, 1985); *"Of Didcot and The Demon"* by Anthony Gibson (Fairfield Books, 2009)

☐ Arthur GILLIGAN

Truly fast bowler, firstly for Surrey in 1919, then for Sussex, and inspiring county captain 1922-29. Fifty years of service to county, later as chairman, marked when The Arthur Gilligan Stand opened 1971 at southern end of Hove Ground. His widow unveiled a memorial plaque to him on the Gilligan Stand at Hove in 1984. England captain for 1924 Tests and Australian tour, but England beaten. Gilligan's bowling diminished by blow over heart while batting and Test career ended. Led the first M.C.C. tour of India and due to take side to New Zealand in 1929-30 when withdrew unfit and retired. Became sports writer and BBC radio commentator. President of M.C.C. 1967. Died at home in Pulborough on 5 September 1976 and buried in neighbouring village, in Stopham churchyard. Headstone is on right-hand side near gate.

St Mary the Virgin church, Stopham *Sat Nav* RH20 1EG
Sussex County Ground, Hove *Sat Nav* BN3 3AN

• When the Gilligan Stand was replaced by a new South Stand at the sea end of Hove's Probiz County Ground, a new plaque in memory of the two Gilligan brothers was unveiled by Harold's daughters, Joanna Turner and Virginia May (wife of the late Peter May). Arthur Gilligan had no biography but he and Harold are included in other sources such as *"The Cricket Captains of England"* by Alan Gibson (Cassell, 1979).

☐ *Harold GIMBLETT*

Fast-scoring opening batsman. After unsuccessful trial for Somerset in 1935, injuries to other players gave last-minute opportunity v Essex at Frome; scored hundred in an hour. Represented county until 1954, fifty centuries in all but picked for only 3 Tests. Coaching at Millfield School. Living in mobile home on site in Verwood, Dorset, when took overdose of tablets night of 30 March 1978. Inquest at Bournemouth returned verdict of suicide. His cremated remains dispersed on the rosebeds of Bournemouth Crematorium's Gardens of Remembrance, without any memorial. However, not only is he featured in large wall display in Somerset Cricket Museum but Gimblett's Hill is a landscaped seating area on the county ground formerly part of the adjacent St James' churchyard.

Somerset Cricket Museum, Taunton *Sat Nav* TA1 1XX

Biography : *"Tormented Genius of Cricket"* by David Foot (Heinemann, 1982)

☐ *Tom GODDARD*

Master off-spinner. Long career with Gloucestershire 1922-52. Started as fast bowler but advised to try off-spin. Sixteen times took hundred wickets in season. Captured 17 Kent wickets in one day at Bristol in 1939. Six hat-tricks in career. Almost 3,000 wickets in career, fifth on all-time list of wicket-takers yet called up only eight times for England. Died at home, 'Dunbolin', in city of Gloucester on 22 May 1966. Funeral at All Saints church, followed by cremation at Coney Hill Crematorium and ashes scattered on Lawn Three. Memorial plaque placed on kerbing of row H at Coney Hill.

Coney Hill Crematorium *Sat Nav* GL4 4PA

☐ *[Sir] Home GORDON*

Writer of statistical work, *"Cricket Form at a Glance"*, and column *"In the Pavilion"*. Knew most cricket personalities of his day and said to have ear of the selectors. Wrote history of Sussex and was club secretary from 1943, president in 1948. Director of publishing and electricity supply companies. Died at home in Rottingdean on 9 September 1956. After funeral at Downs Crematorium, Brighton, ashes interred with memorial in churchyard wall at St Margaret's, Rottingdean.

St Margaret's church, Rottingdean *Sat Nav* BN2 7HA

☐ *Alfred GOVER*

Fast bowler for Surrey through 1930s. Took 4 wickets in 4 balls v Worcestershire in 1935. Won four England caps. His indoor cricket coaching school in London, inherited from Sandham and Strudwick, won a worldwide reputation for correcting technical faults of all, from school children to Test stars. Industrial sheds used for school demolished when it closed 1989, now apartments called Cricketers Mews. Journalist for Sunday Mirror and BBC radio commentator. Manager of Commonwealth team tours to Pakistan. President of Surrey 1980. MBE 1998. Died at age of 93 in south London on 7 October 2001. Funeral took place at Putney Vale Crematorium: the ashes were retained by the family.

Former site of indoor school East Hill, Wandsworth *Sat Nav* SW18 2HD

Biography : *"The Long Run"* by Alfred Gover (Pelham Books, 1991)

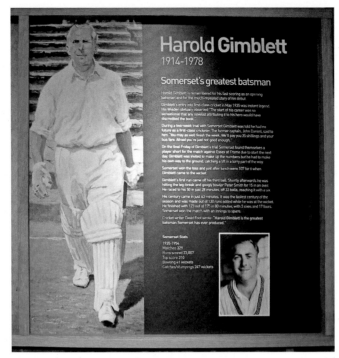

Harold Gimblett display at Somerset Cricket Museum, Taunton.

(below) Broadhalfpenny Down Monument   *Sat Nav*   PO8 0UB.

☐ E.M. [Edward Mills] GRACE

Right-handed batsman known as "The Coroner". Emerged, aged 21, as powerful, highly competitive young batsman by scoring 192 and carrying his bat at Canterbury. Toured America 1863-64 with George Parr's team. Played for county from 1871 until 1894, helping make Gloucestershire pre-eminent county. Scorer of 10,000 first-class runs. Also, county club secretary. Died after a long illness on 20 May 1911 at his home Park House, Thornbury High Street, Gloucestershire. Remains buried in Christ Church churchyard next to Downend Cricket Club ground.

Park House (place of death) *Sat Nav* BS 35 2AR   Christ Church, Downend *Sat Nav* BS 16 5TB

Biography : *"Edward Mills Grace, Cricketer"* by F S Ashley-Cooper (Chatto & Windus, 1916)

☐ Fred GRACE

All three Grace brothers selected for the 1880 Test match against Australia at The Oval, but only two weeks later Fred died from congestion of the lungs at Basingstoke. Buried and memorial inside Christ Church, Downend, Bristol, Gloucestershire.

Christ Church, Downend *Sat Nav* BS 16 5TB

☐ Dr W.G. [William] GRACE

Born Downend House, Mangotsfield, Bristol, 1848. Plaque on birthplace, now offices at 112 North Street. Greatest cricketer of Victorian Age. Died from heart failure 23 October 1915 at 'Fairmount', his residence (1902-15) in Mottingham, south-

east London. G.L.C. placed a plaque there, unveiled by Stuart Chiesman on 2 July 1966. Grace's funeral in Beckenham, Kent, on 26 October attended by large congregation of cricket notables. Buried at Elmers End (now Beckenham) Cemetery. Sir Home Gordon immediately invited to write memorial biography; no other cricketer has had life story told so many times. Cemetery is near to Birkbeck Station and opposite bus garages. Follow tarmac road for 50 metres then veer right on grassy path for further 50 metres. Grave is on right. In 1965, *The Daily Telegraph* published letter from Arthur Gilligan deploring its run-down condition. As a result a fund started to commemorate 50th anniversary of death, and dilapidated grave repaired. Further upkeep of grave took place in 2004. Grace Gates memorial erected at members' entrance to Lord's Ground in July 1922. The gates were designed by HW (later Sir Herbert) Baker and inscribed with Sir Stanley Jackson's suggestion of "The Great Cricketer". The 1948 Gentlemen v Players match at Lord's, played in honour of centenary of his birth, and also a Centenary Exhibition in Gloucester. Also, gates at Gloucestershire's county ground in Nevil Road, which he had purchased in 1889. In 1963 London County Council placed plaque (arranged by The Cricket Society) on wall (now demolished) of No 7 Laurie Park

Road, Sydenham, unveiled by Billy Griffith. When house demolished, the Lawrie Road plaque moved to Fairmount and a new plaque on redevelopment by Laing, saying "W. G. Grace 1848-1915 cricketer lived in a house on this site" Memorial plaque unveiled at Downend church in 1980. The W G Grace memorial ground, home of Downend C.C, pavilion opened in 1922. According to *Playfair Cricket Monthly* even doorstep from his home in Downend placed at Wellingborough School, Northants. Pub in Witham Road, Penge, named The Dr WG Grace (now Grace's Bar & Grill).

(John Wisden's, 1916); "The Memorial Biography of W G Grace" by Lord Hawke, Lord Harris and Home Gordon (Constable, 1919); "WG Grace" by Bernard Darwin (Duckworth 1948); "Cricketing Lives: W.G.Grace" by Clifford Bax (Phoenix House, 1952); "The Great Cricketer" by A A Thomson (Robert Hale, 1957); "W G Grace, His Life and Times" by Eric Midwinter (George Allen & Unwin, 1981); "W G" by Robert Low (Richard Cohen Books, 1997, reissued as "WG Grace : An Intimate Biography" (Metro Publishing 2010); "W. G. Grace: A Life" written and published by Simon Rae (1999) "The Chronicle of W G" by J R Webber (ACS, 1998); "Amazing Grace: The Man who was W.G." by Richard Tomlinson (Little Brown, 2015); "Gilbert: The Last Years of WG Grace" by Charlie Connelly (Wisden, 2015).

Birthplace *Sat Nav* BS16 5SE Beckenham Cemetery *Sat Nav* BR3 4TD Fairmount *Sat Nav* SE9 4RT Lawrie Park Road *Sat Nav* SE26 6DZ Grace Gates, Lord's Ground *Sat Nav* NW8 8QN Christ Church, Downend *Sat Nav* BS 16 5TB Bristol County Ground, Nevil Road *Sat Nav* BS7 9EJ WG Grace Memorial Ground *Sat Nav* BS16 5UE Grace's Bar & Grill, Penge *Sat Nav* SE20 7YA

Biographies: "W G Grace: A Biography" by Methven Brownlee (Iliffe & Son, 1887); "Cricketing Reminiscences & Personal Recollections" autobiography, ghosted by Arthur Porritt (James Bowden, 1899, reprinted Hambledon Press, 1980); "Dr W.G.Grace, the King of Cricket" by F G Warne (pub Bristol, H A Burleigh, 1899); "W G Grace" by Acton Wye (Henry Drane, 1901); "WG Grace, A Record of his Performances in first-class cricket" by F S Ashley-Cooper;

☐ 'Jackie' GRANT

From wealthy Trinidad business background, chosen on batting form at Cambridge University in England to be youngest ever West Indies captain, though he had never played in Caribbean or met team mates before. To Australia 1930-31 and England 1933; 12 Tests, all as captain. Then missionary work with United Church of Christ in Africa until expelled from Rhodesia in 1976. Secretary of Cambridge Christian Aid. Died at Addenbrooke's Hospital 26 October 1978. Funeral at City of Cambridge Crematorium and memorial service at St Columba's, address given by Sir Garfield Todd. Ashes are scattered in the Gardens and an entry made in Book of Remembrance. A small plaque placed on rose garden bed BB3359.

City of Cambridge Crematorium *Sat Nav* CB3 0JJ

☐ C.E. [Charles] GREEN

One of best schoolboy batsmen, coached at Uppingham by H H Stephenson, joined Essex (before it became a f-c county), aged 16. Became captain 1883. Later county club president and, as managing director of Orient Steamship Line, able to save club from financial extinction. Briefly M.C.C. committee and president 1905. Died at Theydon Grove, Epping, on 4 December 1916. Funeral at St Alban's church, Coopersale, near Epping. Grave has kerbing and fallen cross but no headstone. Lies at sw corner of churchyard, two grave spaces left of path to the porch.

St Alban's Church, Coopersale *Sat Nav* CM16 7RB

☐ Andrew GREENWOOD

Member of England's first Test match side at Melbourne in 1876-77. Batsman for Yorkshire 1869-1880. Died in Huddersfield, Yorkshire, on 12 February 1889. Buried at rear of churchyard of St John's church, Kirkheaton. A photo by Patrick Neal in Paine's *Innings Complete* vol 15 shows "the sorry state of the Victorian headstone"; Neal awarded Huddersfield Central Cricket League heritage award for 2006 for leading role played in restoration of Greenwood's grave which has a cricket motif at its top.

St John's church, Kirkheaton *Sat Nav* HD5 0BH

☐ Henry GRIERSON

Was, in 1936, founder of the Forty (XL) Club. In 1976 XL Club gave Lord's two showcases of historic costumes and plaque as memorial to him. Minor county cricketer with Bedfordshire 1909-23. Columnist ("Ramblings of a Rabbit") in *The Cricketer* and *Morning Post*. Died in a Sunbury-on-Thames nursing home on 29 January 1972. Funeral held at Kingston Crematorium. No memorial or plaque; ashes scattered in the Garden of Remembrance.

☐ George GUNN

Brother of John Gunn and nephew of William. Brilliant opening batsman and by far the county's highest scorer (31,592 runs), though commonly-held view is of great ability unfulfilled. Twenty times scored 1000 runs in a season yet never 2000. Rated highly but played only once in a Test in England (in 1909) though 14 Tests overseas, first as reinforcement in 1907-08. Final tour, aged 50, to West Indies in 1930. Retired from Notts. in 1932. Landlord of Bentinck Hotel until 1939. One of first Honorary Life Members of M.C.C. Died on 28 June 1958 at home of son, John, in Cuckfield, Sussex, where had lived since wife died in 1956. Was thought in perfect health and even intending to watch M.C.C. in Australia. Funeral planned for Sussex but abruptly changed to cremation at Wilford Hill, Nottingham, on 4 July. No memorial. Ashes scattered on pitch at Trent Bridge Ground.

Biography : *"The Trent Bridge Battery - The Story of the Sporting Gunns"* by Basil Haynes & John Lucas (Willow Books, 1985)

☐ William GUNN

Started working life in Richard Daft's sports outfitters, calling on experience later for commercial success in bat-making firm partnership Gunn & Moore. Standing 6' 4", he was one of dominant batsmen of the age: nearly 26,000 runs, 48 hundreds, including 102* at Manchester v Australia 1893. Also splendid outfielder. Eleven Tests. Illnesses after WW1. After recuperating in Skegness, came home but died 29 January 1921 at his home in Nottingham. Buried three days later in Church (also called The Rock) Cemetery, Mansfield Road, Nottingham, off Forest Road East. Grave lies in select site C : grave 9100, and is next to path, three back from privet hedge.

Church Cemetery (The Rock) Sat Nav NG1 4HT

☐ Nigel HAIG

Born in Kensington 1887. Fast bowler and hard-hitting batsman with Middlesex, his last five years as skipper. Five Test appearances for England. Died at Eastbourne on 27 October 1966. Member of same family as Field-Marshall Douglas Haig. Ashes buried at Dryburgh Abbey, Scotland. Wall plaque placed in north chapel.

Dryburgh Abbey Sat Nav TD6 0RQ

☐ Schofield HAIGH

Yorkshire debut in 1895 and won a regular team place by slowing pace of his bowling and mastering fast-medium skills. Topped county bowling averages for ten successive seasons. Also, four centuries, and the 'double' once. Twice visited South Africa with M.C.C. Played 11 times for England between 1899 and 1912. In September 1913 announced retirement to become coach at Winchester College, where boys included Douglas Jardine. Died of heart disease at Taylor Hill, Huddersfield, shortly before 50th birthday on 27 February 1921. Interment in Armitage Bridge churchyard. Church burnt down by vandals in February 1987, but graves unharmed. Laid out in date order and Haigh's lies between north-east corner of church and churchyard wall, approximately ten metres in front of a distinctive white angel. Haigh also commemorated as one of "The Great Triumvirate : Hirst - Rhodes - Haigh" on memorial tower at Fartown Ground.

St Paul's church, Armitage Bridge Sat Nav HD4 7PD
Fartown memorial Sat Nav HD2 2QA

Biography : *"William Gunn"* by Albert Craig (All-England Athletic Pub Co, 1899); *"The Trent Bridge Battery - The Story of the Sporting Gunns"* by Basil Haynes & John Lucas (Willow Books, 1985)

☐ Charlie HALLOWS

Stylish, left-handed opening batsman who eleven times scored 1000 runs in season, including 1000 in month of May in 1928. Twice represented England. Coached for the Indian Board, for Worcestershire and, when 70, appointed coach to Lancashire for five more seasons. Died at Bolton, Lancashire, on 10 November 1972. Buried in unmarked grave at St Michael's church, Great Lever, Lancashire.

☐ HAMBLEDON Monument

On Broadhalfpenny Down, opposite Bat & Ball Inn, two miles east of Hampshire village of Hambledon, stands the rough-cut pillar of grey granite, erected to mark 150th anniversary of original cricket ground. Monument is eleven feet tall and has base of two blocks, inscribed "This stone marks the site of the ground of the Hambledon Cricket Club 1750-87." On top is a third upright piece carved with design of curved bats and wicket with two stumps. Special match arranged in September 1908 to mark monument's completion and, in the absence of W.G.Grace, Hampshire's Edward Sprot performed opening.

[from photo inside The Bat & Ball Inn]

☐ Wally HAMMOND

A soldier's son, childhood in Malta. At Cirencester G.S. made 365 in a house match and recommended to Gloucestershire (although born at Dover in 1903). Made debut in 1920. Required to qualify because he was born in Kent. Missed whole 1926 season with disease acquired on West Indies tour, and nearly died. Yet became leading English batsman between Wars; topped first-class batting averages every season from 1933, and three times made 3,000 runs in a season. Also talented as medium-paced bowler, tactician and fieldsman, having brilliant anticipation at slip. Record 78 catches in 1928 season, including ten in one match. On three occasions scored triple century for Gloucestershire, plus once for England. Made 167 centuries in all; on seven occasions made two in a match and scored 15 centuries in 1938 season alone. Played in 85 Tests for England, 20 as captain once he became an amateur. Was for years England's top scorer in Test cricket, until overtaken by Cowdrey. In WW2, with R.A.F. in Middle East. Retired in 1947 but played occasionally until emigration to South Africa, where second wife came from, to be coach-groundsman at University of Natal. Car smash in 1959, fractured skull but recovered well. Died at home in Kloof, near Durban, on night of 1 July 1965 after brief illness. Service at Dove's Funeral Chapel in Durban followed by private cremation. His ashes brought back to England to be scattered on pitch (18 August 1966) at Bristol County Ground in presence of family and officials of Gloucestershire club. The members bar in pavilion at Bristol, refurbished in 2013, named The Hammond Room.

Bristol County (Brightside) Ground, Nevil Road *Sat Nav* BS7 9EJ

Biographies : *"Cricket My Destiny"* autobiography (Stanley Paul, 1946);*"Cricket My World"* autobiography (Stanley Paul, 1947); *"W R Hammond: Cricketer"* by David Moore (Filton Cricket Biographies, 1948); *"Cricket's Secret History"* autobiography (Stanley Paul, 1952); *"Walter Hammond"* by Ronald Mason (Hollis Carter, 1962); *"Walter Hammond"* by Gerald Howat (George Allen & Unwin, 1984); *"The Reasons Why"* by David Foot (Robson

Books, 1996)

• A 1966 cricket magazine reported that a fund was begun for a memorial to Hammond but I have been unable to find out whether this aim was ever achieved.

☐ Joe HARDSTAFF senior

Batsman, born in Kirkby-in-Ashfield 1882. Twelve times appeared for the Players, and 5 England caps on Australian tour of 1907-08. Died at home in Fisher Street, Basford, Nottinghamshire, on 2 April 1947. Wireless message sent to son Joe returning from M.C.C.'s Australian tour on board 'Largs Bay'. Buried in New Cemetery East, Kirkby-in-Ashfield. Grave is no 3285 in Row AA. Name is on kerbing but no reference to cricket. Follow main path before chapel, it is ten graves in on right-hand side.

New Cemetery, Kingsway   Sat Nav   NG17 7FJ

• His son, 'Young Joe' Hardstaff who played 23 times for England, died in 1990 and, after cremation at Mansfield Crematorium, his ashes were interred in *Mansfield Cemetery*.

☐ Lord [George Canning] HARRIS

Took title on father's death in 1872. Attacking batsman, made Kent debut in 1870 while at Eton College. Oxford blue and university captain. Fitzgerald's tour of North America 1872. Led English team in Australia 1878-79, also in first Test played in England 1880, and in 1884. Hon. secretary of Kent, also president and captain in 1875 and leading batsman. No less important in Marylebone club. Having been born in Trinidad, was paradoxically a stickler for birthplace qualifications to play in county cricket. On committee at Lord's from 1875, president in 1895, trustee 1906-16 and treasurer succeeding Ponsonby-Fane, 1916-32. Fearsome reputation for severe manner but held in respect for outstanding service.

By some standards second in influence only to W.G.Grace in annals of English international cricket's development. Last Kent appearance 1911, aged sixty. As late as 1930 batted briefly in club match. Died at his estate of Belmont, near Faversham, Kent, on 24 March 1932 and buried in nearby Throwley church cemetery. A host of memorials to Harris family inside church occupies northern aisle and chapel. Church locked and key obtained from Town Place House next to Belmont Estate. Commemorated in Lord's pavilion by a bust, by Arthur Hacker and by a portrait; and in Memorial Garden (often called Harris Garden) where tablet unveiled May 1934 by Lord Hailsham.

St Michael & All Angels church   Sat Nav   ME13 0PJ   Lord's Cricket Ground   Sat Nav   NW8 8QN

Biography : *"A Few Short Runs"* by Lord Harris (John Murray, 1921); *"Lord Harris"* by James Coldham (Allen & Unwin, 1983)

☐ Lord [Martin Bladen] HAWKE

Debut for Yorkshire, where family home was, as batsman in the Scarborough Festival though not qualified because born in Lincolnshire. Offered captaincy in 1883 while still at Cambridge University. Under him Yorkshire won eight championships and he remained captain for 28 seasons. In 1900 and 1908 seasons not one match lost.

Led six overseas tours with English teams, aiming to broaden the extent of cricket across the world. Captained England in four early Test matches, all won, against South Africa. Elected life-president of Yorkshire 1910. Introduced winter salaries for his county professionals, and white rose on Yorkshire cap. Important 'establishment' figure. Chairman of England selectors. President of M.C.C. 1914 and, because of War, served until 1919. M.C.C. Treasurer from 1932. In 1938 taken suddenly ill at "Glasclune", his North Berwick residence and removed to Edinburgh nursing home where died on 10 October. Funeral at Edinburgh Crematorium and ashes taken away by brother Edward, who later succeeded to title. His ashes later scattered on his wife's grave at West Norwood Cemetery, London. She was buried in her former husband Arthur Cross's grave (number 31528 in square 23). Hawke's name engraved on the side of the memorial, and in 1996 a white rose bush planted there [information from FOWNC newsletter 29].

West Norwood Cemetery Sat Nav SE27 9JU

Biographies : *"Recollections And Reminiscences"* autobiography (Williams & Norgate, 1924); *"Lord Hawke: A Cricketing Biography"* by James Coldham (Crowood Press, 1990) reprinted as *"Lord Hawke: A Cricketing Legend"* (Tauris Parke, 2003)

☐ Ernest HAYES

Professional batsman with Surrey before WW1, then captain as amateur 1919 until return of C.T.A. Wilkinson. Scored more than 27,000 runs with nearly fifty hundreds. Three Tests when South Africa beat England in 1905-06, but none in Australia 1907-08, and only two afterwards. Coach with Leicestershire and re-appeared in championship for them 1926, leading averages at the age of 50. Also coach of Craddock C.C. (South Africa), Winchester College and Surrey 1929-34. Death at West Dulwich nursing home, 30 Alleyn Park,

from pneumonia on 2 December 1953, same day due to be guest of honour celebrating Surrey's second successive championship. Cremation was 2 days later at Camberwell Crematorium in Honor Oak.

Biography : *"Ernest Hayes: Brass in a Golden Age"* by Keith Booth (ACS, 2008)

☐ Arthur HAYGARTH

A plaque (arranged by Roger Heavens) was unveiled on 6 May 2000 at 29 Wellington Square, Hastings, where he was born in 1825. Harrow-educated batsman invited to appear for M.C.C. and other sides. Compiler of the 15 *'Scores and Biographies'* published by Fred Lillywhite between 1850 and 1878. Died at his home 77 Warwick Way, Victoria, on 1 May 1903 and buried in West Brompton Cemetery, London, where his grave marked by a cross of white marble. A green plaque unveiled by Christopher Martin-Jenkins in 2003 at house where Haygarth died.

77-79 Warwick Way (now Enrico Hotel), Victoria *Sat Nav* SW1V 1QP   West Brompton Cemetery *Sat Nav* SW10 9UG   29 Wellington Square, Hastings *Sat Nav* TN34 1PR.

Biography: *"Cricket's Other Chronicler: Arthur Haygarth, 1825-1903"* by Roger Heavens (self-published, 1996)

☐ Tom HAYWARD

Cambridge-born professional batsman for Surrey between 1893 and 1914, relied upon to make 1000 runs every season (did so 20 times). Finished career with better than 43,000 runs. In 1900 scored 1000 runs before end of May. In 1906, his best season, scored four centuries in a week, and in all had 104 in his career. Was responsible for bringing Jack Hobbs, with whom he later opened the batting, to The Oval for trials. Played 35 times for England and only one run short of 2000 Test runs. Died on 19 July 1939 in Cambridge, where lived after retiring from cricket, and buried in Mill Road Cemetery. Entering cemetery at junction of Mackenzie Road and Collier Road, follow path for 100 metres, as far as chimney of Anglia Ruskin College. Grave marked with a simple cross, is on left, near the wall.

Mill Road (Petersfield) Cemetery *Sat Nav* CB1 2AN

□ J.T. ['Old Jack'] HEARNE

Highly-skilled medium-paced bowler. Born and also eventually died and was buried at Chalfont St Giles, Buckinghamshire.. Qualified for Middlsex 1890. Cutting and moving the ball off the seam for many seasons with county in 'Golden Age' of cricket, took more than 3000 wickets against Victorian and Edwardian batsmen of the day, most notably 257 in 1896 season alone. Only three bowlers have taken more wickets. Yet only 12 Test appearances in all. Test hat-trick v Australia in 1899, dismissing Hill, Noble and Gregory for ducks. Honoured by election to M.C.C. Committee 1920. Died on 17 April 1944 and buried in Chalfont St Giles parish churchyard in an unmarked grave: later a celtic cross placed there.

Chalfont St Giles church *Sat Nav* HP8 4JH

Biography : as below

□ J.W. ['Young Jack'] HEARNE

Only distantly related to other Hearnes of Middlesex or Kent. Brilliant, elegant right-handed batsman and leg-break bowler, an England regular before and after WW1. Played 24 times for England. Went to Australia on three M.C.C. tours. Despite indifferent health, made in excess of 37,000 runs with 96 centuries. Five times

did 'the double' during first-class career. Retirement in 1936. In 1949 given Honorary Life Membership of M.C.C. Died at his home in Bagley Close, West Drayton, on 14 September 1965 and body was cremated at Breakspear Crematorium, north-west Ruislip. Cremated remains were dispersed in Gardens of Remembrance and a double lower-cloister memorial tablet (ref P 24) placed.

Breakspear Crematorium *Sat Nav* HA4 7SJ

Biography : *"Wheelwrights to Wickets: the Story of the Cricketing Hearnes"* by J W 'Jack' Hearne (Goostrey: Boundary Books, 1996)

• On 30 May 1966 the Harris Garden at Lord's was filled for a short ceremony at which Walter Robins unveiled a seat in Jack Hearne's honour, calling him "the best all-rounder Middlesex ever produced."

□ [Elias] 'Patsy' HENDREN

Adored by crowds at Lord's and all over the world for the engaging manner of his batting, a hero of every North London schoolboy, yet often forgotten as being one of most efficient scorers in history of game. Only Hobbs and Woolley scored more than his 57,000 f-c runs and only Hobbs made more centuries. His list of 170 centuries includes 22 doubles. Firstly, a member of groundstaff at Lord's. Debut Middlesex match spoilt by rain so had to wait till next summer (1910) for first innings. Most glorious years, when scored more than 2000 runs each season, averaging 60 or better, came after WW1. Had impressive Test cricket record: on three M.C.C. tours of Australia and to West Indies twice, and South Africa once. 51 Test matches in all, scoring 3,525 runs at 47.63. In era of many great batsmen, as near to a Test regular as possible. Senior professional in 1930s. Retired from county cricket in 1937. Coach at Harrow School, then Sussex. Finally, Middlesex scorer. Entered Whittington Hospital, Highgate, in May 1962 and died there 4 October 1962. Interred

9 October in East Finchley Cemetery, East End Road, London N2. Buried in plot number 11 of Lawn Private graves section. His wife, Minnie, who died in 1970, is also buried there and brother Denis in the grave behind. East Finchley was once known as St Marylebone Cemetery.

East Finchley Cemetery *Sat Nav* N2 0RZ

Biography : *"Big Cricket"* autobiography (Hodder & Stoughton,1934); *"Patsy Hendren: the Cricketer and His Times"* by Ian Peebles (Macmillan, 1969)

• Hendren's burial place proved very difficult to trace because Ian Peebles' biography of him had stated that Hendren was buried in London's Kensal Green. When the cemetery staff could not find his name in their records, I remembered that Hendren was a Catholic and thought Peebles must have meant the adjoining RC cemetery of St Mary's. Checks and double checks turned up nothing there either, so I wrote to the Middlesex office at Lord's where the secretary, Arthur Flower, was sure that Hendren had been buried in Highgate Cemetery. Mr Ian Tanner of the Highgate Manpower Services project was very interested in my enquiry; as a north Londoner, Hendren's name had been for him a legend to bracket with Denis Compton and Arsenal's Alex James but he could not find it in the Highgate register. When he pointed out that Highgate is commonly confused with the vast St Pancras Cemetery, I hurried off there; but no sign was to be found of Hendren's grave.

At last it occurred to me to contact someone who might have attended the funeral: E.W.Swanton. While not present himself, he suggested I should try Gubby Allen. It proved to be an excellent lead for Mr Allen still kept meticulous engagement diaries and could at last confirm that Hendren's funeral was on 9 October in East Finchley Cemetery. But contacting the cemetery, I learned that it had been controversially sold off by Westminster City Council and was now being re-sold again. Eventually I traced the management agency to Runnymede Group and luckily the records were intact, showing that Hendren was interred in 'Lawns Private', the spot being marked by a simple headstone. Discovering this location had taken two years.

□ Allen HILL

One of several important early players born in villages around Huddersfield, in his case Kirkheaton. Round-arm fast bowler. In Australia 1876-77 took the first wicket to fall in Test cricket. Died in Leyland, Lancashire, on 29 August 1910 and buried in Leyland churchyard. Enter churchyard through the arch; walk anticlockwise around the church to the first path on the right. His grave is 20 yards down the path on the left; it is under trees, its back facing the path.

St Andrew's church, Leyland *Sat Nav* PR25 3EL

□ George HIRST

Another Test cricketer born at Kirkheaton. Debut county match for Yorkshire aged 18, and a first team regular from 1892. Before that, professional in leagues. Pioneered left-arm 'swerve' bowling, introduced it in 1901 giving him 183 wickets in season. Giant of an all-rounder, best year 1906 when took 208 wickets and scored 2385 runs, completing 'double' in 16th match of season by 28 June (next earliest 12 July, also by Hirst). Also scored 111 and 117* and took two 'five-fors' (6-70 and 5-45) v Somerset at Bath, all four together in one match being unique achievement. For England played 24

Test matches. Benefit was 1904 Roses match raising £3,703, a record until Roy Kilner's benefit. Retained by Yorkshire as coach, widely recognised as one of best. Able to serve as part-time coach at Eton, too, and took hat-trick for Master's XI on farewell 1938. Elected Hon. Life Member of M.C.C. and Yorkshire (1949). On 10 May 1954 died at home in Lindley, nr Huddersfield. Newspaper leaders described him as an example to the nation. Funeral at Holy Trinity church, Huddersfield, followed by cremation at Lawnswood in Leeds. A 10 metre-high clock tower, designed by Geoffrey Rose, was erected as memorial to him at Fartown ground, Huddersfield, and unveiled on 22 October 1955 by Herbert Sutcliffe. Fund set up in 1985 to restore monument but abandoned because of fundraising for the Bradford Fire victims, until re-started in 1990s.

Hirst & Rhodes memorial, Fartown *Sat Nav* HD2 2QA

Biography : *"Hirst and Rhodes"* by A A Thomson (Epworth, 1959; new edition Pavilion Books, 1986); *"George Herbert Hirst"* by Patrick J A Neal (at www.ckcricketheritage. org.uk/northkirklees/mirfield/docs/Book.pdf)

☐ *Bill HITCH*

One of fastest bowlers. Born in Radcliffe, Lancashire, but early in life family moved to Newmarket and spotted by Tom Hayward. Surrey debut 1907. Owing to WW1, went with England on first tour of Australia too young and second too old. In 1934 joined Glamorgan as coach until outbreak of WW2, when worked at Guest & Keen's steelworks. Retired 1945. Died at St David's Hospital, Cardiff, 7 July 1965 and body interred in churchyard in churchyard of St Augustine's, Rumney.

St Augustine's church, Rumney *Sat Nav* CF3 3BA

☐ *[Sir] Jack HOBBS*

Born at Cambridge 1882, eldest in family of twelve. No plaque to mark birthplace at Rivar Place, Sleaford Street. Coached by Tom Hayward and encouraged to make career as professional with Surrey. Widely acknowledged as ablest batsman and finest cricket brain in English cricket. In 61 Test matches, between 1907-08 and 1930, scored 5,410 runs with 15 hundreds and 24 century partnerships to credit. Being professional, destined not to captain England (except to cover illness), but selectors and captains relied on him for advice and approval. Highest-ever scorer of runs (61,237) and most centuries (197) in f-c cricket; when records amended, yet more runs added and 2 further hundreds. Only once (in 1909) could be *Wisden's* Cricketer of Year but afforded Special Portrait in 1926, following exceptional 1925 summer of 3000 runs at an average above 70, with 16 centuries. Owned sports outfitters on The Strand, London. On retirement in 1934, engaged as newspaper columnist. Countless ways found to honour and commemorate him, culminating in knighthood in 1953. The Hobbs memorial in Cambridge is the pavilion (now a Thai restaurant) on Parker's Piece in centre of the

Image courtesy of Julia & Keld © 2009 (cropped)

☐ Eric HOLLIES

Tireless, economical bowler of leg-breaks, for Warwickshire. Capped by England in West Indies, aged 22, but not again till 12 years later. In 1946 took ten wickets in an innings, all bowled or lbw, still a county record. Famously bowled Bradman for a duck in 1948. To Birmingham league cricket in 1958. Played for Halesowen and lived at Cradley Heath. Died 17 April 1981 while staying with his daughter at Chinley, Derbyshire. Funeral at Rowley Regis Crematorium a week later and ashes collected by family. To honour him as Warwickshire's leading wicket-taker, the Rea Bank at Edgbaston Cricket Ground renamed The Eric Hollies Stand in 1989. Its redevelopment in 2003 won a Civic Trust Award.

Edgbaston Cricket Ground   *Sat Nav*   B5 7QU

Biographies : *"I'll Spin You a Tale"* autobiography (Museum Press, 1955); *"Eric Hollies: The Peter Pan Of Cricket"* by Norman Rogers (Warwickshire Cricket Printing, 2002)

city. It was built by the then Town Council in 1930. At The Oval Surrey county cricket club commissioned Louis de Soissons to design a set of gates, declared open by H.D.G.Leveson Gower as The Jack Hobbs Gates on 5 May 1934. Blue plaques erected in 1986 at former home, 17 Englewood Road, London, SW12, and another in 1982 at 13 Palmeira Avenue in Hove, where he and wife Ada had moved in 1946. Died at his last home, Furze Croft, block of flats in Hove on 21 December 1963. Funeral at All Saints church, followed by interment in wife's grave in Hove Cemetery on Old Shoreham Road. To see his gravestone enter main gates of cemetery on south side of A27 road; follow cemetery road round until meeting four quarter circles. Grave lies next to one of these, approx. 100 metres due east of chapel.

Kennington Oval *Sat Nav* SE11 5SS   Englewood Road *Sat Nav* SW12 9PA   Hobbs pavilion, Cambridge *Sat Nav* CB1 1JH   Palmeira Avenue, Hove *Sat Nav* BN3 3GE   Hove Cemetery *Sat Nav* BN3 7EF

Biographies : *"My Cricketing Memories"* autobiography (Heinemann, 1924); *"Between The Wickets"* autobiography (A & C Black, 1926); *"Playing for England"* autobiography (Gollancz, 1931); *"My Life Story"* autobiography (The Star, 1934); *"Jack Hobbs, Gentleman & Player"* by Pat Landsberg (Todd Publishing, 1953); *"Jack Hobbs: A Portrait of an Artist as a Great Batsman"* by Ronald Mason (Hollis & Carter, 1960); *"Jack Hobbs: a Profile of the Master"* by John Arlott (John Murray 1981; Penguin Books, 1982); *"Jack Hobbs"* by Leo McKinstry (Yellow Jersey, 2012)

☐ Jack HOLMES

Born in Surrey and educated at Repton. First appeared for Sussex in 1922, and made 1000 runs in following season. County captain for four seasons. Asked to lead M.C.C. side in India 1939-40, but tour cancelled. Group-captain in RAF in WW2. Member of Test selection committee: chairman from 1946 until ill-health caused him to stand down. Died of a heart attack on 21 May 1950 at his home, Barklye Wood, in Heathfield. Funeral at nearby St Philip's church in Burwash Weald on 25 May when Sussex C.C.C. represented by Duke of Norfolk. Ashes buried in Hastings Cemetery.

Hastings Borough Cemetery   *Sat Nav*   TN34 2AE

Percy HOLMES

Opening batsman, impulsive and lively stroke-maker, joined Yorkshire 1913. Scorer of more than 26,000 runs for county. Formed opening partnership with Sutcliffe in 'twenties; most notable stand was 555 v Essex 1932. Capped for England 7 times. In retirement lived at Marsh, Huddersfield, where died on 3 September 1971. Funeral at Huddersfield Crematorium, attended by old Yorkshire team-mates, including Sutcliffe. No memorial. His ashes strewn in Garden of Remembrance.

Biography: *"Holmes & Sutcliffe: the Run Stealers"* by Leslie Duckworth (Hutchinson, 1970)

A.N. ['Monkey'] HORNBY

Born in Blackburn, son of the Mayor. Dashing opening bat for Lancashire to complement barndoor approach of Barlow. Prominent member of Harris's 1878-79 touring side. Test career only three matches, captain in two. First man to play both Test cricket and rugby for England. Died in Parkfield, Nantwich, of sudden heart failure on 17 December 1925. Buried next to son, who died in Great War, in Acton churchyard, Nantwich, Cheshire. Grave covered by a slab with bat, ball and stumps design and has a large white upright cross.

St Mary's church, Acton, Cheshire *Sat Nav* CW5 8LE

Biography : *"A.N.Hornby: The Boss"* by Stuart Brodkin (ACS Lives in Cricket, 2013)

Geoffrey HOWARD

Cricket administrator. Grandson of Ebenezer Howard (whose garden city ideas so influenced British town planning). As secretary of Lancashire, asked by M.C.C to manage three overseas tours to India (1951-52), Australia (1954-55) and Pakistan (1955-56). Secretary of Surrey 1965-75. Surrey president 1989. Lived at Horsfall House, Minchinhampton. Died there on 8 November 2002, aged 93. Funeral at Holy Trinity church, Minchinhampton followed by cremation at Coney Hill. Ashes scattered in a private location of great personal importance to him, as he wished for no memorial, saying the Fairfield biography sufficed. Shortly after his death, a painting of him was hung in the pavilion at Kennington Oval.

Biography : *"At The Heart Of English Cricket"* by Stephen Chalke (Fairfield Publishing, 2001), which won Cricket Society jubilee award 2002.

Harry HOWELL

In youth a ground bowler at Edgbaston, not tried in county XI until Field's declining years. After War was Warwickshire's premier fast bowler until he left in 1929. Performances like 6 for 7, dismissing Hampshire for 15, and all ten v Yorkshire in 1923 earned two Test tours of Australia with M.C.C. Became publican. Died on 9 July 1932 in Queen's Hospital, Birmingham. Interment in Yardley Cemetery. His grave, which also contains his wife Marion and two children, is number 17B-1611.

Yardley Cemetery *Sat Nav* B25 8NA

Walter HUMPHREY

Born Southsea, Hampshire, 1849. Known at the time as "the last of the lob bowlers". Took 150 wickets for Sussex in 1893, rewarded with tour of Australia 1894-95 when aged 45, but played none of the Tests. After career finished, briefly an umpire, then reverted to trade of shoemaking. His son also played for Sussex. Died Brighton 23 March 1924 and buried in grave C108 in Brighton & Preston (The Downs) Cemetery.

Brighton & Preston Cemetery *Sat Nav* BN2 3PL

☐ Joe HUMPHRIES

Succeeded William Storer as Derbyshire wicket-keeper. Over 670 victims in career. Finest moment with bat: in partnership with S.F.Barnes towards end of innings at Melbourne 1907-08 enabled England to win by one wicket. Died at home in Fairfield Road, Chesterfield, 8 May 1946 and buried in Boythorpe Cemetery.

Boythorpe Cemetery *Sat Nav* S40 2NX

☐ David and Joe HUNTER

Brothers, both born in Scarborough, sons of a builder. Joe was wicket-keeper in Australia for Arthur Shrewsbury 1884-85 and represented Yorkshire until 1888. Injury to hands put end to career and succeeded by brother David who played for Yorkshire until 1909. Joe died, aged only 35, at his home, the Wheat Sheaf Inn, Rotherham, on 4 January 1891. Body taken for interment to Dean Road Cemetery, Scarborough, to be buried in grave number 3 on row 19, section F. Twelve-feet high obelisk marks the grave. David, who had captured nearly 1300 victims behind the stumps but never played for England, died on 11 January 1927 at Northstead, Scarborough, and has a grave adjacent to the West Circle.

Dean Road Cemetery *Sat Nav* YO12 7JH

Biography : *"The Reminiscences Of David Hunter: The Genial Yorkshire Stumper"* (W H Smith, 1909; Red Rose Books, 2001)

☐ Kenneth HUTCHINGS

Kent-born amateur batsman, a brilliant driver of the ball. Enjoyed great season 1906 and, though never again so consistently

good, played seven Tests and scored 126 v Australia on the 1907-08 tour. Accomplished slip or boundary fielder. Plaque at his former home in London Road, Southborough, Kent (now a care home). Was killed in action with King's Liverpool Regiment on 3 September 1916 at La Ginchy in France. His name is on *Thiepval Memorial*, France: Pier and Face 1D, 8B and 8C.

71 London Road, Southborough (private home) *Sat Nav*

TN4 0NS   Thiepval Memorial is off the main Bapaume to Albert road, Somme, France.

☐ Jim HUTCHINSON

Professional for Derbyshire 1920-31. Excelled at cover-point. After cricket lived at Thurnscoe, working as a pit safety officer. Claim to fame: longest lived f-c cricketer when died on 7 November 2000 in Doncaster Royal Infirmary, aged 103. Cremation was at Barnsley Crematorium (Ardsley). Remains interred in lawns (section BB, row 11, plot 242), but there is no memorial to be seen.

☐ [Sir Leonard] Len HUTTON

Great opening batsman for Yorkshire and England. Blue plaque unveiled in 1995 by Sir Lawrence Byford, President of Yorkshire County Cricket Club, on n wall of the house where born in 1916 at 5 Woodland View, Fulneck. First played club cricket for Pudsey in 1931. Memorial gates unveiled at cricket ground at Tofts Road, Pudsey St Lawrence in September 1991. Arguably, the country's finest-ever opening batsman. Debut for Yorkshire 1934 and for England 1937. Scored record Test innings of 364 versus Australia at The Oval 1938, aged 22. During training in WW2 broke left arm badly but, batting remained technically as good as ever. 79 Test matches with 6,971 runs for England and became first professional captain of

England between 1952 and 1954/55. Back injury enforced retirement with more than 40,000 first-class runs to his credit. Knighted for services to cricket in Birthday honours 1956. Moved to London and worked for engineering firm J H Fenner, became director. Newspaper columnist, England selector 1975-76 and Yorkshire president. Died in Kingston Hospital, Surrey, on 6 September 1990. Funeral at Putney Vale Crematorium. Memorial service at York Minster. Memorial gates designed by Kate Maddison officially opened at Headingley on 15 August 2001. John Major was invited to perform ceremony but withdrew after objections because he was president of Surrey C.C.C. The brick structure just inside the Hobbs Gates at The Oval, sculpted by Walter Ritchie, unveiled by Hutton's wife on 27 May 1993.

Birthplace 5 Woodland View, Fulneck   *SatNav*   LS28 8NT   Tofts Road, Pudsey St Lawrence   *Sat Nav*   LS28 7SQ   Headingley Cricket Ground   *Sat Nav*   LS6 3BU   Kennington Oval   *Sat Nav*   SE11 5SS

Biography :   *"Cricket is My Life"* autobiography (Hutchinson, 1949) ; *"Len Hutton - The Story of a Great Cricketer"* by J M Kilburn (Pitkins, 1952); *"Cricketing Lives – Len Hutton"* by Laurence Kitchen (Phoenix House, 1953); *"Just My Story"* autobiography (Hutchinson, 1956); *"Fifty Years in Cricket"* autobiography with Alex Bannister (Stanley Paul, 1984); *"Len Hutton - A Biography"* by Gerald Howat (Kingswood, 1988); *"Len Hutton Remembered"* by Donald Trelford (Witherby, 1992).

☐ Jack IDDON

Hard-hitting but reliable right-handed batsman who, for 15 years prior to outbreak of WW2, played for Lancashire. Selected for M.C.C. Test tour of West Indies in 1934-35 and given a county benefit in 1936. After War, went into engineering. Returning from business meeting in London to home in Stockport, was killed in accident on 17 April 1946. Car in which was a passenger collided with a bus near Madeley, and Iddon died immediately from skull fracture. Buried in Leyland churchyard, Church Road, next

door to town museum.

St Andrew's church, Leyland   *Sat Nav*   PR25 3EL

☐ John IKIN

Image © 2015 David Eardley

Left-handed bat and leg-break bowler. Debut for Staffordshire in Minor Counties championship, aged 16. Qualified for Lancashire, first appearing in 1939 but War intervened. Dependable batsman for Lancashire and Test career of 18 matches. Returned to Staffs 1958 as captain till 1967. Briefly coach with England team in Australia 1965-66. League cricket and coaching at Denstone School. Died at home, The Knoll, Bignall End, on 15 September 1984, ten days after suffering heart attack. Funeral at Halmer End, followed by interment in Audley Methodist Cemetery, which is at Bignall End. Cyril Washbrook, Jim Laker and Cedric Rhoades were among mourners.

Audley Methodist Cemetery   *Sat Nav*   ST7 8QE

(above) The Len Hutton Gates at Headingley (© Rich Tea, licensed for re-use under Creative Commons License)

Grave of F.S. (Sir Stanley) Jackson in Welton Cemetery, near Hull

☐ Colin INGLEBY-McKENZIE

First played for Hampshire as a 17 year-ol;
scorer of some 12,000 runs. Cricket writers'
Young Cricketer of Year 1958. In 1961 led
Hampshire with dash and daring to its first
county championship title. Retired in 1965
to go into insurance business. President of
M.C.C. 1996-98; oversaw rule change during
term of office whereby women allowed to
become members. OBE in birthday honours
2005. Died of cancer on 9 March 2006. Colin
Ingleby-McKenzie Stand named after him
at the Ageas Bowl, Southampton.

The Ageas Bowl   *Sat Nav*   SO30 3XH

Biography: *"Many A Slip"* autobiography (Oldbourne, 1962)

☐ [Sir Stanley] F.S. JACKSON

Born in Chapel Allerton, near Leeds, in
1870. Memorial window placed by his
family in Chapel Allerton church. Middle-
order batsman. Educated Harrow and
Trinity College. 'Jacker' was a success from
start. Test debut for England 1893 while
undergraduate. Returned from South
African Army service to Ashes series of
1905 (known as "Jackson's Year"); won
all 5 tosses, headed batting and bowling
averages, and won series against Australia.
M.C.C. president 1921. Unionist MP for
Howdenshire 1915-26 when appointed to
Privy Council, Financial Secretary to War
Office, Governor of Bengal for five years,
during which assassination attempt made
in 1932 at Calcutta. Died on 9 March 1947
at home in Cadogan Square, London. Heart
failure after several weeks' illness. Private
cremation at Golders Green, and buried
in Welton Cemetery, Brough, Yorkshire
(extension to St Helen's graveyard). Joined
on her death in 1958 by his wife Julia, who
was born in Welton. Cemetery is in Common
Lane, where Stanley Jackson Way turns off,
opposite Humber Growers' old offices on
south side of A63. Grave is large flat slab
surrounded by iron railings 30 metres from
cemetery gates.

Welton Cemetery   *Sat Nav*   HU15 1PS   St Matthew's
church, Chapel Allerton   *Sat Nav*   LS7 3QF

Biography : *"The Hon F S Jackson"* by Percy Cross
Standing (Cassell & Co, 1907); *"F S Jackson: A Cricketing
Biography"* by James Coldham (Crowden, 1989)

☐ John JACKSON

Born in Bungay, Suffolk, 1833. Fast bowler
with Notts. Took part in first-ever overseas
cricket tour which sailed for Canada
and United States in 1859; and with All-
England Eleven to Australia in 1863-64.
Called 'Foghorn' Jackson, supposedly
for way he used to blow his nose loudly
after taking a wicket. Died in infirmary at
Brownlow Hill workhouse, Liverpool, on 4
November 1901. Buried in pauper's grave in
Toxteth Park Cemetery, Smithdown Road,
Liverpool. Grave is no 256 in consecrated
section 8. A proper headstone was not laid
until September 2009.

Toxteth Park Municipal Cemetery   *Sat Nav*   L15 2HD

• This is an very impressive Victorian cemetery but it
covers an enormous area. Detailed plans of the cemetery
to locate his grave may be found online.

Biography: *"John Jackson: The Nottinghamshire Foghorn"*
by Gerald Hudd (ACS Lives in Cricket, 2015)

☐ Douglas JARDINE

Born in Bombay where father engaged in legal career. Upright, fearless right-handed batsman, product of Winchester School but coached since prep school days. Strong on leg-side and in back play. Oxford blue and amateur for Surrey in 'twenties, his weight of runs earning Australian tour 1928-29. England captain 1931 and on 1932-33 tour, beating Australia 4-1 by use of bodyline tactics to counter Bradman. Gave up county cricket after leading M.C.C. to India 1933-34 but re-appeared in occasional festival matches after WW2. Died of cancer at nursing home in Montreux, Switzerland, 18 June 1958. Body flown home after cremation and ashes dispersed on Cross Craigs Mountain, near Loch Rannoch, Scotland.

Biography : "Douglas Jardine: Spartan Cricketer" by Christopher Douglas (Allen & Unwin, 1984)

☐ C.L.R. JAMES

Trinidadian, Marxist activist and cricket writer: 'Beyond a Boundary' (1963). Moved to Lancashire 1932, then London and in 1938 to America. Died on 31 May 1989 at 165 Railton Road, Brixton, where plaque unveiled by Darcus Howe in 2004. His name commemorated also at Dalston Library, Hackney, London. Buried in Tunapuna, St Augustine, Trinidad.

Railton Road, Brixton   *Sat Nav*   SE24 0LU

Biography : "C L R James: Cricket, Caribbean and World Revolution" by Farrukh Dhondy (Weidenfeld, 2001; republished as "C L R James: A Life" by Pantheon Books, 2002) "C L R James: The Enigma of Cricket's Philosopher" by Dave Renton (Haus Publishing, 2007)

☐ 'Roly' JENKINS

Leg-spinner who used to bowl in a cap. To South Africa with MCC 1948-49 (replacing Hollies who withdrew) and topped tour bowling averages. Two hat-tricks in match against Surrey 1949. Nine Test appearances. For Worcestershire 1938-58, "…, full of artistry, thought, endeavour, anecdotes and cheerful aggression" [David Lemmon], then Birmingham League for 15 year. Plaque was placed on Ombersley cricket pavilion (photo in Paine's "Innings Complete" volume 14) He died on 20 July 1995. After cremation at Astwood Crematorium his ashes were scattered on the outfield at New Road Ground, Worcester. Portrayed on montage, which his wife Olive describes as "a good likeness", that commemorates Worcestershire greats at rear of D'Oliveira Stand.

New Road Cricket Ground, Worcester *SatNav* WR2 4QQ   Ombersley Cricket Club   *Sat Nav* WR9 0ET
• A photograph of the Jenkins plaque at Ormbersley cricket club may be found in Philip Payne's "Innings Complete" volume 14

☐ Digby JEPHSON

As a boy, a fast bowler for The Wanderers. Took up underarm lob bowling in his third year at Cambridge University. Middle-order batsman with Surrey. Succeeded Kingsmill Key as captain 1900-02. In Gents v Players 1899 took 6-21, and hat-trick v Middlesex 1904. After WW1 coaching at Cambridge. Member of Stock Exchange. Author of poems *"A Few Verses"*. Died at Cambridge 19 January 1926. Funeral at Old Cherry Hinton church, Cambridge, and interred in unmarked grave in parish churchyard.

Biography : *"The Demon & the Lobster : Remarkable Bowlers in the Golden Age"* by Anthony Meredith (Kingswood, 1987).

☐ Gilbert JESSOP

Plaque on wall of birthplace, 30 Cambray Place, Cheltenham. Apart from genius as fieldsman, "The Croucher" was throughout 20-year career fastest scorer in cricket history. A schoolmaster, made Gloucestershire debut 1894, then four years at Cambridge University. County captain 1900. Only 18 England appearances, perhaps owing to impetuosity, but celebrated for innings of 104 in 75 minutes at The Oval 1902 to win Test match by one wicket. Captain of 14th Manchester Regiment in WW1 until invalided out with heart trouble, also ended sporting career. Lived with son at St George's vicarage in Dorchester, where died of heart dropsy on 11 May 1955. Buried in St George's churchyard, Fordington, Dorset. Grave has shield design with small cross over it. House at Cheltenham Grammar School is named after him. In 1957 blue plaque placed on 3 Sunnydale Gardens, the house where he lived in Mill Hill, London, between 1924 and '36.

30 Cambray Place, Cheltenham *Sat Nav* GL50 1JP   3
Sunnydale Gardens, Mill Hill   *Sat Nav* NW7 3PD   St
George's churchyard *Sat Nav* DT1 1LB

Biography : *"A Cricketer's Log"* autobiography (Hodder & Stoughton, 1922); *"The Croucher"* by Gerald Brodribb (Constable, 1985)

• Jessop's grave is hard to find.....["I thought I would never find the final resting place of 'The Croucher'. But then, right next to the path leading to a gate on to a main road and by a small privet hedge I found the grave. It was overgrown, surprisingly small and quite sad really." - from Mike Farley, goodkinghal blog]

☐ Brian JOHNSTON

Wicket-keeper for Eton 2nd XI and at university for Oxford Authentics. Grenadier Guards in WW2, awarded Military Cross. Joined BBC 1946, broadcaster of In Town Tonight, Down Your Way, etc. Became BBC cricket correspondent 1963. TV commentary until 1970, then radio's *Test Match Special* until 1992. OBE 1983 and CBE 1991. Lived in Boundary Road, St John's Wood, London. Tulip tree planted in St John's Wood church gardens in 1994 by the St John's Wood Society in memory of their former president. Died of heart failure on 5 January 1994 at King Edward VII Hospital for Officers in Marylebone, London. Interred in Godlingston Cemetery in seaside town of Swanage where had bought house, Seawall, in 1973. Headstone has a bat, ball, stumps and microphone motif. Local cricket club's pavilion, and a wildflower meadow in Durlston Country Park named after him. The Brian Johnston Memorial Trust founded by widow, Pauline, and son, Ian, in 1995. Managed by the Lord's Taverners it awards scholarships to promising young cricketers, and supports blind cricket.

St John's Wood church gardens   *Sat Nav* NW8 7PF
Godlingston Cemetery, Swanage   *Sat Nav* BH19 3DJ
Croxley Road, Maida Vale *Sat Nav* W9 3HL

Biography : *"It's Been a Lot of Fun"* autobiography (WH Allen, 1974), *"Someone Who Was"* autobiography (Methuen, 1992), *"Summers Will Never Be The Same"* by Christopher Martin-Jenkins and Pat Gibson (Partridge Press, 1994); *"Brian Johnston : The Authorised Biography"* by Tim Heald (Methuen, 1995); *"Johnners - the Life of Brian"* by Barry Johnston (Hodder, 2004).

• The Westminster Society for People with Learning Disabilities had a cherry tree planted in Croxley Road in his memory but the tree died. The M.C.C. then realised the plaque failed to mention Johnston's CBE and Military Cross, so the club planted a new tree, and an updated plaque was officially unveiled by Pauline Johnston.

☐ A.O. [Arthur] JONES

At Cambridge University in same team as Ranji and Jackson. It was said he won his blue because of his fielding. First game for Notts as opening bat in 1892. Forceful, rapid scorer. Once enjoyed stand of 391 for first wicket with Shrewsbury in 1899, year before he succeeded J.A.Dixon as county captain. England captain in 1907-08 but chest illness from which never fully recovered. Gave up cricket. Retired to nursing home in New Forest 1914. Died of tuberculosis at home of brother, Lanark House, Dunstable, on 21 December 1914. Body interred at West Street Cemetery, Dunstable. Buried in grave space E235, which lies 250 metres from road against northern fence of cemetery. Gravestone was paid for by Nottinghamshire C.C.C

West Street Cemetery   *Sat Nav*   LU6 1QD

☐ John JUNIPER

Born Southwick 1862. Left-arm fast bowler with Sussex. Known as 'one-eyed Jack'. Died of typhoid on 20 June 1885, shortly after his final f-c match, at Southwick and buried in St Michael's churchyard, Southwick, nr Brighton.

St Michael & All Angels, Southwick *Sat Nav* BN 42 4GD

☐ Harry JUPP

Opening batsman from Dorking. Known as 'young Stonewall' for defensive skills. Prolific scorer for Surrey, member of early English teams to Australia and played in first-ever Test match. Died at Bermondsey 8 April 1889 and buried on 13th at Nunhead Cemetery, S.E.London. Difficult to find his grave (Con / 19473 / 20) in far SW corner of cemetery, as memorial stone hidden by trees and undergrowth.

Nunhead Cemetery   *Sat Nav*   SE15 3LP

• I joined a tour of the cemetery given by the Friends of Nunhead Cemetery one Sunday afternoon but the route did not include Jupp's grave, so all I can do is quote David Frith: "It is on the outskirts of the cemetery where water accumulates in low ground."

☐ Vallance JUPP

Energetic all-rounder, right-handed bat and off-spin bowler. Initially, professional with Sussex (he was born at Burgess Hill) but, on moving on to Midlands for business reasons, joined Northants as amateur and started a second, more successful career. Appointed county secretary and then captain. Chosen for M.C.C's 1922-23 tour, won 8 England caps. In 1932 took all ten wickets in an innings. Ten times completed 'the double' in a season, exceeded only by Rhodes and

Hirst. Retired from cricket 1938. Died of heart attack while gardening at home, 'Threeways', in Spratton, Northants, on 9 July 1960. Funeral at Counties Crematorium, Milton, Northampton. Ashes interred in rosebed immediately beside brick shelter on right-hand side of main drive. Rose planted and memorial plaque set up.

Counties Crematorium *Sat Nav* NN4 9RN

Biography : A 2011 article by Martin Wilson *"Vallance Jupp: A Forgotten Superstar"* in ACS journal 154, p11-17

☐ *Alec KENNEDY*

From an Edinburgh family that moved to Southampton when a child. Appeared in Hampshire 1st XI, batting no 11, aged only 16, but not a regular until 1909. During 30-year career took more than 2,500 wickets for Hampshire, county record (later exceeded by Shackleton) with bowling based on attributes of length, accuracy and swing. Only five men took more wickets but he never appeared in a Test in England, though went on two overseas tours. Also scored over 16,500 runs. In retirement coach at Cheltenham College and at a school in Johannesburg; also, licensee and tobacconist. During long illness taken to Hythe Hospital, Southampton, where died on 15 November 1959. Funeral service at Highfield church. Body interred in Hollybrook Cemetery, Lordswood Road, Southampton. Follow main path from lodge including round the chapel. It is 12th block along on left-hand side, just after second path from chapel: grave number K12/127, inscribed on kerbing.

Hollybrook Cemetery *Sat Nav* SO16 6LP

☐ *Walter KEETON*

Batsman from Shirebrook. From debut in 1926 became third highest scorer for Notts after George Gunn and Hardstaff. Hit 100 versus every other f-c county. Run over by lorry in Mansfield in 1935 but a nervous temperament more than his lengthy recuperation limited England appearances to two. Picked for his last in 1939, after scoring 312* against Middlesex. Played again after WW2 making 22 more centuries before retirement in 1951. Sports goods business and voluntary worker with disabled children. Died in Forest Town 9 October 1980 and funeral held at Mansfield and District Crematorium after service at local methodist church. No memorial. Cremated remains were strewn in Garden of Remembrance.

☐ *Don KENYON*

Worcestershire opening batsman, scorer of more f-c runs for his county than anyone. 8 Tests for England. Captain of first Worcestershire side to win county

championship in 1964 and '65. Appointed England selector 1965 until 1972. Retired from playing 1967, and following March his career commemorated by planting a copper beech on the ground. Became county president in 1980s. Collapsed and died on 12 November 1996 in the very room named after him at Worcester's New Road County Ground. Plaques in the Garden of Remembrance at Claines church and in memorial garden on Worcester's ground, where his ashes were scattered on the outfield.

Kenyon Room, New Road Cricket Ground *Sat Nav* WR2 4QQ St John's church, Claines *Sat Nav* WR3 7RN

Biography : *"Don Kenyon - His Own Man"* by Tim Jones (Amberley Publishing, 2015).

☐ J.M. 'Jim' KILBURN

Born Sheffield and educated at Barnsley's Holgate Grammar School which closed 2012 when merged to become Horizon Community College. Senior cricket writer for *Yorkshire Post* 1934-76. Founder member of the Cricket Writers Club. *"Sweet Summers"*, edited by Duncan Hamilton, is anthology of his writing [pub Great Northern, 2008]. Elected a Life Member by Yorkshire CCC. Died in Harrogate on 28 August 1993.

Biography : *"Overthrows - A Book of Cricket"* (Stanley Paul, 1975);

☐ Roy KILNER

Childhood home was The Halfway House in Wombwell, south Yorkshire, where father Seth was landlord. Yorkshire debut at Taunton 1911. Integral member of championship XI in 'twenties, relied upon for 1000 runs and 100 wickets each season. Nine England caps, including tour of Australia 1924-25. Returned from winter coaching in India suffering from enteric fever and died in Kedray Fever Hospital, Barnsley, 5 April 1928. Interred in Wombwell Cemetery, Yorkshire, on 20 April. More than 10,000 people present on funeral route, including many famous past Yorkshire players. Grave is no. 396 in new consecrated section 16 (map at entrance to cemetery). Beside the Mitchell & Darfield sportsground is Roy Kilner Road.

Wombwell Cemetery *Sat Nav* S73 8HY   Roy Kilner Road *Sat Nav* S73 8DY

Biography *"The Laughing Cricketer of Wombwell"* by Mick Pope (Darf Publishers, 1990).

• Coming across a photo on flickr of a rail track engineer in the Barnsley area working on cable troughs in 'Tunnel Roy Kilner', I thought I'd found a most unusual way to commemorate a cricketer. In fact the tunnel in question had nothing to do with Roy Kilner the cricketer, and was named after the project manager on site who coincidentally had the same name!

☐ Jack KING

Left-handed batsman and slow left-arm bowler from Lutterworth (north of Rugby). On only Test appearance was asked to open bowling, having scored 60, yet never picked again. In his first Players v Gents match scored 100 in each innings. Once took 7 for 0 in 20 balls to win match v Yorkshire. Double 1912. In 1923 when aged 52 and oldest man in f-c cricket made 205 in a day v Hampshire, and in 1925 scored fastest century of summer. Umpire 1926-31. Died at his daughter's home in Denbigh on 20 (or 18?) November 1946. Funeral at St Mary's church and buried in plot A of Lutterworth churchyard. Grave is in third row and 4 spaces in from path. Headstone not erected until 2003.

St Mary's church, Lutterworth *Sat Nav* LE17 4AN

Biography : *"J.H.King: Leicestershire's Longaevous Left-Hander"* by A.R.Littlewood (ACS Lives In Cricket, 2009)

Wombwell Cemetery, Barnsley: Roy Kilner's memorial is the tall cross

(Below) Jack King's grave in Lutterworth churchyard

☐ KING COLE

Real name - 'Brippokei'. Member of team of Australian Aboriginal cricketers which toured Britain in 1868. After match at Lord's, taken ill with respiratory problems caused by tuberculosis and died of pneumonia at Guy's Hospital on 24 June 1868. Buried at Victoria Park Cemetery (now a park called Meath Gardens) in Tower Hamlets, east London. Commemorative Australian aborigine team visited in 1988, and unveiled a brass plaque and planted eucalyptus tree in his memory. Plaque stolen within days but replaced with another commemorative inscription set in concrete. Follow main tarmac path until crossroads, veer right towards metal benches and the distorted eucalyptus tree.

Meath Gardens *Sat Nav*   E2 0QD

Biography : No biography, but information in *"Cricket Walkabout: The Australian Aborigines In England"* by John Mulvaney and Rex Harcourt (Macmillan Australia 1988) or *"Lord's Dreaming"* by Ashley Mallett (Souvenir Press, 2002)

Image © Ken Goldfinch, Bethnal Green Photo Archive

• A memorial to the whole 1868 aboriginal cricket team stands in western Victoria (Australia). Unveiled by Vic Richardson on 13 October 1951, an eight-foot high granite block with bronze plaques giving the names of the players. It stands in the grounds of the Edenhope Secondary College, beside Lake Wallace, where Tom Wills coached the team.

The Johnny Mullagh Cricket Centre in Harrow, Victoria, tells the story of the aboriginal team. Mullagh, the leading player, lies in Melbourne General Cemetery.

☐ Albert KNIGHT

Forcing opening bat for Leicestershire. Chosen for first M.C.C. tour of Australia 1903-04, played 3 Tests. The bat he scored 70* with is now at Highgate School, but failed in five other innings. Wrote *'The Complete Cricketer'* (1906). Retired 1912 to coach at Highgate School until 1941, living at 24 Hampstead Road next to cricket ground for which also groundsman. His portrait once hung in pavilion. On retiring, widowed, he lived in Muswell Hill. Died in North Middlesex Hospital, London, same day as Joe Vine, 25 April 1946.

Highgate School Museum (visitors by appointment) *Sat Nav*   N6 4AY

☐ Neville KNOX

Outstanding at Dulwich College. Surrey debut 1904. Hobbs thought him best fast bowler he saw, but appeared in only two Tests. Long run-up led to shin soreness and, after missing most of 1908 and 1909 seasons, caused early retirement from the f-c scene in 1910. In WW1 and afterwards served as a Major in Observer Corps. Became stock broker. Died at home, 56 Ditton Road, Surbiton, on 3 March 1935 and cremated at Golders Green Crematorium where ashes dispersed on lawns, without memorial.

Charles KORTRIGHT

In the opinion of many, the fastest bowler there has been. Story goes that he once hurled ball so fast, it bounced once and went clean out of the ground: "This makes me the first cricketer to bowl six byes," he said. Only thirteen when represented Brentwood 1st XI. Invited to appear for Essex and played as amateur for 13 seasons, but never for England. After leaving cricket an enthusiastic golfer and, thanks to an inheritance, "never did a day's work in my life". Died on 12 December 1952 at home, 'Earlywood', in South Weald, Essex, and buried in Fryerning churchyard, Essex, in newer part of churchyard. Beyond three pine trees turn left off main path and five metres along side path. Grave is on left, its inscription facing north-east.

Church of St Mary the Virgin, Fryerning *Sat Nav* CM4 0NL

Biography : *"Korty, the Legend Explained"* by Charles Sale (Ian Henry, 1986); *"The Demon & the Lobster : Remarkable Bowlers in the Golden Age"* by Anthony Meredith (Kingswood, 1987).

[Sir] Frances Eden LACEY

For 28 years Secretary of M.C.C. and, on retirement in 1926, first man to be knighted for services to the game. Restored declining finances of club. In 1902 initiated Easter coaching classes. Previously, was forcing batsman for Hampshire and for some time captain. Made record score in minor county cricket of 323* v Norfolk in 1887. Died at Sutton Veny House, near Warminster, Wiltshire, on 26 May 1946 and cremated at Bristol. There is no memorial but large portrait of him hangs in Lord's pavilion.

Jim LAKER

Brought up in Saltaire and played local club matches. Side street named after Laker in the district of Shipley. Yorkshire coached him but no f-c cricket. In North Africa during WW2 developed his off-spin and after demobilisation settled in Catford, south London, so registered with Surrey 1946. Took almost 1400 wickets for Surrey to 1959, as well as 550 in other f-c cricket. With Tony Lock formed deadly strike partnership, key to Surrey winning a run of county championships. 46 England caps including, most famously, against Australia at Old Trafford 1956 when returned match figures of 19-90. Essex 1962-65 as an amateur, then became BBC TV commentator. Died at his home in Putney on 23 April 1986. Funeral held at Putney Vale Crematorium. By request of his wife, Lillie, ashes were scattered on pitch at Kennington Oval, watched over by Micky Stewart.

Jim Laker Place, Shipley *Sat Nav* BD18 4SR

Biography : *"Spinning Round the World"* autobiography (Muller, 1957); *"Over To Me"* autobiography (Muller, 1960); *"Laker: Portrait of a Legend"* by Don Mosey (McDonald Queen Anne Press, 1989); *"Jim Laker: A Biography"* by Alan Hill (Andre Deutsch, 1998); *"Jim Laker: 19 for 90"* by Brian Scovell (Tempus, 2006)

Harold LARWOOD

Fast bowler with Nottinghamshire and England. Born at Nuncargate, north of Nottingham: plaque depicting a bowler's hand gripping a cricket ball outside house at 17 Chapel Street where grew up. Worked in coal mining aged 14 to 18, then professional cricket. 21 Test appearances and 78 wickets. Never picked again for England after 1932-33 bodyline series. Played league cricket in Blackpool in 1939: plaque on pavilion at Blackpool Cricket Club, Stanley Park, West Park Drive. From 1946-50 when Jack

Fingleton helped arrange for his family to emigrate to Sydney, owned confectioner's in Blackpool at corner of Victory Road and Caunce Street. Awarded MBE 1993. Died 22 July 1995 at Randwick, Sydney, New South Wales, and ashes interred in wall next to Holy Trinity Church, Kingsford, NSW where he attended services. His Sydney home now demolished.

Bronze statue by sculptor Neale Andrew in Kirkby-in-Ashfield town centre unveiled on 3 June 2002 by Larwood's daughter, Enid. In 2009 she again travelled across world to Blackpool to unveil a plaque where sweet shop once stood; and in 2014 a small park on the site renamed 'Harold Larwood Park'.

Chapel Street, Nuncargate *Sat Nav* NG17 9EE   Blackpool Cricket Club   *SatNav*   FY3 9EQ   Harold Larwood Park *SatNav* FY1 3JP   Larwood Statue, Kirkby-in-Ashfield *Sat Nav* NG17 7BQ

Biography : *"Bodyline?"* autobiography (Elkin Matthews and Marrot, 1933); *"The Larwood Story"* by Kevin Perkins (W H Allen, 1965); *"Blackpool Cricket Club Professional"* by Gerry Wolstenholme (2003; Red Rose Books 2009); *"Harold Larwood, Nottinghamshire and England"* by Raymond Smith (self-published 2006); *"Harold Larwood"* by Duncan Hamilton (Quercus, 2009).

☐ [Sir] Walter LAWRENCE

Founder in 1934 of The Lawrence Trophy, awarded with prize of 100 guineas, now £3000, for fastest century of season. Director of building contractor and joinery business. Owned his own cricket field at Hyde Hall, Herts. Knighted 1924. Died at Hyde Hall after 3 months of illness on 15 November 1939. Ashes brought from Golders Green for interment in the churchyard at Great St Mary's parish church, Sawbridgeworth, Herts. Hyde Hall was divided into flats in 1978.

Great St Mary's parish church   *Sat Nav*   CM21 9AH
Hyde Hall   *Sat Nav*   CM21 9JA

☐ Walter LEES

Yorkshire-born,   fast-medium   bowler for Surrey. In 1905 England 12th man at Nottingham but never played against Australia. Five Tests on M.C.C.'s 1905-06 tour of South Africa. Professional with West Hartlepool CC 1921. Died at The Good Intent Inn, West Hartlepool, on 10 September 1924. At time of death, coach to Durham C.C.C. Buried in Stranton Grange Cemetery: the grave in consecrated section has reference 14.B.11

Stranton Cemetery Lodge   *Sat Nav*   TS25 5DD

☐ Geoffrey LEGGE

An Oxford University and Kent amateur batsman, and county captain 1928-30. Five Test appearances on tours of South Africa 1927-28 and New Zealand 1929-30. In WW2 Lt Commander in volunteer reserve on H.M.S. Vulture. Killed on training flight at Bramford Speke, Devon, on 21 November 1940. His name appears on chapel war memorial at Malvern College. Buried in St Merryn churchyard, Cornwall.

St Merryn church, nr Padstow   *Sat Nav*   PL28 8ND

Charles LENNOX

2nd Duke of Richmond and grandson of Charles II. Cricket's first patron, he ran a team drawn from best cricketers in west Sussex to whom he gave employment on Goodwood estate. Shaped the game and spread cricket in early 18th century. Died 8 August 1750 and buried in family vault in Chichester Cathedral.

Chichester Cathedral   *Sat Nav*   PO19 1PX

Biography :   *"The Duke Who Was Cricket"*   by John Marshall (Frederick Muller Ltd. 1961)

Henry LEVESON GOWER

"Shrimp" was Surrey captain 1908-10 who took an M.C.C. team to South Africa in 1909-10. Test selector and chairman. Had from 1898 served on several committees at Lord's. Chairman of Surrey 1929-49. Organiser of Scarborough Festival from Thornton's death until 1950s. In recognition of long service to cricket, knighted 1953. Died in St Mary Abbot's Court, Kensington, on 1 February 1954. Funeral at Holy Trinity, Sloane Square, followed by interment in churchyard at St James's, Titsey, on family estate near Limpsfield, Surrey. Memorial a few paces from lych-gate below window. A large block surmounted by cross. Inscriptions worn.

St James's church, Titsey   *Sat Nav*   RH8 0SD

Biography: *"Off and On the Field"* autobiography (Stanley Paul, 1953)

Maurice LEYLAND

Played as boy with Harrogate C.C. and given a trial with Yorkshire in 1920. Regular member of Yorkshire's team that won eleven championships between Wars. Won 41 caps for England as middle-order batsman and especially good record v Australia, where he made three tours. Scorer of nearly 34,000 runs with 80 centuries. Following death of Roy Kilner, called on to bowl left-arm spinners more frequently. Hat-trick in 1935 against Surrey. Occasional appearances after War (during which was in command of anti-aircraft battery) then Yorkshire coach before ill-health enforced retirement. Hon membership of M.C.C. 1949. After several months in Scotton Bank Hospital, near Knaresborough, died there on 1 January 1967. Funeral at Trinity Methodist church on 4 January then to Harrogate Crematorium, the cremated remains being scattered in the gardens of rest at Stonefall Cemetery. The Leyland Gates were erected in tribute to him in north-east corner of St George's Road cricket ground, Harrogate in 1965 but removed after being repeatedly damaged by vandals.

Harrogate Cricket Club Ground   *Sat Nav*   HG2 9BP

[A.F.A.] 'Dick' LILLEY

Despite lack of records, was in selectors' view premier wicket-keeper in England for a decade and kept in 35 Tests. Brought up in Birmingham. Working as packer at Cadbury's, played for works team, nicknamed 'Dick' after likeness to founder Richard Cadbury. Best season for Warwickshire (to whom recommended by John Shilton) in 1895, their first in first-class cricket, scoring one run short of 1,400 runs and capturing 60 victims. Played until 1911. On giving up cricket, went to Bristol as landlord of the Talbot Hotel in Knowle. Died at his home in Brislington on 17 November 1929 and buried in Brislington Cemetery, grave number 888 Green.

Brislington Cemetery   *Sat Nav*   BS4 4LT

Biography : *"Twenty Four Years of Cricket"* autobiography (Mills & Boon, 1912)

☐ James LILLYWHITE junior

Born Westhampnett, Sussex, 1842, nephew of William Lillywhite. Professional cricketer for 22 seasons as left-arm bowler with Sussex. Toured Australia with W.G.Grace in 1873-74 and again, as captain, in 1876-77 when first Test Match played at Melbourne. Arranged four more tours in 1880s with Shaw and Shrewsbury, until unprofitable to continue. England's first Test captain and last survivor of the team on his death at Westerton, near Chichester, West Sussex, on 25 October 1929. Buried in St Peter's churchyard at Westhampnett. Headstone stands on northern side of church, approx. ten metres from wall. On church's southern inside wall is a chart to help locate grave.

St Peter's church, Westhampnett   *Sat Nav*   PO18 0NT.

☐ James LILLYWHITE senior

Son of William Lillywhite; born 1825 at Hove. A lesser player than his cousin, James junior (above), turned to coaching at schools like Eton, Westminster and eventually Cheltenham College where introduced the Cricket Festival in 1872. Conceived the 'James Lillywhite Cricketers' Annual', published from 1872-1900, usually referred to as "Red Lilly" because of colour of its cover. Owned a sports goods shop at 3 Queens Circus, Montpellier, and his household lived in rooms above. Died on 24 November 1882 and his remains interred in Cheltenham Cemetery on 29 November, the funeral attended by masters and boys of the college, his cousin James Lillywhite and E.M.Grace among others. Grave number is O 2070.

Cheltenham Cemetery, Bouncers Lane   *Sat Nav*   GL52 5JT

Biography : included in *"Lillywhite's Legacy: A History of the Cheltenham Cricket Festival"* by Grenville Simons (Wisteria 2004)

• The Lillywhite Family Museum is located in Palm Coast, Florida.

☐ William LILLYWHITE

From Westhampnett, Sussex, became landlord of Royal Sovereign Inn at Brighton, and played little cricket until age of 30 when appeared more frequently for Sussex. In 1844 employed as ground bowler at Lord's and played as required for M.C.C. or The Players. Instigator and renowned exponent of round-arm bowling style: "The Nonpareil". In 1851 coach at Winchester College. Died of cholera at home of one of his sons in Islington, London, on 21 August 1854. At first buried in common grave at Highgate Cemetery but in 1855 reburied at place where M.C.C. put up obelisk in his memory. William's grave also contains body of his wife and 4 of his 14 children (not son Fred, the first man to print scorecards and editor of Lillywhite's Guide). The pillar has collapsed, the engraving worn and the scene become dilapidated yet it remains of interest on guided cemetery tours, the only way allowed to see it. On the memorial was an upset wicket and the word "Bowled".

Highgate Cemetery   *Sat Nav*   N6 6PJ

Biography :   *"Lillywhite, the First Modern Bowler"* by Martin Wilson (Christopher Saunders, 2011)

☐ [Charles] 'Buck' LLEWELLYN

South African batsman and slow left-armer, born at Pietermaritzburg in 1876. On Major Poore's recommendation in 1899 joined Hampshire as professional. Qualified 1901 and in England Test squad 1902. Toured Australia with South African team 1910-11, and England in 1912. Made fifteen Test appearances, once incorrectly thought to be first Cape Coloured to play in Test cricket. In 1911 first Test player to join a Lancashire League club (Accrington). Inactive since breaking thigh in 1960, died at Northcroft Hospital, Chertsey, Surrey, 7 June 1964. Funeral at St John's Crematorium, Woking, Surrey. Ashes strewn on south-east side of orchard lawns beside three parrotia trees.

Biography : *"C.B.Llewellyn: A Study in Equivocation"* by Neil Jenkinson (ACS Lives in Cricket, 2012)

☐ Bert LOCK

Born into a family of market-gardeners. In 1920s bowler on Surrey staff, then played for Devon. Demobilised from RAF in 1945 and restored The Oval from wartime use by the military, all mud and barbed wire to newly-turfed ground. Groundsman at The Oval for 20 years until in 1967 chosen as TCCB's Inspector of Pitches. Died at his south-east London home on 19 May 1978 and funeral at Honor Oak Crematorium.

Honor Oak Crematorium *Sat Nav* SE23 3RD

☐ Tony LOCK

Fiery left-arm spin bowler who won 49 Test caps for England. Played for Surrey 1946-63 and in partnership with Laker helped Surrey to win county championships 1952-58. Left for Leicestershire, becoming captain

in 1966. Captain of Western Australia 1967-71 and led state to its first Sheffield Shield title since first winning it 22 years before. Only seven bowlers have taken more than his 2,844 f-c wickets and only two players took more catches than this fearless short-leg fielder's 831. Died of cancer in a hospice in Perth on 29 March 1995. Funeral held at Anglican Cathedral, Perth. His ashes and those of his wife taken by daughter Jackie home to Melbourne to be laid beside a favourite flowering plum tree in her garden. The Lock Stand at Kennington Oval redeveloped in 2015.

Biography : *"For Surrey and England"* autobiography (Hodder, 1957); *"Put Lock On"* by Kirwan Ward (Robert Hale, 1972); *"Tony Lock: Aggressive Master of Spin"* by Alan Hill (The History Press, 2008)

☐ Bill LOCKWOOD

In his first county match for Notts up against W.G.Grace. Unable to retain first XI place and joined Surrey in 1889, despite new offer from Notts. Fast bowler with sharp break-back, lethal on wet wickets. During 1894-95 Australian tour, bowling skills deserted him and dropped out of county cricket only to begin new career, as good as ever, after taking the pledge. From 1898 until 1904 partnership with Tom Richardson flourished. On retirement back to Nottinghamshire. Died at home in Radford on 27 April 1932. Buried in unmarked grave in Beeston Cemetery, Notts.

☐ George LOHMANN

Born at Kensington in 1865, and thus qualified for Middlesex but, having learnt cricket at Wandsworth, made debut with Surrey in 1884. In 1885 took 150 wickets at 14 runs each and in best season (1888) took 209 wickets at 11 each. Brilliant exponent

of medium-paced cutters, with devastating fast yorker. Health broke down after 1892 and missed two seasons but back to best form and regained England place in 1896, his benefit year. Spent winters in dry South African climate for his health and employed by cricket enthusiast J.D.Logan. Died of tuberculosis on 1 December 1901 at Matjesfontein [pronounced 'Mikeys fontyne'] and buried in local cemetery with elaborate monument paid for by Surrey C.C.C. and South African friends.

Biography : "George Lohmann: The Beau Ideal" by Ric Sissons (Pluto Press, 1991); "George Lohmann: Pioneer Professional" by Keith Booth (Sports Books, 2007)

□ Thomas LORD

Born in Thirsk, Yorkshire, but family moved and schooled in Diss, Norfolk. Attendant at White Conduit Club in London. Acquired lease to first cricket ground, now Dorset Square, in 1787 but obliged to move (with the turf) to a second ground in 1811, and thirdly to present site at St John's Wood, London. Retired with his profits to Hampshire in 1825. There died on 13 January 1832 and buried in West Meon churchyard. In 1951 M.C.C. paid for a new flat slab of Portland limestone to cover the elevated tomb, which rests in lower part of graveyard below steps. Commemorative plaque unveiled 9 May 1973 in Dorset Square to mark site of his first ground. M.C.C. placed another plaque, unveiled in 2006 by England captains Andrew Strauss and Charlotte Edwards, on site of second ground where Park Road bridge crosses canal. Also plaque on house next door to his birthplace in 16 Kirkgate, Thirsk. In 1977 numbers 14 and 16 Kirkgate became local history museum, including the Thomas Lord Room of cricket memorabilia, where new plaque unveiled by MCC Secretary Roger Knight in 2004.

Lord's 1st ground (Dorset Square) *Sat Nav* NW1 6QJ
Lord's 2nd ground (Park Road) *Sat Nav* NW8 7RH St John's church, West Meon *Sat Nav* GU32 1LF Kirkgate, Thirsk *Sat Nav* YO7 1PQ

• A further memorial to Lord is the wall tile with his profile in relief placed on north-bound platform of St John's Wood underground station, London.

□ LORD'S Memorial Gallery

Wooden memorial board is tribute to M.C.C. members who died in WW1; was mounted on wall of pavilion's top staircase at Lord's Cricket Ground. The Imperial Cricket Memorial Gallery was opened by HRH the Duke of Edinburgh on 27 April 1953 to commemorate cricketers who died in two World Wars. Sited on a disused racquets court. Exhibits donated by individuals and from all the cricket-playing Commonwealth countries filled the gallery space on two floors. Most treasured exhibit was urn containing The Ashes. Redesigned in 2002 as the M.C.C. Museum, and open daily.

Lord's Cricket Ground *Sat Nav* NW8 8QN

Alfred LUCAS

Amateur batsman with Surrey. Member of Lord Harris's 1878-79 team to Australia. Five Test appearances. Joined Essex as captain and, despite calls of business, scored 10,000 runs opening the batting. Died at Great Waltham, Essex, on 12 October 1923 and buried, as was Kortright, in Fryerning church cemetery, Essex.

Church of St Mary the Virgin, Fryerning *Sat Nav* CM4 0NL

Frederick LUCAS

Born Warnham, Sussex, in 1860. His cousin 'Bunny' (Alfred) represented England. Left-hander, emerged in 1885 with magnificent 215 not out which W.G. described as best innings he had ever seen. It was Sussex's first double-century. Died on 7 November 1887, aged 27. Impressive memorial tablet inside St Margaret's church, Warnham, records he "died suddenly of cholera at Surat, India, while travelling round the world."

St Margaret's church, Warnham *Sat Nav* RH12 3QW

Brian LUCKHURST

Right-handed opening batsman. Played for Kent and England between 1958 and 1976, scoring 22,000 first-class runs. Then captained 2nd XI and was club coach. Awarded office of Kent County Cricket Club's president 2004. Died from cancer of oesophagus on 1 March 2005. Funeral held on 14 March at St Anthony's church in Alkham village, where he lived near Dover. After cremation at Barham Crematorium, the ashes taken in October to St Lawrence ground at Canterbury to be scattered on the cricket field.

St Anthony's church, Alkham *Sat Nav* CT15 7DF

Biography : *"Boot Boy to President"* autobiography (KOS Media, 2004)

Hon Alfred LYTTELTON

Took up wicket-keeping at Eton College. Cambridge blue 1876-79. Was also in 1880s among best bats in England but declined captaincy of 1882-83 Australian tour. In 1884, with pads still on, he captured 4 for 19 with underarm lobs. All-rounder playing football for England, and among best tennis players in country. President of M.C.C. in 1898. Barrister and Unionist politician, Colonial Secretary 1903-06. Died following an operation at Marylebone, London, on 5 July 1913. Buried in St John the Baptist churchyard, Hagley Hall (Worcestershire). Large plaque in memory of him close to the altar inside St John the Baptist church, Wittersham, Kent.

St John's church, Wittersham *Sat Nav* TN30 7EA   St John the Baptist, Hagley Hall Park *Sat Nav* DY9 9LQ

Biography : *"Alfred Lyttelton, an Account of His Life"* by Edith Sophy Balfour Lyttelton (Hard Press Publishing, 2013)

George MACAULAY

Born in Thirsk, Yorkshire, 1897: memorial plaque on birthplace in Town End. Portrait and inscription in Barnard Castle School hall; included, too, in names on chapel's War memorial. Joined Yorkshire aged 22 after serving with Artillery in WW1 and briefly bank clerk. Between 1920 and 1921 slowed down bowling to ensure unremitting accuracy. Fiercely enthusiastic and competitive. Determined fielder off own bowling, which led to eventual retirement when finger damaged fielding a drive from

Geary. Only three Yorkshiremen had taken more wickets, yet he played in only eight Test matches, and only once v Australia. League cricket until joined R.A.F. in 1939. Pilot Officer in Volunteer Reserve. Killed on 13 December 1940 in flying accident [also reported as pneumonia?] over Sullom Voe. Buried 'away from home' in Lerwick New Cemetery, Shetland: terrace 9, grave 35.

Lerwick New Cemetery *Sat Nav* ZE1 0YB.

Image © 2008, courtesy of Philip Paine

☐ Jack MacBRYAN

All-round games player, including Olympics hockey. Amateur batsman for Somerset. His sole Test appearance for England in 1924 blighted by rain and he never got on the field. Lived in Cambridge, and was 90 when he died on 14 July 1983. Funeral was a week later at City of Cambridge Crematorium and his ashes scattered in the crematorium gardens.

City of Cambridge Crematorium *Sat Nav* CB3 0JJ

Biography : *"Cricket's Unholy Trinity"* by David Foot (Stanley Paul, 1985)

☐ Ted McDONALD

Outstanding Australian fast bowler on 1921 tour of England. Test career of 43 wickets in 11 Tests in two-year period. Returned to qualify for Lancashire and in first full season (1925) took over 200 wickets. Left county cricket 1931. Proprietor of Raikes Hall Hotel in Blackpool. Driving home from charity cricket match, involved in minor traffic accident on Blackrod by-pass near Bolton on 22 July 1937. While assessing damage by roadside, struck by third vehicle and killed with neck and skull fractures. Cremated at Blackpool's Layton Cemetery. Ashes interred in a wall niche under the

Columbarium - in bottom row of back wall, thirty two from right-hand side.

Layton Cemetery *Sat Nav* FY3 7BD

Biography : *"The Silk Express"* by Nick Richardson (Ken Piesse Football & Cricket Books, 2015)

☐ Charlie McGAHEY

With Perrin, one of the 'Essex twins'. Cheerful character and attractive batsman for 28 seasons. Captaincy 1907-11. Fearing tuberculosis would cause him to give up cricket, travelled to Australia in 1897-98 and health much improved. Then, following best season and Wisden C of Y, chosen for MacLaren's 1901-02 Australian tour where played his only Tests. From 1930 Essex scorer, including Holmes & Sutcliffe partnership of 555 in 1932. Died at Whipps Cross 10 January 1935 due to accident on Christmas Day when slipped on a greasy pavement, received septic poisoning to finger. Funeral on 15 January at West Ham Cemetery. Grave number NE1/ H/ 7.

West Ham Cemetery *Sat Nav* E7 9DG

Biography : *"Cheerful Charlie"* by Jan Kemp (self-published, 1989)

☐ Francis MacKINNON

Born Kensington 1848, then lived at Acrise Park, nr Folkestone, and represented county of Kent for 4 years. Invited by Lord Harris on 1878-79 Australian tour and played in only 'Test'. President of Kent C.C.C. and first president of The Cricket Society. Clan chief of the Mackinnons. Died at Drumduan, on the edge of Forres in Morayshire on 27 February 1947, one month short of 99th birthday, this being longest life-span of any Test cricketer at the time. Buried on 1 March at Cluny Hill Cemetery, Forres, in grave 1095 with his wife Emily who died in 1934. His cricket bat donated to Falconer Museum, Forres.

Cluny Hill Cemetery   *Sat Nav*   IV36 1DW   Falconer Museum *Sat Nav*   IV36 1PH

☐ Archie MacLAREN

Stylish Edwardian batsman and formidable presence as captain. Debut for Lancashire 1890 while still at Harrow School when made 108, enabling Lancashire to win match. Also finished career with a large score: double century in New Zealand 1922-23 at age of 52, but then knee injury prevented him playing again. In between, scorer of more than 22,000 f-c runs, including 424 for Lancashire v Somerset 1895 - only score above 400 made in county championship until 1988. Represented England in 35 Test matches, in 22 of which captained the side. Arranged his own third tour of Australia 1901-02, the last before M.C.C. took responsibility. Relinquished coaching post at Old Trafford in 1923 and, apart from managing Joel's 1925-26 South African tour, no further connection with cricket. In 1938 wife inherited legacy, bought Warfield Park estate in Berkshire and built new house. Here MacLaren died on 17 November 1944. Funeral held at St Michael The Archangel, parish church of Warfield, north of Bracknell. Buried in approximate centre of cemetery opposite parish church. Low headstone and grave surrounded by iron railing. Grave renovated 2004.

St Michael's church, Warfield   *Sat Nav*   RG42 6EG

Biography : *"Archie: A Biography of A.C.MacLaren"* by Michael Down (Allen & Unwin, 1981); *"Archie Remembered"* by Malcolm Lorimer (self-published 2004 in limited edition of 424 copies)

☐ [J.E.P.] Emile McMASTER

Born County Down, Ireland 1861. Educated at Cambridge, winning a tennis blue. Barrister. Invited on Major Warton's tour of South Africa 1888-89 where played sole Test and failed to score. Had he been a better batsman, would not have become well-known. Last lived at Freshwater, Isle of Wight, but died in Bloomsbury in London 7 June 1929. Buried in Highgate Cemetery.

Highgate Cemetery   *Sat Nav*   N6 6PJ

Biography: chapter in *"Brief Candles"* by Keith Walmsley (ACS Lives in Cricket, 2012)

☐ Gregor MAGREGOR

A child prodigy from Edinburgh, took a hat-trick and scored 65 in match when only nine, won colours in second year at Uppingham School. 'Mac' was finest wicket-keeper of his day. Retired 1908 with 8 Test caps and an Australian tour to his credit. Member of Counties Advisory Committee. Also, rugby international for Scotland, winning 13 caps 1896-99. Died 20 August 1919 in a Marylebone nursing home and buried in West Hampstead Cemetery. To find the grave, walk through gates, follow perimeter path to left and Magregor lies in grave 06 62 on right side of path.

West Hampstead Cemetery   *Sat Nav*   NW6 1DR

☐ Harry MAKEPEACE

Born Middlesbrough 1881, but family from Liverpool. Dour opening batsman for Lancashire, stepping into Barlow's tradition ("no fours before lunch"). Four Tests and one tour of Australia, making century and two fifties, yet never picked for England again. Lancashire county coach until War. Died at home in Spital, Bebington, Cheshire, on 19 December 1952. Funeral at Landican Crematorium, Birkenhead. Ashes collected to be scattered on pitch at Old Trafford.

☐ [R.H.] Harry MALLETT

All-round athlete representing Durham at rugby, football and track events as well as cricket, as a batsman and in 1897 captain. Only one f-c appearance (for M.C.C.) in 1901 but a leading administrator, helping form the Minor Counties Association in 1895 and serving as hon secretary. Great friend of West Indies cricket, guiding formation of a Board of Control and their membership of the I.C.C. Managed their first Test-playing parties to England 1928 and Australia 1930-31 as well as M.C.C. in the Caribbean. Arranged programmes for Test sides touring England through 1930s (always ensuring Durham was on the fixture list). Died on 29 November 1939 at his home in Ickenham (Middlesex) and funeral at Golders Green Crematorium. Ashes dispersed without commemoration.

• Harry Mallett's name may not be widely known but, in researching Test cricket tours, I realised how much the M.C.C. and Imperial Cricket Conference called on him to make arrangements for and manage tours between the Wars. His was an interesting life in cricket.

☐ Frank MANN

Attacking batsman for Middlesex 1909 to 1931. Won county championship in his first season as captain (1921). Invited to take M.C.C. side to South Africa in 1922-23 for 5 Test matches, as did son George in 1948. Director of family brewing business Watney Mann. Died on 6 October 1964 at Upper Farm House, Milton Lilbourne, Wiltshire. His body taken back to Norfolk family seat of Thelveton Hall, near Diss, for interment on Saturday 10 October in the family plot on south side of St Andrew's church, Thelveton.

St Andrew's church, Thelveton *Sat Nav* IP21 4EP

Biography: *"Frank and George Mann: Brewing, Batting and Captaincy"* by Brian Rendell (ACS Lives in Cricket, 2015)

(above) The Leyland Gates at Harrogate   (Below) Geroge Mann's grave in West Woodhay churchyard

☐ George MANN

Batsman for Middlesex. Won a Military Cross in Italy 1943. Appointed to lead M.C.C. touring side in South Africa 1948-49 and won the series 2-0, scoring hundred in fourth Test. Chairman of T.C.C.B. Appointed CBE 1983. Lived nr Newbury in West Berkshire for 40 years. Director of family brewing business. Died in Dalecare nursing home on August 8, 2001. Family funeral at West Woodhay on 16 August at church of St Laurence, and interred in wife's grave in churchyard. On RHS of path from porch to church. Also, inside church, entry made in the book of remembrance.

St Laurence's church, West Woodhay   *Sat Nav*   RG20 0BL

Biography: *"Frank and George Mann: Brewing, Batting and Captaincy"* by Brian Rendell (ACS Lives in Cricket, 2015)

☐ [Charles Stowell] 'Father' MARRIOTT

Born Heaton Moor (Stockport) 1895. Played 3 seasons for Lancashire before transferring to Kent when became schoolmaster in charge of cricket at Dulwich College. Leg-spinner, made only one Test appearance, taking 11 for 96 v West Indies at age of 37 but, after touring India with M.C.C. in 1933-34, not selected again. Swanton wrote that his fielding was bad and his batting worse but was a beautiful bowler. Retired to Kilmington, Wiltshire. Died in hospital at Dollis Hill on 13 October 1966. Funeral and requiem at St Peter's church, Streatham. Buried in family plot on northern side of St Mary's Church, Cotesbach, Leicestershire [photo of location on cricketarchive]

St Mary's Church, Cotesbach *Sat Nav* LE17 4HX   St Mary the Virgin, Kilmington   *Sat Nav*   BA12 6RD

☐ Howard MARSHALL

London-based journalist and broadcaster, once thought the most famous voice on British radio. Originator of modern cricket commentary who devised ground rules, still obeyed eighty years later. During WW2 a Director at Ministry of Food but also broadcasting, including D-Day landings. Last cricket commentaries: the Victory Tests of 1945. Died at home in village of Easton, nr Newbury, 27 October 1973 and buried in Welford parish churchyard, West Berkshire. Grave lies beside main path of churchyard, on left as church is approached.

St Gregory's church, Welford   *Sat Nav*   RG20 8HR

Biography : *"Reflections on a River"* autobiographical (H.F. & G. Witherby, London, 1967)

Malcolm MARSHALL

Great West Indian fast bowler of the 1980s. Captured 376 Test wickets at average cost of only 20.94, including five in an innings 22 times. Succeeded Andy Roberts as Hampshire's overseas professional for 14 years. Invited in 1996 to assist the declining Windies team as coach but driven often to desperation by the team's outlook. Unable to continue in March 1999 while undergoing treatment for colon cancer. Died in hospital in Bridgetown on 4 November 1999. Funeral on 14 November conducted by Rev Wesley Hall at St Bartholomew's church at Charnocks, Barbados. Memorial in churchyard is a black stone, with poem written by his son Mali engraved on the marble. Road leading into Southampton's Ageas Bowl ground was named Marshall Drive in memory of both Malcolm and unrelated Roy Marshall.

Marshall Drive, Southampton   *Sat Nav*   SO30 3XH

Biography : *"Maco: The Malcolm Marshall Story"* by Patrick Symes (Parrs Wood Press, 2000)

Frederick MARTIN

Left-arm fast bowler, chosen for Kent in 1885 and for England against Australia in 1890, year he took 190 wickets. Joined Read's tour of South Africa 1891-92. Called "Nutty" but had no idea how nickname started. Died with a sudden seizure on night of 13 December 1921 at his home in Dartford. Interred in East Hill Cemetery (The Brent), Dartford, Kent, in grave number 3500.

East Hill Cemetery, Dartford   *Sat Nav*   DA1 1RZ

Jack MASON

Opening bat or lower down, strong in a crisis. Also, notable slip fielder. Played in all 5 matches of 1897-98 series for Stoddart's team v Australia but never in a Test in England. In 1901 first Kent cricketer to do the 'double'. Invited by M.C.C. to lead 1905-06 tour of South Africa but declined. Headed f-c batting averages 1909. Died at Cooden Beach, Sussex, on 15 October 1958. Buried in Bexhill Cemetery in plot FEF01 with his wife who died 1950. Memorial on the grave.

Bexhill Cemetery, Turkey Lane   *Sat Nav*   TN39 5HT

Biography: *"Test of Time: Travels in Search of a Cricketing Legend"* by John Lazenby (John Murray, 2005)

Peter MAY

Born in Reading and educated at Charterhouse, where coached to a perfect batting technique by George Geary. At Cambridge University was among a formidable batting line-up. Cricket Writers' *'Young Cricketer of Year'* 1951. Amateur for Surrey throughout 1950s, winning five consecutive championships under Surridge and two more when made captain himself in 1957. Noted for his on-drive, the finest post-War batsman in country by standards of power, concentration, technical correctness. First chosen for England in 1951 when scored century on debut. Succeeded Len Hutton as England Test captain and went undefeated in any series until Australia 1958-59. Shyness and charm concealed toughness as skipper; led the side in then record number of 41 Test matches. Scored 285 not out against West Indies at Edgbaston 1957, then the record score for an England captain. Retired 1962 when aged only 32, partly for health and partly business reasons as insurance broker at Lloyds. Test selector from 1965 to 1968 and again as chairman 1982-88. CBE

1981. Lived at Cranleigh before moving to Liphook. Was due to take on presidency of Surrey C.C.C. in 1995 for 150th anniversary year but died at Liphook of a brain tumour on 27 December 1994. Funeral at Guildford Crematorium after which family collected ashes. The first round match between Surrey and Berkshire on 27 June 1995 dedicated to him. The Peter May Enclosure and Lock Stand on eastern side of The Oval being redeveloped as a new Peter May Stand from 2015. Otherwise no memorial is known.

Kennington (Kia) Oval   *Sat Nav*   SE11 5SS

Biography: *"Living biographies for young people: Peter May"* by Robert Rodrigo (Phoenix House, 1960); *"A Game Enjoyed"* autobiography (Stanley Paul, 1985); *"Peter May - The Authorised Biography"* by Alan Hill (Andre Deutsch, 1996);

☐ *Phil MEAD*

Joined groundstaff at The Oval but moved to Hampshire. Left-handed batsman, change bowler and superb slip fielder. Debut v 1905 Australians at Southampton, scoring 41* ; century in next match. Went on to career spanning 32 years with Hampshire. With 153 centuries, Mead is fourth on all-time list of hundreds, as well as fourth for run-making: scored slightly more than 55,000 runs, behind only Hobbs, Woolley and Hendren. Is highest run-scorer in county championship. Uniquely, he took part in century partnerships for all ten wickets for his county (Rhodes and Hammond did so in all cricket). Made 1000 runs in a season 27 times. With M.C.C. touring sides went twice each to Australia and South Africa but only 17 Tests in all despite a batting average of nearly fifty. On retirement in 1936, played for Suffolk. In old age lost his sight. Died at Boscombe Hospital, near Bournemouth, on 26 March 1958. Buried in North Cemetery, Bournemouth. Grave is in plot 4, row S, and 17 grave spaces from drive. Mead was depicted on pub sign of 'The Centurion' pub at Barton-on-Sea, now renamed 'The House Martin'.

North Cemetery, Bournemouth   *Sat Nav*   BH8 9HX

Biography: *"C P Mead: Hampshire's Greatest Run-Maker"* by Neil Jenkinson (Paul Cave, 1993)

☐ *William MIDWINTER*

Right-handed batsman and medium-paced spin bowler. Family emigrated from Forest of Dean to Australia at age of nine. Played for Victoria and chosen for the first Test match in 1876-77. Selected to join 1878 Australian tour of England but quit tour midway to play for Gloucestershire. In 1881-82 included in Shaw's English cricketers to Australia, then in 1884 in Australian team to England, so became first man to play for and against both countries in Test matches. A fine all-round cricketer. Following loss of his wife, committed to Kera Asylum, Melbourne, where he died on 3 December 1890. Buried in R.C. section of Melbourne General Cemetery. Was the first Australian Test cricketer to die. No memorial known in England. In 1982 members of Australian Cricket Society arranged restoration of his grave, unmarked for a hundred years, by placing a headstone.

☐ *Colin MILBURN*

From childood, lived in Park View, Burnopfield. Attacking batsman who played intermittently for England, his excessive weight and slow fielding counting against him. In nine Test appearances he made two superb hundreds. Put out of the game after road accident robbed him off an eye. Brief unsuccessful comeback. Died on 28 February 1990 when collapsed with a heart attack in a pub car park at Newton Aycliffe, and pronounced dead shortly after arriving at Darlington Memorial Hospital.

(above) Philip Mead's grave, Bournenouth North Cemetery

(Below) Colin Milburn Lounge at Riverside, and memorabillia in the bar at Burnopfield cricket club

Funeral held at Methodist chapel in his home village, on Monday 5 March 1990, followed by cremation at Mountsett; ashes scattered. Housing development on the former cricket club ground in Burnopfield is

named Milburn Green. New cricket ground opened 2014 above the village; pavilion has a Milburn Bar. At Chester-le-Street's Riverside ground (Emirates Durham) the Colin Milburn Lounge is a conference suite.

Milburn Green *Sat Nav* NE16 6QL Burnopfield Cricket Club *Sat Nav* NE16 6ED Riverside Stadium *Sat Nav* DH3 3QR

Biography : *"Largely Cricket: An Autobiography"* (Stanley Paul, 1968); *"Cricketing Falstaff: A Biography Of Colin Milburn"* by Mark Peel (Andre Deutsch, 1998)

• For a long time I had been unable to find the whereabouts of Colin Milburn's grave. The website www.findagrave said that he was buried at Newcastle-under-Lyme (simply confusion with Newcastle on Tyne), while wikipedia said he was buried in Burnopfield so I made a trip to Tyneside to search the cemetery of St James's church as the most likely spot. There are some recent graves but not Milburn's. I tried the methodist chapel, where fortunately a welcoming coffee drop-in is held on Thursday mornings. A local man kindly showed me where Milburn lived and where they played as boys. 'Milburn Green' is being built on the old cricket ground (the soil had become eroded and the underlying surface of clinker too rough to field on). He confirmed there is no grave and the ashes were scattered, and also pointed me to the new cricket ground where, luckily again, the club treasurer was just arriving and showed me the memorabilia that is being placed in their Milburn Bar.

☐ *Frank MILLIGAN*

Pictured from website:
http://www.haroldpark.info/
photo03112008104934/1225722639.jpg

Hard-hitting amateur batsman, fast bowler and enthusiastic fielder. One of five Yorkshire team players invited on Lord Hawke's 1898-99 South African tour, later given Test status. Army Lieutenant, killed during sortie by mounted troops at Ramathelebama, South Africa, on 31 March 1900 during relief of Mafeking. His remains identified by Archdeacon Upcher and a wooden cross placed over his grave. Yorkshire committee met at Headingley on 3 July 1900 to inaugurate with 100 guineas fund for Milligan's memorial and asked Yorkshire public to subscribe. Had been employed at Low Moor forge works (south Bradford) so tablet unveiled by Lord Hawke in 1901 at Low Moor church, St Mark's; renovated 1988, but church closed 2002 and became a private residence. Also, commemorated on north face of sundial war memorial, erected 1902, at Harold Park rose garden in Low Moor.

Harold Park, Low Moor *Sat Nav* BD12 0DL Old St Mark's church *Sat Nav* BD12 0UT

☐ *Arthur 'Ticker' MITCHELL*

Dour, resolute batsman, great close fieldsman, personified Yorkshire team spirit in 1930s. Summed up by opening partner

Sutcliffe : "...as grim and steadfast as a piece of stone from the Baildon Moors". Called up literally from garden at home to play for England in 1935. Six Tests. County coach 1945-70. Died on Christmas Day 1976 in St Luke's Hospital, Bradford. Funeral at parish church in Baildon, the town of his birth, on 31 December, followed by cremation at Nab Wood Crematorium.

☐ Frank MITCHELL

Captain and leading batsman at Cambridge University but unable to play more than two full seasons for Yorkshire, both successfully. On Hawke's 1898-99 tour of South Africa played his two Tests for England. Remained in South Africa in Boer War. Captain of South African touring teams to England in 1904 and 1912. Director of tin mining company. During retirement lived in Blackheath and, while wife absent at mother's bedside in South Africa, died at home, 'Heathend', on 11 October 1935. Buried in Charlton Cemetery, Kent, in grave 799, section C, row 33.

Charlton Cemetery *Sat Nav* SE7 8DZ

Biography : *"Frank Mitchell: Imperial Cricketer"* by Anthony Bradbury (ACS Lives in Cricket publications, 2014)

☐ R.A.H. 'Mike' MITCHELL

Batsman at Oxford University, then schoolmaster-coach at Eton College. His insistence on orthodox strokemaking forced fun out of the game for some boys, but turned out batsmen such as Thornton, the Lytteltons and Studds. Died 19 April 1905 at Mayford House, Woking, Surrey. Commemorated at his old college and has grave in Worplesdon churchyard.

St Mary the Virgin church, Perry Hill *Sat Nav* GU3 3RE

☐ Tommy MITCHELL

Former miner, spotted while playing a colliery match. Leg-spinner for Derbyshire 1928-39. Last man to take all ten wickets for county (v Leics in 1935); his 168 wickets in that season are a county record. Five Test caps. After WW2 played only club cricket. At death on 26 January 1996 at age of 93, was living in a home for the elderly at Hickleton. Last survivor of the 1932/33 bodyline touring team. Funeral on Mon 5 Feb at Barnsley (Ardsley) Crematorium; his ashes were collected by the family with no memorial there.

☐ Arthur MOLD

Oxfordshire-born at Middleton Cheyney. Fast bowler with Lancashire from 1889, formidable partnership with Briggs. Regularly considered for place in England team but played only 3 Test matches. No-balled for throwing in 1902 but had by then decided to retire anyway. Died at home, the Dolphin Inn, in his native village on 29 April 1921 after two years' illness. Buried in All Saints churchyard, Middleton Cheyney, near Banbury. Grave is on northern side of church. White headstone erected in affection and admiration by old friends in Lancashire C.C.C.

All Saints church. Middleton Cheyney *Sat Nav* OX17 2NR

Fred MORLEY

Fast-medium bowler for Notts but light-heartedly known as worst batsman ever. Made one tour - Ivo Bligh's to Australia in 1882-83. Injured ribs on voyage and struggled through 4 Tests but health deteriorated afterwards. Died at birthplace from congestion of lungs and dropsy on 28 September 1884. A benefit match for him, started day before death, continued with players wearing black crepe armbands. Buried next day, 29 September, in cemetery of St Mary's parish church at Sutton-in-Ashfield, his birthplace.

St Mary Magdalene church, Sutton-in-Ashfield   *Sat Nav*
NG17 2EB

William MORTLOCK

Batsman and underarm bowler. Surrey professional. Member of first cricket tour of Australia by an English team, promoted by Melbourne caterers Pond and Spiers in 1861-62. Lived at 23 Monckton Street, Lambeth (no blue plaque - a request for one was turned down). Died at Acre Lane, Brixton, 23 January 1884. Buried in grave 19684, square 122, of West Norwood Cemetery. Base is present but cross missing [information from FOWNC newsletter 58].

West Norwood Cemetery *Sat Nav* SE27 9JU

Billy MURDOCH

Leading early Australian batsman and in 16 of his 18 Tests was captain, including first Test match in England, played at The Oval 1880. Led Australia on four overseas tours. In 1891-2 he and John Ferris joined W.W.Read's South African tour, so he played matches (retrospectively Tests) for England, too. In 1893 represented Sussex and captain. Played with W.G.Grace's London County until age of 50. Died at Melbourne 18 February 1911, suffering apoplectic fit (stroke) while watching a Test match. Body returned to England in May for burial in Kensal Green Cemetery, London. His grave, number 42962 in row 2, plot 175, is a simple dark cross, near grave of 'Spy'.

Kensal Green Cemetery   *Sat Nav* W10 4RA

Alfred MYNN

'The Lion of Kent', a man of huge stature, weighing 19 stones. A hop merchant by trade but patronised by Cavendish was able to play cricket as amateur for thirty years. Coached by John Willes, first noteworthy round-arm bowler. Speed from short run-in and extreme accuracy helped make Kent pre-eminent county. Many appearances for the Gentlemen and Clarke's All-England XI. Lived at Ware Street in Bearsted and features on current village sign. Died of diabetes on 1 November 1861 at brother's residence near London Bridge. Buried at Thurnham churchyard, near Maidstone, with full military honours, being a Volunteer of the 31st (Leeds Castle) Rifle Corps. In March 1862 committee formed to promote a Mynn memorial decided on an elaborate headstone. Stands on north side of church, next to old graveyard wall, now demolished to allow expansion of cemetery.

St Mary the Virgin church, Thurnham *Sat Nav* ME14 3LH
Bearsted village sign *Sat Nav* ME14 4EJ

Biography : *"Alfred Mynn and the Cricketers of His Time"*
by Patrick Morrah (Constable, 1986)

Billy NEWHAM

Stroke-making batsman associated with Sussex cricket (he was from Shrewsbury but had attended Ardingly College) for more than sixty years since first appearance in 1881. Captain 1892 but from 1905 too busy as assistant secretary to appear regularly. Died at Worcester Villas, Hove, on 26 June 1944, and funeral held at St Leonard's church, Aldrington, Hove. Interred in Hove New Cemetery in plot no 2 - 79.

Also known as Hove Cemetery North *Sat Nav* BN3 7EF

Richard NEWLAND

Left-hander, regarded as finest English batsman of the age. Born at Slindon, near Chichester, in 1718. Captain of Slindon, the Duke of Richmond's team - see Charles Lennox - which dominated cricket in 1740s. Died on 29 May 1791 at Bath, Somerset. Marble tablet inside porch of Slindon parish church, placed by his son to commemorate Newland. Plaque on Slindon's village sign (dated 2000) says: "This sign … depicts the shape and size of the bat and wicket that was first used in Slindon in 1731". Sign stands in village centre, on Reynolds Road.

© Roger Pagram - licensed for reuse under the Creative Common license.

St Mary's church, Slindon *Sat Nav* BN18 0RB   Slindon village sign *Sat Nav* BN18 0QX

[Morris] Stan NICHOLS

Tall and tireless fast bowler for Essex between Wars. Achieved 'the double' eight times and winner of race to do so each year 1935-39. Highest score 205; best bowling 9-32 v Notts 1936. Made tours of NZ and India and appeared in 14 Tests. Physical fitness instructor in Army, moved to Newark early in War. After WW2 played Birmingham League, while an ice cream and brewery sales rep. Died at home in Newark on 26 January 1961. Funeral on 30 January at Newark parish church, and buried in London Road Cemetery, Newark. His grave, number 386-W-West, has no headstone. Follow main path past lodge, mortuary cemetery and circles to end; turn right and right again. Nichols' grave is 50 yards down on left-hand side.

Newark Cemetery *Sat Nav* NG24 1SQ

Richard NYREN

A left-handed all-rounder. Leading light of England's principal 18th century club, Hambledon, he joined in 1772 after moving from Slindon to be landlord of 'The Hut', subsequently re-named The Bat and Ball Inn. Respected as most knowledgeable man about cricket. Acted as secretary, treasurer, organiser and captain; the club broke up soon after he left it. Died 25 April 1797 at Lee, Kent.

John NYREN

Born in Hambledon 1764, son of Richard, also a left-hander. Important for compiling recollections of Hambledon club, gathered since he was 11, in 'The Cricketers of my Time', to appear later as 'The Young Cricketer's Tutor' (published 1833, with illustrations by James Crowden Clarke: a new edition issued by John Arlott in 1974). His likeness was portrayed on the Hambledon Bat and Ball Inn sign. Nyren set up in business as a calico printer in Bromley-by-Bow, London, where he died on 30 June 1837. "...and was buried in Bromley St Leonard churchyard" [D.N.B], now laid out as a public garden on an island in busy Bow Road so the grave site cannot be found.

Hambledon Bat & Ball Inn   *Sat Nav*   PO8 0UB   St Leonard's churchyard, Bow   *Sat Nav*   E3 3AH

• Once gravestones are removed from a churchyard this old, burial records don't give a precise enough location to find a person's grave site. It was suggested to me that Nyren would likely have been exhumed with all the others in the road widening and removed to City of London Cemetery.

☐ Charles OLLIVIERRE

Born at Kingstown on St Vincent [on grave it mistakenly says Kingston, Jamaica] in 1880. After touring England with West Indians 1900, never returned home. Qualified for Derbyshire 1902 and played seven seasons as opening batsman. In 1904 scored 229 and 92* v Essex. His career ended by eyesight problems. Yorkshire League cricket with Featherstone C.C. From 1924-39 annually to Holland for coaching. During War worked in food control unit. Died at home of 25 years in Tanshelf Drive, Pontefract, on 25 March 1949. Interred at St Stephens Old Churchyard (now redundant), Fylingdales Thorpe, Yorkshire, near Robin Hood's Bay where close friends lived. On B1447 road. Grave lies six spaces from western boundary, next to boundary path.

St Stephen's church, Fylingdales Thorpe   *Sat Nav*   YO22 4PF

☐ George PAINE

Left-arm spinner, started on Lord's groundstaff. As a Londoner, played for Middlesex in 1926 before qualifying for Warwicks. 4 Tests on West Indies tour of 1934-35. Dismissed without scoring in each innings of benefit match. Disagreement with county over terms in 1938, played only once afterwards. 20 years at Solihull School as groundsman/coach, retired 1974. Died at home in Warwick Road, Solihull, on 30 March 1978. After funeral service at St Alphege church, cremation at Robin Hood Crematorium, in Streetsbrook Road.

☐ Lionel PALAIRET

Elegant batsman who set the benchmark for style. Won blue at Oxford University 1890 to 1893, joined Somerset and with Herbie Hewett set a record first-wicket partnership of 346 against Yorkshire in 1892. Widely

admired but appeared in only two Tests (in 1902). County captain 1906. Lived in Bath, came to Exmouth when wife died 3 years before. For 20 years steward for the Earl of Devon's estate. Keen fox-hunter and represented Devon at golf. Died while walking in garden of his Exmouth home, Dodhill, on 27 March 1933. Funeral at St Margaret & St Andrew's church, Littleham on 30 March: grave is in northern corner of plot V. It is inscribed: "Life a pathway, Death a gateway, Beyond a garden." Plan of this huge church cemetery on wall of Sexton's office / store.

St Margaret & St Andrew's church cemetery   *Sat Nav*   EX8 2RQ.

Note - Lionel's brother Richard Palairet was financial manager on M.C.C.'s 1932-33 (bodyline) tour and about to return from Australia when he heard of the death. 'Dick' died on 11 February 1955 at Budleigh Salterton, where he was buried in St Peter's churchyard.

• I knew that Littleham was the location of Lionel Palairet's funeral from his death notice in *The Times*; contemporary newspapers reported his well-attended funeral but none actually confirmed that he was interred in the church cemetery. Not until I consulted burial registers in the Devon Heritage Centre could I verify that his grave was indeed in the cemetery but, looking at its huge extent on Google Earth, I realised I needed a precise grave location. There is a plan of the cemetery on the wall of the sexton's hut but it does not identify any specific people's graves. There was no further information inside St Margaret & St Andrew's church either, except to say that "God's Acre" at this church was 13 acres in extent! I readied myself for hours of wandering round in optimistic searching. Yet within a few minutes, I was unexpectedly lucky and very pleased to stumble on it. I then went to Douglas Avenue to find his old house "Dodhill" but it was no longer there; it must have been demolished to make way for Mayfield Drive.

☐ *Charles PALMER*

Worcestershire amateur until invited to become secretary and lead Leicestershire in 1950. Took county to third in championship in 1953. He scored 1000 runs for eight successive seasons. One Test appearance. Fulfilled most roles at county including captain, paid and hon secretary, chairman (for 25 years), president (for six), as well as chairman of TCCB and president of M.C.C. Awarded C.B.E. 1984. Died in Leicester on 31 March 2005. The Charles Palmer Suite is a large conference room at Leicestershire's Grace Road.

Grace Road Ground   *Sat Nav*   LE 2 8EB

Biography :   *"More than Just a Gentleman"* by Douglas Miller (Fairfield, 2005)

☐ *Sydney PARDON*

No cricketer, but sound judge of game and acquired vast knowledge as *Times* correspondent and editor of sports section of Press Association. Formed Cricket Reporting Agency. Appointed editor of *Wisden Cricketers Almanack* 1891 on death of brother Charles and took charge for 35 years. Taken ill in Fleet Street offices, rushed to St Bartholomew's Hospital, where died 20 November 1925. Cremated at Golders Green Crematorium. Ashes placed in niche 3362 of Ernest George columbarium.

Golders Green Crematorium   *Sat Nav*   NW11 7NL

☐ *Charlie PARKER*

Club cricket for Cheltenham G.S. and Tewkesbury C.C. Debut as seam bowler 1903. Brilliant but temperamental left-armer for Gloucestershire between 1907 and 1935, capturing 3278 f-c wickets (only Rhodes and Freeman took more), yet only one Test appearance owing to upset with selectors. Added spin to repertoire after WW1. Many remarkable bowling achievements, especially on wet wickets. Had six hat-tricks and, against Yorkshire in 1922, struck the stumps with five consecutive balls.

Two separate hat-tricks taken in match v Middlesex 1924. Died at Cranleigh, Surrey, where worked as school coach, on 11 July 1959. Buried in Cranleigh Cemetery, which is off Ewhurst Road, the B2172. Grave number 252 is 100 metres from entrance porch, beside main path on left-hand side.

Cranleigh Cemetery *Sat Nav* GU6 7AE

Biography: *"Cricket's Unholy Trinity"* by David Foot (Stanley Paul, 1985)

□ 'Ciss' PARKIN

Off-spinner. One appearance for Yorkshire in 1906 before was realised his birthplace Eaglescliffe (County Durham) just outside boundary. For Lancashire 1914-1926. Off-spinner. Played in ten Test matches and made tour with M.C.C. in 1920-21. But publicly criticised England captain in 1924 which ended Test career. Left county 1926 after disagreement with committee. Went to Staffordshire League. Died of throat cancer in Manchester Northern Hospital 15 June 1943 and funeral at Manchester Crematorium. His ashes scattered on pitch at Old Trafford Cricket Ground. No memorial is known.

Biography : *"Cricket Triumphs And Troubles"* autobiography (C Nicholls, 1936); *"Cricket's Unholy Trinity"* by David Foot (Stanley Paul, 1985)

□ Jim PARKS senior

Opening batsman for Sussex. Career began 1924 and became all-rounder. Scored 1000 runs a season every year, bar one, 1927 to '39. Only man to score 3000 runs and take 100 wickets in a season; in final innings of 1937 needed a further 60 runs and got them. Won sole Test cap in that season. Wartime policeman, then league cricket. Notts coach,

first-class umpire and coach at Sussex until 1968. Died at Cuckfield Hospital 21 November 1980 and buried in Cuckfield churchyard cemetery. Brother Harry and son Jim also played for Sussex.

Holy Trinity church, Cuckfield   *Sat Nav* RH17 5JZ

Biography: none ; referred to in son's biography *"Young Jim"* by Derek Watts (Tempus, 2005)

□ George PARR

One of nine children, born in Radcliffe-on-Trent. Tremendously strong leg-side hitter, professional for Notts: 'The Lion of the North'. For ten years after Pilch leading batsman in country. Member of All-England XI, of which became manager. Pioneered cricket in United States and led second tour of Australia 1863-64. Dropped out of cricket 1871 and settled in native village. Died from gout (?) in 66th year on 23 June 1891. After funeral at St Mary's church, buried in Radcliffe Cemetery and a branch from 'Parr's Tree' laid on grave. Grave is 100 metres beyond the wrought iron gates on left-hand side of path. Has slender black headstone with clear inscription. Tall old elm called 'Parr's Tree' inside walls of Trent Bridge. "..A double-decker concrete stand was erected in front of the tree in 1955 and was duly christened Parr's Stand." [history.trentbridge.co.uk] Trunk had metal plaque some six feet above ground level but in 1976 tree blew down in a gale.

Radcliffe-on-Trent Cemetery *Sat Nav* NG12 2FB

□ Eddie PAYNTER

Combative batsman joined Lancashire 1926, regular in 1930s and heavy scorer in his 20 Test appearances. In 1932-33 roused from sick bed to bat for England at Brisbane and helped to win match. Made only two M.C.C. overseas tours and omission from 1936-37 Australian tour one of selectors' regrettable mistakes. In WW2 worked in brickyard where lost top joints of two fingers. First-class umpire, and scorer on Commonwealth tour. League cricket for Enfield, Keighley and others, until aged 53. Invited to be Hon Member of M.C.C. 1949. Licensee of Roebuck Inn at Utley (nr Keighley). Died at home in Idle (north Bradford) 5 February 1979. Funeral at Rawdon Crematorium, Leeds.

Biography : *"Cricket All The Way"* autobiography with Alan Buckley (Richardson, 1962)

☐ *Ted PEATE*

Leeds-born spin bowler. Spotted in club match in 1879 and given trial for Yorkshire in match v Notts, became first in line of Yorkshire left-arm spinners: Peate, Peel, Rhodes, Verity and Wardle. In 1883 took 8 for 5 against Surrey, criticised for ending match early and ruining gate! Career ended abruptly in 1887 owing to Hawke's dislike of him. Had also played 9 times for England. Died of liver disease and pneumonia at home in St Michael's Road, Headingley, 11 March 1900 and buried in Town Cemetery at Yeadon where family had lived since Peate was six years old. Lies in grave A241 but no headstone to be seen.

☐ *Ian PEEBLES*

Aberdonian leg-break bowler, learnt his cricket at Uddingston and in Western League of Scotland. Coach at Faulkner's London cricket school. F-c debut at age 19 for Gentlemen. Chosen for two M.C.C. South African tours. Oxford blue and Middlesex cap but shoulder injury limited number of Test caps to 13. County captain 1939. Lost sight in one eye in WW2 and retired. Journalist and author, wrote six cricket books. Lived at Speen and died 28 February 1980 after returning home from hospital in High Wycombe. Funeral at Chilterns Crematorium: ashes scattered in gardens of remembrance area 2. Only memorial is his entry in Book of Remembrance, which may be viewed online.

Biography: *"Spinner's Yarn"* autobiography (Collins, 1977); *"Batter's Castle: A Ramble Round the Realm of Cricket"* some autobiographical (Souvenir Press, 1958)

● Ian Peebles' death was reported in the local paper, the Free Bucks Press, but without any mention of the whereabouts of his funeral and thus his possible grave and memorial. I searched the steep churchyard in the village of Speen but all the time the answer was lying there on the website www.findagrave : that he was cremated at Amersham and his ashes scattered.

☐ *Bobby PEEL*

Left-arm spinner, taken on by Yorkshire with view to succeeding Ted Peate, and took nine wickets in first match 1882. Chosen 20 times for England, selected for 4 Australian tours, bowling economically and with high strike rate. Unusual record of three pairs in Tests but in fact talented batsman, with 7 centuries to name. Bowed out of Tests in 1896 with 6 for 23 and his 100th wicket. Yorkshire employment abruptly terminated in 1897 by Lord Hawke, who accused him of being drunk. Unfortunately, Peel tried to disprove it with a trial ball and sent it in wrong direction. Therefore aggregate of first-class wickets for county (1330) exceeded by lesser bowlers. Died at home of son-in-law at Morley, Leeds, on 12 August 1941. Interred in an unmarked grave in Morley Cemetery.

Frank PENN

Round-arm bowler and attacking batsman with Kent from 1875. In short but brilliant career played 8 times for Gentlemen v Players. Lord Harris's tour of Australia 1878-79 and Oval Test 1880, when he made winning hit. But heart condition and in 1881 forbidden to run, so gave up game. President of Kent county cricket club 1905. Died at home, 'Bifrons', on Boxing Day 1916. Funeral at St Mary's church, Patrixbourne, nr Canterbury, Kent. Large cross over grave in churchyard.

St Mary's church, Patrixbourne   *Sat Nav*   CT4 5BP

died at home, Waterside Cottage, Hickling, on 20 November 1945. Funeral held at St Faith's Crematorium near Norwich, and his ashes scattered on pitch at Lord's Ground.

Biography: *"P.A.Perrin: His Record Innings by Innings"* by David Jeater (ACS Famous Cricketers Series No 95, 2006) .

• Perrin is one of only four cricket people (Falcon, Tylecote and Frank Mann are the others) who would be regarded as nationally significant and whose last resting place I know of in my home county of Norfolk. Any trips to look at cricket graves or research in London always mean for me a long journey, but Norwich is a fine city to live in. I was not born in Norfolk but have lived here since 1975 (so I'd be regarded as just a newcomer).

Richard (or Robert) PERCIVAL

Never a famous cricketer yet for many years in *Wisden Almanack's* records section for throwing the cricket ball 140 yards and 2 feet at Durham Sands Racecourse on Easter Monday 1884. Left-handed all-rounder, professional in Cheshire with New Brighton C.C. Then coal miner. Died from pneumonia in South Shields, 13 May 1918, buried in Harton Cemetery. Grave destroyed in air raid in WW2. No known memorial.

Harton Cemetery   *Sat Nav*   NE34 6EU

Hylton ['Punch'] PHILIPSON

Excelled at wicket-keeping and other sports at Oxford University 1887-89. Toured Australia with Sheffield's and Stoddart's teams, and played in five Tests. Some matches with Middlesex. Purchased the Stobo Estate, Peebleshire, and laid out Japanese water gardens. Died in Sussex Square, London, on 4 December 1935 and funeral held at Stobo estate. His grave is in top corner of graveyard of Stobo Kirk.

Stobo Kirk   *Sat Nav*   EH45 8NU

'Peter' PERRIN

Powerful and safe batsman with Essex, almost good enough to play for England but slow fielding let him down. Hit nearly 30,000 first-class runs with 66 centuries, including two in match four times, and innings of 343* v Derbyshire in a match which Essex managed to lose. Test selector from 1926 and served until 1939 when chairman. Retired to Norfolk Broads and

Fuller PILCH

Born at Horningtoft, nr Fakenham, Norfolk. A pioneer of modern cricket technique, best batsman of century until W.G. came on scene. Left Norfolk for higher standard of cricket in Kent and, while groundsman at Town Malling, in single-wicket matches. Later managed Kent side and groundkeeper at St Lawrence 1847-69. Sports business in Canterbury and publican of Saracens Head Inn. Died of dropsy at home of nephew in Canterbury on 1 May 1870. Funeral at St Gregory's church, Canterbury, where admirers had stone obelisk erected. In 1922 Kent C.C.C. added to base of cenotaph a bronze plaque showing Pilch at his stance. Design also shown on village sign at birthplace, Horningtoft, Norfolk, which copied the bronze plaque. St Gregory's church closed in 1960s. Now used by Christ Church University as a music venue, once assurances given that grave would not be disturbed by building works. The Pilch Memorial, less obelisk, taken to St Lawrence Ground and positioned close to turnstiles. Bronze plaque and other Pilch relics, such as bats, may be seen in Chiesman Pavilion. In 2008 new granite headstone erected to mark original burial site in churchyard.

St Gregory's Music Centre (old churchyard) *Sat Nav* CT1 1QU   The Spitfire Ground, St Lawrence, Canterbury *Sat Nav* CT1 3NZ   Horningtoft village sign   *Sat Nav* NR20 5EA

Biography : *"Fuller Pilch: A Straightforward Man "* by Brian Rendell (ACS Lives In Cricket, 2010)

☐ Dick PILLING

Born in Bedfordshire, of Lancashire parents. Given trial by Lancashire (in same match as Allan Steel) 1877. Wicket-keeper for Lancashire and England between debut and 1889. Twice toured Australia in 1881-82 and 1887-88. Benefit in 1889 realised £1700, a record at time. In 1890 wintered in Australia owing to ill-health. Died from inflammation of lungs at Old Trafford on 28 March 1891 a few days after returning home. Interred in Brooklands Cemetery, Sale, Manchester. Grave number I/539. His wife and sons also buried there.

Brooklands Cemetery, Sale *Sat Nav* M33 7UN

☐ Winston PLACE

Batsman for Lancashire, mostly opening innings with Cyril Washbrook. After ten centuries in 1947 season, chosen to tour West Indies with M.C.C. in 1947-48 and played 3 Tests. Became newsagent in town of his birth, Rawtenstall. Died in Burnley on 25 January 2002. Buried in Rawtenstall Cemetery, Lancashire - grave 1128 is right at back of cemetery.

Rawtenstall Cemetery *Sat Nav* BB4 8EW

☐ Christopher POND

Met Felix Spiers at time of Australian gold rush in 1850s. Made fortune with catering establishments like Café de Paris in Melbourne and providing refreshments on railway route to gold rush towns. Pond & Spiers organised first cricket tour of Australia by an English team 1861. Retired to Herne Hill, London. Died at Updown House, Margate, 30 July 1881. Has splendid Grade II-listed mausoleum (plot 18718, square 88) at West Norwood Cemetery. A sundial later erected by his widow at the Cemetery [information from FOWNC newsletter 58].

West Norwood Cemetery *Sat Nav* SE27 9JU

☐ Spencer PONSONBY-FANE

Appeared in few matches for Surrey or Middlesex but influential member of game's establishment. Member of M.C.C. for record 75 years (since broken), committeeman, treasurer from 1879 to 1915 and founder of M.C.C. art collection. Laid foundation stone of Lord's pavilion. Declined presidency several times. Founder of I Zingari club and instigated Old Stagers week at Canterbury. Public service in Foreign Office, and authority on etiquette and ceremonial in Lord Chamberlain's office. Died on

Image from Somerset Cricket Museum at Taunton County Ground

1 December 1915 at home, Brympton D'Evercy (stately home opened to public 2013), and buried at Brympton D'Evercy church, nr Yeovil. His portrait displayed in Somerset Cricket Museum.

St Andrew's church, Brympton d'Evercy   *Sat Nav*   BA22 8TD   Somerset Cricket Museum   *Sat Nav*   TA1 1XX.

☐ 'Dick' POUGHER

Career began in 1885 as medium-paced bowler and several remarkable anlyses led Shrewsbury to take him to Australia in 1887-88. Much to do with Leicestershire's elevation to first-class status. In 1895 first from county to take 100 wickets in season and in 1896 first to score 1000 runs. After

ankle injury in 1897 never back to best and gave up game in 1901. Landlord of Old County Ground Hotel, where died 20 May 1926. Interred in Welford Road Cemetery, Leicester, without headstone. Buried in unconsecrated section 01 in grave number 760, seventh row down and third in from boundary path.

Welford Road Cemetery Visitor Centre   *Sat Nav*   LE2 6BB

☐ A.W. PULLIN ("Old Ebor")

Originally from Carmarthenshire, cricket writer, mostly for *Yorkshire Post*. His 'Talks with Old English Cricketers' brought to public attention plight of retired professionals living in dire straits. Based in Leeds but came to London to report Lord's Test match, collapsed on bus bound for ground and died at Royal Free Hospital, 23 June 1934. Buried in Wakefield Cemetery (consecrated portion, section H, grave 1759).

Wakefield Cemetery   *Sat Nav*   WF1 5LF

☐ Willie QUAIFE

Born at Newhaven, Sussex, in 1872. Diminutive batsman, one match for Sussex 1891, then for Warwickshire. Also, medium-paced or spin bowler and reliable fielder. Went on MacLaren's Australian tour in 1901-02. Played in 7 Tests. Only seven men scored more than him in county championship. Scorer of 72 centuries, including a hundred in final innings in 1928. On retirement joined firm of bat-makers. Died on 13 October 1951 at home in Edgbaston after short illness. Funeral at Perry Barr Crematorium, West Midlands. Ashes scattered on plot AA12. No memorial.

☐ *Kumar Shri RANJITSINHJI*

Born Sarodar 1872. Promise shown at Cambridge University fulfilled with Sussex and England at turn of century. In August 1896 v Yorkshire, scored two centuries on same day. Toured Australia 1897-98. Appeared in 15 Test matches and scored 989 runs with two classic centuries. Exceptional eyesight and flexibility of wrist helped to perfect cuts, glances and other delicate strokes. Sussex captain. Lost an eye in shooting accident so last match 1920 but had in any case returned to throne of Jamnagar in 1907. Died in Palace of Jamnagar of heart failure, following pneumonia, on 2 April 1933. Procession of half-mile to royal burning ghat for cremation. Ashes taken to Allahabad to be scattered in River Ganges. Only memorial in England is old scoreboard at Hove ground. For years he took rooms above a baker's shop in Sydney Street, Cambridge, but no plaque. On centenary of birth, signed portrait presented to Memorial Gallery at Lord's.

Sussex County Ground, Hove   *Sat Nav*   BN3 3AN

Biographies: *"Ranjitsinhji, Prince of Cricket"* by Percy Cross Standing (Arrowsmith, 1903); *"The Land of Ranji and Duleep"* by Charles A Kincaid (Blackwood & Sons, 1931); *"The Biography of Colonel His Highness Shri Sir Ranjitsinhji"* by Roland Wild (Rich & Cowan,, 1934); *"Ranji, the Legend and the Man"* by Vasant Raiji (1963); *"Ranji: Prince of Cricketers"* by Alan Ross (Collins, 1983); *"Ranji: A Genius Rich and Strange"* by Simon Wilde (Kingswood Press, 1990); *"Ranji, Marharajah of Connemara"* by Anne Chambers (Roli Books, India, 2004)

and stumps design but the lead letters of his name have fallen away [information from Philip Paine's *Innings Complete*, Vol 8].

Greasbrough Cemetery, Town Lane   *Sat Nav*   S61 4JH

☐ *Maurice READ*

Nephew of H.H.Stephenson, born in 1859. First-class debut for Surrey 1880 as batsman. Four tours of Australia but relatively unsuccessful in 17 Tests. Retired prematurely in 1895 to superintend and play in matches at Sir Henry Tichborne's superb cricket ground at Tichborne Park, Hampshire. At age of sixty still knocking up centuries. Died in Winchester Hospital, Hampshire, on 17 February 1929 and buried in St Andrew's churchyard, Cheriton-cum-Tichborne.

St Andrew's church, Tichborne   *Sat Nav*   SO24 0NA

☐ *John RAWLIN*

Yorkshire-born fast bowler who joined Lord's groundstaff 1887 and able to play for Middlesex. Member of G.F.Vernon's team in Australia 1887-88. Died 19 January 1924 and buried in Greasbrough Cemetery, north of Rotherham. His grave has a crossed bats

☐ *Walter READ*

In his day greatest batsman produced by Surrey. In youth assisted at his father's school so unable to play in earlier half of season but in 1881 appointed to administrative office at The Oval. Played till 1897. Appeared

18 times for England, including twice as captain on South Africa tour, also taking part in two tours of Australia. He once scored 117 going in at number ten, to save a Test match for England. Over 22,000 runs in career, also took occasional wicket with his lobs. Died at home in Addiscombe Park, Croydon, on 6 January 1907 and buried in churchyard of St. John the Evangelist, Shirley (Surrey). There is a stone celtic cross over grave.

St John's church, Shirley *Sat Nav* CRO 5EE

Biography : *"Annals of Cricket"* by W.W. Read. London 1896; *"Walter Read: A Class Act"* by Keith Booth (ACS Lives in Cricket, 2011)

☐ *Wilfred RHODES*

Like Hirst, born in Kirkheaton, near Huddersfield, Yorkshire. Greatest wicket-taker of all time. In career between 1898, when Peel's abrupt sacking assured Rhodes of left-arm spinner's place in Yorkshire side, and final match in 1930 captured 4204 f-c wickets. Chosen for England in his second season and won 58 Test caps, with 127 wickets. Final Test match 1930. Post-WW1 was senior adviser to the selectors. Also a distinguished batsman, playing in all positions in batting order from 1 to 11 for England, and finishing career with both Test and f-c average of more than 30. Achieved 'the double' in 16 seasons, more times than anyone else. On retirement, coach at Harrow School until eyesight failed. After wife died, lived in Bournemouth with daughter. Outlived her, moved into Broadstone (Branksome Park) nursing home where died on 8 July 1973, aged 95. Private funeral : cremation in Bournemouth and his ashes conveyed to Leeds, laid to rest in wife's grave in Lawnswood Cemetery. When the Hirst memorial clock tower unveiled at Fartown Ground, near Huddersfield, Yorkshire, in 1955, planned

to engrave a stone at base with Rhodes's name. Although this was not then done, it was henceforth known as the Hirst and Rhodes Memorial. [see entry for George Hirst]; then in 1996 as memorial to 'The Great Triumvirate' (Hirst, Rhodes and Haigh), repaired and rededicated. At Kirkheaton the cricket pavilion has foundation stone bearing his name.

Hirst, Haigh & Rhodes Memorial, Fartown *Sat Nav* HD2 2QA Lawnswood Cemetery *Sat Nav* LS16 6AH

Biography: *"Wilfred Rhodes: Professional and Gentleman"* by Sidney Rogerson (Hollis & Carter, 1960); *"Hirst & Rhodes"* by A A Thomson (Epworth, 1959; new edition Pavilion Books, 1986)

● The website 'Kirkheaton Curiosities' reveals that Wilfred Rhodes's parents and brother are buried in Kirkheaton cemetery under an unusual headstone with a depiction of a railway engine. It also pictures Kirkheaton Cricket Club's pavilion and its two foundation stones, one laid by Hirst and one by Rhodes in August 1950.

☐ *Tom RICHARDSON*

Fast bowler with Surrey 1892-1904, taking 809 wickets in three consecutive seasons, including 290 in one English summer (1895), record for a fast bowler. Immensely strong and willing. Despite brief peak, may be regarded as best of his time. Represented England in only 14 Tests, taking 88 wickets, including five wickets in innings on 11 occasions. Towards end of career lost form and suffered weight increase. Died at St Jean d'Arvey in French Alps on 2 July 1912. Found dead of heart attack (not suicide as was rumoured at time) beside Bout du Monde Cascade, near Chambery. *Sporting Life* started fund to bring body back to England, and funeral held at Richmond Cemetery in Grove Road. Richardson buried next to path in block C, in grave 629, which has cricketing motif showing a middle stump knocked down.

Richmond Cemetery *Sat Nav* TW10 6HP

Biography : *"Tom Richardson: A Bowler Pure and Simple"* by Keith Booth (ACS Lives in Cricket publications, 2012)

☐ Jack ROBERTSON

Middlesex opening batsman. A bench placed at Lord's in his memory. Career started with a duck in only appearance in 1937 but scored 1000 runs a season every year 1946-58, and nine times exceeded 2000. Yet played intermittently for England in only 11 Tests, mostly on two M.C.C. tours. His omission one of several mistakes by selectors of side to Australia in 1950-51. Retired 1959 to become coach, and then ran hotel in Cornwall. Moved to Suffolk to be nearer his family. Died in Bury St Edmunds on 12 October 1996, and cremated at West Suffolk (Risby) Crematorium. His ashes were scattered on lawn G4, without memorial or plaque.

Biography : *"More than just the warm-up act"* by Chris Overson (ACS Lives in Cricket publications, 2013)

☐ R.C.ROBERTSON-GLASGOW

Played for Oxford University. Gained blue for 4 years. Fast-medium bowler as amateur with Somerset 1920-37 but 1923 was only full season. Schoolmaster at Hindhead, cricket correspondent on *Morning Post* after Warner stood down. Occasional BBC radio summariser; chairman of Cricket Writers Club; after-dinner speaking. On 4 March

1965 took overdose of barbiturate tablets at home in Pangbourne, Berkshire, and was dead on arrival at Park Hospital. Was buried in churchyard of Holy Trinity, Buckhold.

Holy Trinity, Buckhold *Sat Nav* RG8 8QB

Biography : *"Forty-Six Not Out"* autobiography (Hollis & Carter, 1948)

● Buckhold church was declared redundant and became a private dwelling. To find it, take the A340 to Tidmarsh and follow signs 'Upper Basildon'. The grave lay to east of former chapel and had black marble headstone; but even when I photographed it in the early 1980s it had toppled and was lying flat.

□ Walter ROBINS

Gifted all-rounder: powerful batsman and, from university days, leg-break and googly bowler. From Cambridge to Middlesex and England, made rapid rise to prominence. Achieved 'double' at age of 23. Owing to business reasons, able to make only one tour with M.C.C. (1936-37 as vice-captain) and missed playing in several seasons at home. 19 Tests for England. Test selector in 1947 - same year as skipper of county championship side - and again in 1960s when chairman and apostle of brighter cricket. M.C.C. tour manager in West Indies 1960. Died of pneumonia at St John's Wood home on 12 December 1968. Funeral at Golders Green Crematorium. In 1970 Middlesex CCC placed five wooden memorial benches in gardens at Lord's Cricket Ground with inscriptions to cricketers including Robins.

Lord's Cricket Ground *Sat Nav* NW8 8QN

Biography : *"Walter Robins: Achievements, Affections and Affronts"* by Brian Rendell (ACS Lives in Cricket, 2013)

• Brian Rendell's biography reveals that Robins's wife strolled around the playing perimeter at Lord's secretly dispersing his ashes on the outfield from a torn plastic bag!

□ Fred ROOT

Played for county of birth (Derbyshire) before joining Worcestershire in 1921, bowling medium-paced inswing. Speeded up and bowled form of 'leg theory' from 1923, taking 542 wickets in three seasons, and won 3 England caps. No overseas tours except West Indies 1925-26. Professional with Dudley C.C. Wrote *"A Cricket Pro's Lot"* in 1937. Leicestershire coach and sports columnist. Died at Royal Hospital, Wolverhampton, 20 January 1954, after month's illness. Buried in New Cemetery, Dudley. Buried in plot C1339 but there is no headstone.

New Cemetery, Dudley   *Sat Nav* DY1 2DA

Biography : *"A Cricket Pro's Lot"* autobiography (Arnold, 1937)

• Many visit this cemetery to see the grave of footballer Duncan Edwards, a shrine for Man United supporters and usually adorned with red and white flowers.

□ Vernon ROYLE

Oxford University and Lancashire batsman, ambidextrous, celebrated for cover fielding prowess. One Test on Lord Harris's 1878-79 tour about which Royle compiled a diary, since published. President of Lancashire C.C.C. 1928. Gave up cricket to become clergyman and later headmaster of boys' preparatory school at Stanmore Park House from 1901 until his death there on 21 May 1929. When school moved to Hertford in 1937, mansion was demolished; plaque to Royle on one of original school gate piers on Uxbridge Road. To the south is Stanmore parish church where his funeral took place, and he was buried in the churchyard. During service, according to Royle's wishes, boys at the school played cricket until a bell tolled when they stood silently to remember him. Buried beside main path in St John's churchyard, Stanmore.

Kingsmead Ground, South Africa, for each of the M.C.C. touring team, including Russell. Died at Leytonstone Hospital on 23 March 1961 and funeral at City of London Cemetery, Aldersbrook Road. Ashes placed in bed 1412 of the Memorial Gardens. Dedication expired in May 1981 and was not renewed.

City of London Cemetery   *Sat Nav* E12 5DQ

Image © Graham Hill 2015

St John The Evangelist's church, Uxbridge Road, Stanmore
Sat Nav HA7 4AQ

Biography: *"The Diary of Vernon Royle"* (1878-79 tour record) (pub J.W.McKenzie, 2001).

● Stanmore Tourist Board answered my enquiry about the plaque on the old school gate piers They were interested to hear that Royle's grave was in the churchyard and located it, in front of librettist W.S. Gilbert's imposing white angel grave.

☐ *Andrew SANDHAM*

Batsman, made Surrey debut in 1911. Long and fruitful opening partnership with Hobbs, including 66 century opening stands. Scorer of over 41,000 runs and one hundred hundreds. 'The Little Master'. Seven overseas tours, including West Indies 1929-30 when scored 325 in Kingston, then highest score in a Test. 14 Test appearances. Retired 1937. Hon Life Membership of M.C.C. in 1949. Post-War Surrey coach and from 1958 until 1970 county scorer. Died in hospital in Westminster 20 April 1982; at time of death oldest England player, aged 92. Streatham-born he now lies "in an unmarked plot in Streatham Park Cemetery" – [Philip Paine]

Streatham Park Cemetery   *Sat Nav* SW16 5JG

Biography : *"Cricket"* autobiography (W & G Foyle, 1957)

☐ *'Jack' RUSSELL*

Born in 1887, son of Essex wicket-keeper who kept to Kortright. Reliable opening batsman, first appeared for Essex 1911. Career interrupted by War, when served in Royal Army Corps. Best years in early 20s, including two M.C.C. tours but only 10 Test match appearances, scoring 910 runs; restricted by presence of Hobbs & Sutcliffe. Coach at Westminster School. In 1922-23 a plaque was placed on a tree at Durban's

☐ *Geoffrey SAULEZ*

England scorer on a succession of overseas tours in the 1970s and 1980s. Lived in Camberley, and died in Frimley Park Hospital 23 Dec 2004, aged 88. Funeral at St John's Crematorium, Woking.

St John's Crematorium, Woking   *Sat Nav* GU21 8TJ

☐ William SCOTTON

Played his first club cricket, like Shrewsbury, with Meadow Willow club. After initial appearance for Notts aged 19, became a dependable opening batsman, renowned for slow but sure approach. Was nicknamed "Old Everlasting". Went to Australia three times with Shaw & Shrewsbury's teams. Retiring comparatively young in 1890, settled for club cricket and umpiring. Following his divorce, committed suicide by cutting throat at lodgings in St John's Wood Terrace, London, on 9 July 1893. He was 37. Buried close to his father's grave in Nottingham General Cemetery, just below top chapel.

Nottingham General Cemetery   *Sat Nav*   NG7 3ND

☐ John SELBY

Born 1849, son of a Nottingham club player. Batsman with county 1870-87. Toured Australia twice, played in first-ever 'Test' match and five others. Stylish and particularly good with fast bowling. Admitted to Nottingham General Hospital on Standard Hill with paralysis and exhaustion owing to a stroke. Died two months later on 11 March 1894. Funeral in Nottingham General Cemetery, close to grave of old Notts keeper Biddulph.

Nottingham General Cemetery   *Sat Nav*   NG7 3ND

☐ E. H. D. [Edward] SEWELL

Born in India 1872. Cricket writer. As pupil at school, played for Bedfordshire (1891). Next year went to serve in Indian civil service. Prodigious hitter, playing for Madras cricket club. Once in 1896 against a regimental team scored 74 out of team score of 78 in first innings and 51 out of 56 in the second. Essex CCC signed him as a professional, also played for London County and M.C.C., then in 1908 coach at Surrey for 3 years. Writer of *From a Window at Lord's* (1937), *Who Won the Toss?* (1940) etc. In and out of hospital for a year before death in Paddington Hospital, London, on 20 September 1947.

Biography *'The Log of a Sportsman'* autobiography ? (T.F. Unwin Ltd, 1923); *'An Outdoor Wallah'* autobiography (Stanley Paul, 1945)

☐ James SEYMOUR

Stylish middle-order batsman. Was coached as a youth at Tonbridge, joined Kent 1902 until 1926, making over 27000 runs with fifty centuries. Thought of as best slip catcher in England, helped bring him close to Test selection. Benefit of £2000 in 1920; brought court case contesting demands of Inland Revenue and won cricketers' right to tax-free benefit as reward for long service. Died at his home, 'Howlands', in village of his birth, Marden, Kent, on 30 September 1930 and buried in Marden parish churchyard.

St Michael & All Angels church, Marden   *Sat Nav*   TN12 9HS

☐ John SHARPE

Son of an old Notts cricketer, Samuel Sharpe. Lost one eye in childhood. Unable to get into county eleven, became successful fast-medium bowler with Surrey, taking nearly 500 cheap wickets, then returned to Notts but for only 5 matches. Played 3 Tests on tour of Australia with Sheffield's team. Died at his birth village, Ruddington, on 19 June 1936 and buried in Shaw Street Cemetery, which is accessed from Vicarage Lane.

Ruddington cemetery   *Sat Nav*   NG11 6HB

☐ Alfred SHAW

A pioneer of the international game. Played in first Test match in 1877. Having organised three tours of Australia in association with Lillywhite and Shrewsbury, arranged the 1891-92 tour on behalf of his employer Earl of Sheffield. As player, supremely accurate right-arm medium-pacer; as tactician led Notts to title of champion county, and led England on 4 occasions in Australia in 1881-82. Died in Gedling, east of Nottingham, on 16 January 1907 (four years after his business partner Shrewsbury) and buried in same churchyard of All Hallows, Gedling. Grave marked by Celtic cross. Inscription faces away from church, which lies to its west. Idea was that his grave would be 22 yards away from Shrewsbury's.

All Hallows church, Gedliing   *Sat Nav*   NG4 4BG

Biography : *"Alfred Shaw Cricketer: His Career And Reminiscences "* by A.W.Pullin [Old Ebor] (Cassell & Co, 1902)

☐ THE EARL OF SHEFFIELD

Benefactor of cricket who, once he had engaged W.G.Grace, sponsored the 1891-92 English tour of Australia. Lost £2000 on tour but donated Shield for which colonies (now states) could compete. Owned, among 6000 acres of Sheffield Park, Sussex, his

ALSO TO THE MEMORY OF
HER SON
HENRY NORTH HOLROYD,
EARL OF SHEFFIELD,
BORN 18TH OF JANUARY 1832,
DIED 21ST OF APRIL 1909.
"REQUIESCANT IN PACE"

own cricket field where touring teams played. Died 21 April 1909 at Beaulieu in France, where recuperating from illness. Body returned for burial in family vault, Fletching church, East Sussex. Inside church of St Andrew & St Mary is the Sheffield mausoleum. However, the interior door is always locked and outer door in north wall sealed up.

St Andrew & St Mary's church, Fletching   *Sat Nav*   TN22 3SS

Biography : *"Cricket in the Park"* by Roger Packham (Methuen, 2009)

☐ Rev David SHEPPARD

Outstanding opening batsman, picked for Sussex while 18 and made Test debut while in first year at Cambridge University. Taken to Australia 1950-51. Modest tour, but came back to top national averages in 1952. Led Sussex to runners-up in 1953 championship; seen as a potential England skipper but only captained twice when Hutton was ill in 1954. Ordained as a minister of church in 1953 and, working at the Mayflower Family Centre in East London, found less time for cricket. Persuaded to turn out in 1962 to be considered for Australian tour, possibly as captain. Retired at end of tour. Prominent in opposing cricket contacts with South Africa at end of 'sixties. Bishop of Woolwich, and then Bishop of Liverpool in 1975. On retiring, appointed to House of Lords. Died of cancer on 5 March 2005 at West Kirby, his home in retirement on The Wirral. Funeral at St Bridget's Church in West Kirby. His ashes interred beneath a slate slab on floor at rear of Liverpool Anglican Cathedral. The Sheppard memorial, dedicated by Justin Welby in May 2011, is an abstract sculpture by Stephen Broadbent of white portland stone embedded in the sandstone wall. Broadbent also designed memorial (see inside back cover) on Hope Street, Liverpool, unveiled 2008, portraying

Sheppard 'in conversation' with Derek Worlock, Catholic Archbishop at the Metropolitan, standing halfway between the two cathedrals, opposite Hope Place.

Anglican Cathedral, Liverpool   *Sat Nav*   L1 7AZ
Hope Street   *SatNav*   L1 9BG

Biography : *"Parson's Pitch"* autobiography (Hodder & Stoughton, 1964) ; *"Steps Along Hope Street"* autobiography (Hodder & Stoughton, 2002)

☐ *Mordecai SHERWIN*

From being a ground bowler at Lord's, became the regular wicket-keeper with Notts and county captain in 1887. Chosen for Shrewsbury's 1886-7 tour of Australia and 3 Tests. In his prime weighed 17 stones but was ill for months and shrunken figure almost unrecognisable at death on 3 July 1910 at The Craven Arms, Nottingham. Funeral held at Church Cemetery (The Rock), Nottingham. Entrance at junction of Forest Lane East and Mansfield Road. Has grave 3359, a plot on 'Church Back'. Headstone has fallen. Next to the path, 34 graves along.

Church (The Rock) Cemetery   *Sat Nav*   NG1 4HT

☐ *Arthur SHREWSBURY*

Nottinghamshire-born in 1856, became second greatest cricketer (after W.G.) of the Victorian age, renowned for eminently skilful batting on all kinds of pitch. Organised four tours of Australia, captain on three of them, and in all appeared in 23 Test matches. Lived always in dread of fatal illness although doctors could diagnose no trouble, and ended his own life by shooting himself at home of sister in Gedling, Nottinghamshire, on 19 May 1903. Burial was at All Hallows church, Gedling, where an elevated tomb stands near churchyard entrance (beside the public footpath) with its inscription still sharp.

All Hallows church, Gedliing   *Sat Nav*   NG4 4BG

Biography : *"A Biographical Sketch of Arthur Shrewsbury"* by S.W.Hitchin (1890); *"Give Me Arthur"* by Peter Wynne-Thomas (Arthur Barker, 1985)

☐ *John SHUTER*

An opening batsman for Surrey, he was also captain from 1885 onwards. Though had made just one Test appearance, became a Test selector. Business in cycle manufacture. He died on 5 July 1920 at Blackheath and was interred in Crayford parish churchyard, Kent. Buried in grave number E216, belonging to his wife Constance Horner, who came from one of Crayford's leading families. Only kerbs carrying inscriptions with his name until an enthusiastic incumbent arranged small headstone in 2011 revealing Shuter's celebrity.

St Paulinus church, Crayford   *Sat Nav*   DA1 4RW

George SIMPSON-HAYWARD

Changed his name from Simpson in 1898. One of the last underarm bowlers in f-c cricket, delivering brisk off-breaks. Chosen for M.C.C. tour of South Africa in 1909-10; took 6-43 in debut Test, and 23 victims in the series. Died on 2 October 1936 at his home, Icomb Place, Gloucestershire, where he had laid out an arboretum and a celebrated rock garden (not open to the public). His grave in St Mary's churchyard, Icomb, nr Stow-on-the-Wold. Also, a wooden plaque to him inside church.

St Mary's church, Icomb   *Sat Nav* GL54 1JE

Alex SKELDING

His playing accomplishments were modest and was aged nearly forty when gave his best bowling performances. E.E.Snow reckoned him fastest bowler in country. After retiring, became a first-class umpire, universally well-liked and good at his job. M.C.C. allowed him to continue until he was 71, but never asked to stand in a Test. Died on 17 April 1960, and buried in Welford Road Cemetery, Leicester. His grave, number 942, lies in plot MA con, next to the railway fence, surrounded by graves with coincidental cricketing connotation (Underwood, Worrell, Tate). No headstone. Grave lies behind a stone lying flat on Blakemore's plot.

Welford Road Cemetery and Visitor Centre *Sat Nav* LE2 6BB

Wilf SLACK

Born on St Vincent 1954. Family migrated to High Wycombe when aged 11. Batsman for Middlesex and in 3 Tests for England. Died of a heart attack while at the crease on 15 January 1989 in Banjul, The Gambia. Plaque in Banjul to commemorate his death. Funeral cortege passed by Lord's on way to Greenford Park Cemetery: buried wearing his England blazer. One of Middlesex's outgrounds at East End Road, Finchley, was renamed The Wilf Slack Sports Ground.

Greenford Park Cemetery *Sat Nav* UB6 9DU   Wilf Slack Sports Ground   *Sat Nav* N3 2LE

John SMALL

In a long career with Hambledon, Hampshire and the All-England XI, was a left-handed batsman in days of curved bats. Became adept at using the straight bat when introduced in the 1770s. Died on 31 December 1826, and buried in St Peter's churchyard, near entrance from Jubilee Square in town centre of Petersfield, Hampshire. There have been no burials in the churchyard since 1856 and all stones were lifted in 1950, save one - John Small's. Its famous inscription recut in the 1960s: "Praises on tombs are trifles vainly spent; a Man's good name is his own monument."

St Peter's church, The Square   Sat Nav GU32 3HS

C.Aubrey SMITH

Born in London, spent his childhood in Sussex. The president of M.C.C. unveiled a plaque at his home (now flats), 19 Albany Villas, Hove, in April 1987. Fast-medium bowler with a 'round-the-corner' run-up. Led England touring teams to Australia and South Africa, and remained in South Africa on business. Acting career followed and Hollywood cinema in the 1930s and 40s. Named his Hollywood home 'Round The Corner' and died there on 20 December 1948. His ashes returned to England nine months later for interment in mother's grave, C7.2, in cemetery of St Leonard's church, Aldrington, Hove.

St Leonard's church *Sat Nav* BN3 4ED   19 Albany Villas *Sat Nav* BN3 2RS

Biography: *"Aubrey Smith: A Biography of C Aubrey Smith"* by David Rayvern Allen (Elm Tree, 1982)

☐ [C.I.J.] 'Big Jim' SMITH

One of two Test players (Kinneir was the other) born at Corsham, Wiltshire. On Lord's groundstaff, minor cricket for native county, then joined Middlesex as fast bowler and big hitter: hit fifties in 14 minutes v Kent 1935 and in 11 minutes v Gloucs 1938. Five Tests. Died at Mellor, nr Blackburn, on 8 February 1979. Funeral at St Mary's church, Mellor, followed by cremation at Pleasington Crematorium. No memorial. His ashes scattered on Gardens of Remembrance.

Biography: *"Corsham's Two Test Cricketers"* by D T Smith (the author, 2000)

☐ [Ernest James] 'Tiger' SMITH

Born in 1886, his whole life was devoted to cricket. Was a wicket-keeper and opening bat for Warwickshire (1904-30); he was picked for England for eleven Tests and two overseas tours; became a first-class umpire; was the county coach until aged 83 ; and even then remained an enthusiastic spectator. Died at home in Northfield on 30 August 1979. Last surviving pre-WW1 player. Service and cremation were at Lodge Hill Crematorium, Birmingham, on 6 September but there was no memorial : his ashes were scattered on Edgbaston Cricket Ground.

Biography: *"'Tiger' Smith of Warwickshire And England"* by Patrick Murphy (Lutterworth Press, 1981)

☐ Fred SPOFFORTH

An Australian fast bowler nicknamed 'The Demon' by his opponents, he had all the virtues of accuracy, cut, pace, tactics and cunning. Was a member of first five Australian touring teams to England in 1878, '80, '82, '84 and '86. He proved, except when injured, more than a match for the English batsmen. In 1886 married a Derbyshire girl and settled in England. Died at home in Ditton Hill, Surbiton, on 4 June 1926 and buried in grave number 191361, on plot 28 of Brookwood Necropolis, Surrey. Grave is approx. 60 metres from the Bent Memorial along St Margaret's Avenue, a low, pink granite tombstone opposite Dashwood's.

Brookwood Cemetery *Sat Nav* GU24 0BL

Biography: *"The Demon Spofforth"* by Richard Cashman (Walla Walla Press, Australia, 1990)

☐ Reginald SPOONER

Joined Lancashire as an amateur from Marlborough College, but business interests interrupted cricket career and prevented him from playing more than ten Tests for England. Manner of his batting made his name; with Palairet's, it became byword for Edwardian style. He was land agent to Lord Londesborough on Blankney estates for 25 years, and died on 2 October 1961 at the Golf Hotel, Woodhall Spa. Grave is in Woodhall Spa Cemetery, Lincolnshire. Cemetery in Kirkby Lane, a half-mile from village. Follow main cemetery path towards a hedge looking for a grave surmounted by a large cross. In Marlborough College chapel an inscription records Spooner's name, his dates at school, and the word 'Cricketer'.

Woodhall Spa Cemetery   *Sat Nav*   LN10 6YE

□ R.T. ['Rony'] STANYFORTH

His cricket was mostly played for The Army. Before playing any f-c cricket, chosen to captain England and keep wicket in South Africa. Made only 3 appearances for Yorkshire. Not realised until ten years after his death that was not even born in

Yorkshire, as tradition required. After 1947 he was Equerry to Duke of Gloucester. Died at his home, Kirk Hammerton Hall, near York, on 20 February 1964. Buried in Kirk Hammerton parish churchyard opposite the Hall. A tall, sandstone memorial cross marks the grave, about 20 metres south-west of the church.

St John the Baptist church, Kirk Hammerton   *Sat Nav*
YO26 8DL

□ Sam STAPLES

Nottinghamshire's medium-paced off-break bowler. From Newstead Colliery village, though not a miner like several players from midland counties. Three Test appearances, then selected for 1928-29 Australian tour but withdrew unwell. Retired from cricket in 1933, became coach to Notts and Hampshire. Died on 4 June 1950 at Standard Hill hospital, Nottingham. Buried in *Redhill Cemetery, Arnold,* Nottinghamshire. Plot contains the bodies of himself, his wife and son. But headstone on grave 3477 at 'class B. Cons' records only his son Roy, killed in action in 1944.

Redhill Cemetery   *Sat Nav*   NG5 8LS

□ Brian STATHAM

Mancunian who made Lancashire debut on his 20th birthday. Formed fast bowling partnerships for England with Frank Tyson and Fred Trueman and ended with 252 wickets. Awarded CBE in 1966 New Year honours and retired in 1968. County president 1997-98. After cricket employed in public relations by Guinness. Died of leukemia at Stockport on 10 June 2000. Funeral was at Manchester Crematorium. Was commemorated at Old Trafford ground in the Washbrook-Statham Stand; also, Trafford Council renamed a road, Warwick Way, alongside the ground as Brian Statham Way.

Emirates Old Trafford Ground   *Sat Nav*   M16 0PX

Biographies : *"Cricket Merry-Go-Round"* autobiography (Stanley Paul, 1956) ; *"Flying Bails"* autobiography (Stanley Paul, 1961); *"A Spell At the Top"* autobiography (Souvenir Press, 1969); *"Bowled Statham: the Authorised Biography"* by Brian Derlien (Breedon Books, 1990); *"Glory Lightly Worn"* by Malcolm Lorimer (Parrs Wood Press 2001).

☐ Allan STEEL

A brilliant natural cricketer, fast accumulator of runs and in his early days skilful spin bowler able to conceal direction of turn. Went on Bligh's tour of Australia but called to the Bar in 1883, limiting his Test appearances to 13. Four times he captained England, and was M.C.C. president in 1902. Died of heart failure at his home near Hyde Park on 15 June 1914. Funeral at St James's church, Paddington, was attended by a large congregation, and followed by interment at the fashionable Kensal Green Cemetery, London. His grave is number 44280 in plot 152, row 2. Memorial proclaims he was Recorder of Oldham.

Kensal Green Cemetery, London   *Sat Nav*   W10 4RA

Biography: *"Cricketing Sketch of Mr A.G. Steel"* by P Y Lodge (self-published, Liverpool, 1895)

☐ Heathfield STEPHENSON

The term "hat trick" apparently gets its name from Stephenson's feat of taking three wickets in consecutive balls with his round-arm bowling in an All-England match at Sheffield, and being awarded a hat as a prize. Had taken to wicket-keeping by the time of pioneering 1861-62 Australian tour : the first tour made there by an English side, of which Stephenson was captain. Retired to coach at Uppingham School. His tombstone was inscribed "beloved and regretted by masters and boys of Uppingham School whose high traditions he nobly upheld for 24 years. Cricketer, wise teacher and loyal friend...." Died after a long illness on 17 December 1896 and buried in Uppingham parish church cemetery. The rector at time of his death was not in the habit of recording graves; but is found in farthest of three graveyard extensions from church.

St Peter & St Paul's church cemetery, Uppingham   *Sat Nav*   LE15 9TJ.

Biography : *"H H Stephenson: A Cricketing Journey from Kennington Oval to Uppingham School"* by Roy Stephenson (Uppingham Local History Study Group, 2009)

☐ 'Lumpy' STEVENS

Mid-eighteenth century bowler, very successful though assisted by laws which allowed fielding side to choose pitch to bowl on. Formerly gardener on Earl of Tankerville's estate. As an early patron of cricket, Tankerville employed him as professional cricketer. In single wicket match 1775 bowled John Small three times but ball passed between the two-stump wicket, so a middle stump added thereafter. Died at Walton-on-Thames 1819, and buried in St Mary's churchyard. Tombstone erected by employer Earl of Tankerville but has become worn and tilted.

St Mary's church, Walton   *Sat Nav*   KT12 2QS

☐ Andrew STODDART

Born in South Shields where a street is named after him. Highly accomplished all-round sportsman, having won an international cap for rugby before concentrating on cricket. Scored 485 runs in match for Hampstead CC in 1886, then highest score ever made. Small bronze of him batting by Neale Andrew (son of England player, Keith) unveiled by Andrew Strauss at Hampstead C.C. on 100th anniversary of Stoddart's death. Joined two touring teams to Australia before organising his own tours in 1894-95 and 1897-98; won the Ashes on first tour, lost them on second. Gave up cricket for business in 1900, after scoring 221 in final county innings. Took his own life at his home in St John's Wood, 4 April 1915. After funeral at Golders Green Crematorium, ashes conveyed to Coventry for burial in his wife's family grave at Radford parish churchyard.

St Nicholas church, Radford *Sat Nav* CV6 1QT   Stoddart
Street, South Shields *Sat Nav* NE34 0JS

Biography : *"My Dear Victorious Stod: A Biography of A E Stoddart"* by David Frith (self-published 1970, Lutterworth Press, 1977); *"Stoddy: England's Finest Sportsman"* by David Frith (Von Krumm Publishing, 2015).

☐ George STREET

A wicket-keeper/batsman for Sussex from 1909. Called up to reinforce M.C.C. in South Africa in 1922-3, he appeared in one Test match when the regular 'keeper was injured. His best season was 1923 when he notched up 95 dismissals. Killed in a motorcycle accident at Portslade, Sussex, 24 April 1924. Was buried in Warnham churchyard and grave marked with a bright, wide, white marble headstone.

St Margaret's church, Warnham *Sat Nav* RH12 3QW

☐ Herbert STRUDWICK

Surrey wicket-keeper from 1902. Not a complete number 11, but batting was not one of his strengths. In all first-class cricket he had 1497 victims and held the record until broken by John Murray. Said never to appeal unless he knew it was out, and he was keen enough sometimes to chase the ball as far as the boundary. One of the crowd's idols at The Oval, always ready with a joke or an autograph. For England he played in 28 Tests. On retirement in 1927, content to be Surrey's scorer until 1958. Died at home in Shoreham-by-Sea on 13 February 1970, shortly after his 90th birthday. Funeral at St Mary's church was followed by interment at Mill Lane Cemetery, Shoreham: grave 10, row 60, extension A.

Mill Lane Cemetery   *Sat Nav* BN43 5NA

Biography: *"25 Years Behind the Stumps"* autobiography (Hutchinson, 1926)

☐ C.T. [Charles] STUDD

Batsman from Spratton, Northants, represented Eton and Cambridge University, and played in 1882 Test at The Oval when England lost. Also, in 1882-83 series in Australia where Ashes regained. Became missionary in China and India and subsequently in 1913 to Belgian Congo while wife Priscilla (died 1929) remained in England organising the Worldwide Evangelisation Crusade. Studd died from untreated gallstones on 16 July 1931 and buried at Ibambi, now in Democratic Republic of Congo.

Biography : *"Charles T Studd, Cricketer and Missionary"* by T B Walters (Epworth, 1930); *"C T Studd: Cricketer and Pioneer"* by Norman Grubb (Religious Tract Society, London, 1934); *"Well Played, Sir! - a Biography of Charles T Studd"* by C J Davey (Edinburgh House, 1950); *"Millionaire for God - the Story of C T Studd"* by JT Erskine (Lutterworth Press, 1968)

● A photo of Charles Studd's grave in the Congo taken by David Stewart may be seen in *'Innings Complete, vol 15'* by Philip Paine. Charles's brother George Studd was a batsman for Middlesex and was also chosen for the 1882-83 tour of Australia. He played no cricket after 1886 when he accompanied his brother to China. In 1891 he went to California to preach among the poor, and opened a mission. After his death in Pasadena, California, he was buried in Mount View Cemetery, Altadena, Los Angeles.

☐ Frank SUGG

Batsman who played for Yorkshire 1883, Derbyshire 1884-86, then 13 seasons with Lancashire. In 1896 v Somerset hit 50 runs off three overs. Retired 1899 to run sports business with brother Walter; chain of shops did not close till 2001. All-rounder: football, weight-lifting, swimming, billiards, throwing the cricket ball, etc. Also f-c umpire and coach at Merchant Taylor's school, Crosby. Died Waterloo, Liverpool, on 29 May 1933. Survived Walter by only a week. Buried in churchyard of St Luke's, Crosby. Interred in a public grave in area next to fence and York Road houses but no headstone; exact location cannot now be identified. By contrast parents have an impressive obelisk monument in Sheffield's Burngreave Cemetery.

Biography : *"Frank Sugg: A Man For All Seasons"* by Martin Howe (ACS Lives In Cricket, 2011)

George SUMMERS

Nottinghamshire batsman, regarded as a promising cricketer, killed at the crease by a fast ball when batting v M.C.C. at Lord's: hit on temple by delivery from Platt in match on 19 June 1870. M.C.C. then paid £30 for his gravestone in Nottingham General Cemetery, inscribed "...to testify their regret at the untimely accident on Lord's ground, which cut short a career so full of promise."

© image courtesy Philip Paine

Nottingham General Cemetery *Sat Nav* NG7 3ND

Stuart SURRIDGE

Fast-medium bowler for Surrey, aged nearly 30 when first chosen. Appointed captain 1952-56 and through bold, attacking leadership and inspirational close catching won five consecutive county championships. At this time lived at Greatlake Farm, Horley; nearby is now a Surridge Court off Whittaker Drive. Retired to run family bat-making and sports goods business. Made president of Surrey in 1981. On 13 April 1992 collapsed while visiting his factory in Glossop and died. His ashes interred at Putney Vale Cemetery, two months after cremation, in block D5, grave 59, a plot purchased in 1912 for the family by his grandfather. Ground redevelopment at The Oval included a Surridge Gate on western side.

Kennington (Kia) Oval *Sat Nav* SE11 5SS Surridge Court, Horley *Sat Nav* RH6 9FB Putney Vale Cemetery *Sat Nav* SW15 3DZ

Biography : *"Stuart Surridge, Skipper of Surrey's Golden Era"* by Jerry Lodge (The History Press, 2008)

• Surridge's wife Betty was the first Lady President of any county cricket club, taking over from Paul Getty at The Oval in 1997. She was also one of the original Lady Taverners.

• It was through Bill Gordon at The Oval and his contact with Surridge's son that I was able to hear about this burial plot. The records of neither crematorium nor funeral director gave sufficient information to locate it, but Su Foster of Wandsworth's public service organisation identified it for me. The names of Surridge's grandparents are on the kerbing but, alas, Stuart's name has not been added.

Herbert SUTCLIFFE

An opening batsman of technical correctness and extreme skill on poor wickets, making 1000 runs or more for Yorkshire in every season between the Wars, and forming with Percy Holmes the county's best-ever opening partnership. Similarly, he and Jack Hobbs were England's best opening pair. Immaculately turned out and very correct, Sutcliffe remained throughout his life one of most popular Yorkshire cricketers. He died in hospital at Crosshills on 22 January 1978. The funeral held at Otley United Reform Church was followed by cremation at Rawdon, after which his ashes were strewn on lawns and an entry made in Book of Remembrance. There was no family memorial but the 'Herbert Sutcliffe Gates' had been officially inaugurated at Headingley in 1965 by Yorkshire president Sir William Worsley.

Headingley Cricket Ground, Leeds   *Sat Nav* LS6 3BU

Biography : *"For England and Yorkshire"* autobiography (Edward Arnold, 1934); *"Sutcliffe: Yorkshire and England 1919-39"* by E L Roberts (Hudson, 1945); *"Herbert Sutcliffe: Cricket Maestro"* by Alan Hill (Simon & Schuster, 1991)

☐ E.W. 'Jim' SWANTON

Cricket writer, born in Forest Hill, London. Joined *Evening Standard* 1928 and then *Daily Telegraph*. OBE 1965. Formed his own wandering club, The Arabs. Retired from journalism in 1975 but continued to contribute articles. Kent President 1981. CBE 1994. Lived in Delf Street, Sandwich, for 35 years. Died on 22 January 2000 in Chaucer Hospital, Canterbury. Funeral at St Clement's church on 1 February attended by PM Sir John Major, and former players including Kent's Denness, Cowdrey and Luckhurst. His and wife Ann's ashes interred in Gardens of Remembrance in St Clement's churchyard and marked by a small memorial plaque.

St Clement's church *Sat Nav* CT13 9EH

Biography : *"Sort of a Cricket Person"* autobiography (Collins, 1972); *"Follow On"* autobiography (Collins, 1977); *"Jim : The Life of E.W.Swanton"* by David Rayvern Allen (Aurum Press, 2004)

• I'm grateful to the Rector of St Clement's church, Revd Canon Mark Roberts, who conducted the funeral in 2000 ("one of the largest gatherings I ever remember in our church....how we accommodated so many I'm not sure") for providing information about the memorial.

☐ Fred TATE

Medium-paced bowler. First played for Sussex once in 1887, then regularly. Took 1300 wickets. At Tonbridge in August 1888 took 5 for 0 when Kent needed 4 runs to win with six wickets left. In 1902 took 15 for 68 in a single day to bowl out Middlesex at Lord's and chosen for Test side at Old Trafford, where England's disastrous defeat unfairly blamed on him. Retired 1905. From 1922 Derbyshire coach and subsequently back at Sussex. Died at home 'Oak View' in Burgess Hill on 24 February 1943, and buried in St Andrew's churchyard, Burgess Hill.

St Andrew's church, Burgess Hill *Sat Nav* RH15 0LG

☐ Maurice TATE

Had a distinguished career for Sussex, starting as off-spinner and batsman but after 1922 concentrating on fast-medium bowling. Strongly-built with pendulum-smooth body action, became a master of seam and swing. Maintained batsmanship with 1000 runs in eleven consecutive seasons. Only player to achieve the "double" of 1000 runs and 100 wickets in an overseas season (1926-27). Played in 39 Test matches for England, firstly in 1924 (taking a wicket with his first ball), and eventually 155 Test wickets. Most successful bowler of his time, finished playing in 1937. Due to attend coaching at Butlin's Holiday Camp in Clacton when suffered heart attack at his Wadhurst home (the Greyhound pub) and died on 18 May 1956. Funeral was

(above) Stuart Surridge was buried in the family grave in Putney Vale Cemetery but is un-named on kerbs

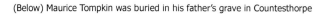

(Below) Maurice Tompkin was buried in his father's grave in Countesthorpe

at Wadhurst parish church, East Sussex. Buried in cemetery beyond the churchyard, on right-hand side of path, three graves in and 29 grave spaces along: a white marble headstone. Commemorative blue plaque at childhood home, 28 Warleigh Road, Brighton. The Duke of Norfolk officially opened the Tate Memorial Gates at Sussex's Hove Ground on 17 May 1958 with Jack Hobbs and Arthur Gilligan present. In 2011 the pillars and gates were removed to make the new Probiz ground "more open and appealing".

St Peter & St Paul's church, Wadhurst   *Sat Nav*   TN5 6AA
Warleigh Road, Brighton   *Sat Nav*   BN1 4NT

Biography : *"My Cricket Reminiscences"* autobiography (Stanley Paul, 1934); *"Maurice Tate"* by John Arlott (Phoenix House, 1951); *"Maurice Tate"* by Gerald Brodribb (Readers Union, 1976); *"Then Came Massacre: the Story of Maurice Tate, Cricket's Smiling Destroyer"* by Justin Parkinson (Pitch Publishing, 2013)

□ [Hon] *Lionel TENNYSON*

The spirited skipper of Hampshire, was tried as captain of England in 1921 to save the series against Australia. Later organised four overseas tours by his own teams, lastly in 1937-38 playing unofficial Tests in India. Died at the Normanhurst Hotel, Bexhill-on-Sea, 6 June 1951. Funeral at Golders Green Crematorium and his ashes interred in family plot at Freshwater, Isle of Wight, where wife of his grandfather, the Poet Laureate, is also buried (Alfred Lord Tennyson himself lies in Poets' Corner).

All Saints church, Freshwater   *Sat Nav*   PO40 9PE

Biography : *"From Verse to Worse"* autobiography (Cassell, 1933); *"Sticky Wickets"* autobiography (Christopher Johnson, 1950); *"Lionel Tennyson: Regency Buck. The Life and Times of a Cricketing Legend"* by Alan Edwards (Robson Books, 2001)

□ *Francis THOMPSON*

Originally from Preston, Lancashire, Thompson abandoned medical studies at college in order to write essays and poetry in London. Published three volumes of poetry, little of it recalling the cricket watched at Old Trafford in youth, apart from immortal lines of *'Run Stealers'*. Died London 13 November 1907 and buried in St Mary's R.C. Cemetery, Kensal Green. Memorial at Owens College, Manchester, where was student 1877-84.

Kensal Green Cemetery   *Sat Nav*   W10 4RA   Owens College (since 1904 merged into University of Manchester)   *Sat Nav*   M13 9PL

□ *George THOMPSON*

Best all-rounder in England for a while, and chosen for six Tests. Was the power behind Northamptonshire's entry into first-class cricket, and first professional to captain the county. Became coach at Clifton College. Died at the Chesterfield nursing home, Bristol, on 3 March 1943. Funeral at St Paul's church, Clifton, was followed by cremation at Arnos Vale Cemetery,

Bristol. His cremated remains were strewn in the Gardens of Rest and a wall plaque commemorates him and his wife, Charlotte. On 8 August 1946 Pelham Warner unveiled

at Northampton County Ground a plaque to honour Thompson as the county's finest all-rounder. In June 2014 a further plaque to mark house in Station Road, Cogenhoe where Thompson lived was unveiled by Mal Loye on behalf of Cogenhoe cricket club.

Arnos Vale Cemetery, Bristol *Sat Nav* BS4 3EW   The Elms, 168 Station Road, Cogenhoe *Sat Nav* NN7 1NG

☐ Charles THORNTON

In an 1868 Eton v Harrow match 'Buns' hit a ball onto the roof of Lord's pavilion, making his reputation as a big hitter. Founded Scarborough Festival in 1873 and made it an annual event. Silver casket and scrolls, presented to Thornton in 1921 when given Freedom of the Borough of Scarborough, now held by Scarborough C.C. On 10 December 1929 collapsed in a London theatre and died later at home, in Montagu Mansions, Marylebone. Buried in St Marylebone Cemetery, East End Road, off London's North Circular Road (now called East Finchley Cemetery). Grave is number 11 in block T3, next to pathway. Has a cricket stump design on headstone.

St Marylebone (East Finchley) Cemetery *Sat Nav* N2 0RZ

☐ Maurice TOMPKIN

Right-handed batsman for Leicestershire, who made f-c debut in 1938, aged 19. Died of cancer on 27 September 1956, less than four weeks after his last match when scored 64* in Torquay Festival. Funeral held at Baptist chapel on Church Street, Countesthorpe, Leicestershire. Interred in the cemetery on Foston Road, Countesthorpe, in the same grave as his father, with inscription "One day we will understand". Walk past

chapel to a circle where paths divide with a bush at its centre. Grave is number 1130, immediately to SE of circle.

Foston Road Cemetery *Sat Nav* LE8 5QP

Biography : *"Maurice Tompkin: More Than Just Runs"* by Richard Holdridge (ACS Lives in Cricket publications, 2011)

☐ [Sir] Fred TOONE

He had no distinction as a player, but was secretary of Leicestershire C.C.C., then of Yorkshire. A popular manager on three England tours of Australia. Was knighted in 1929 for promoting Commonwealth relations. Died at his home, The Grange, in Harrogate on 10 June 1930, and interred in Harlow Hill Cemetery, at Otley Road, Harrogate. Headstone, now collapsed and lying flat, is in section F, 353.

Harlow Hill Cemetery *Sat Nav* HG3 1PZ

☐ Albert TROTT

Born in Melbourne in 1873, an all-rounder, who played only three Tests for Australia, despite averaging over 100. Joined Lord's groundstaff when omitted from 1896 tour party and played for Middlesex. At Lord's struck a ball from Noble of 1899 Australian XI clean over the pavilion. Shortened his own benefit match against Somerset at Lord's by taking two hat-tricks! Represented Hawke's XI in South Africa 1898-99 (retrospectively giving him two Test caps for England). Retired in 1910 as health declined. In 1914 found dead, having shot himself through the head at lodgings in Denbigh Road, Willesden Green, aged 40. It seems he was broke. His funeral was on 5 August 1914 at Willesden 'New' Cemetery. Interred in

IN
Loving Memory
of

C. I. THORNTON
BORN MARCH 20TH 1850
DIED DECEMBER 10TH 1929.
"TO THE GLORY OF GOD."

Section P, in grave 613, which was owned by John Hearne of Lord's Cricket Ground. No marker until 22 May 1993 when headstone paid for by Middlesex CCC unveiled there.

Willesden Cemetery   *Sat Nav* NW10 9TE

Biography : *"Blighted Lives: the Story of Harry and Albert Trott"* by Rick Smith (Apple Books, 2010)

☐ Fred TRUEMAN

Born in a terraced house now demolished, 5 Scotch Springs, Stainton near Maltby, South Yorkshire, in 1931. Fast bowler for Yorkshire and England. CWC Young Cricketer of Year 1952. First bowler to capture 300 Test wickets (1964). Retired from cricket 1968 apart from six one-day matches for Derbyshire in 1972. Summariser for *Test Match Special* radio commentary. OBE 1989. Died of lung cancer in Airedale General Hospital on 1 July 2006 and buried in cemetery to eastern side of Bolton Abbey. Life-sized bronze statue by sculptor Graham Ibbeson at Skipton canal basin, unveiled by his widow Veronica in March 2010.

Bolton Abbey *Sat Nav* BD23 6AL   Skipton Canal Basin
Sat Nav BD23 1LH

Biographies :   *"Fast Fury"* autobiography (Stanley Paul, 1961); *"The Freddie Trueman Story"* autobiography (Stanley Paul, 1965); *"Ball of Fire"* autobiography (Dent, 1976); *"As It Was"* autobiography (Macmillan, 2004) ; *"My Most Memorable Matches"* autobiography (Stanley Paul, 1982) ; *"Fred: Portrait of a Fast Bowler"* by John Arlott (Methuen, 1971 and Simon & Schuster, 1990); *"Fred: Then and Now"* by Don Mosey (Kingswood Press, 1991); *"Fred Trueman: The Authorised Biography"* by Chris Waters (Aurum Press, 2012).

• An excellent photograph of Trueman's grave capturing the light well, taken by Ivor Hunt, may be found at https://www.flickr.com/photos/ihpics/379252789

☐ Maurice TURNBULL

Glamorgan batsman who played in nine Test matches for England as well as winning two rugby caps for Wales in 1933. County skipper and Secretary in the 1930s and Test selector for 1938-39. Died near Montchamp, Normandy, on 4 August 1944, killed during an attack on tank column by Welsh Guards in Normandy D-Day campaign. Buried in Bayeux's War Cemetery. Grave is in the Military Cemetery, number 3 on row 20 of plot C.

Biography :   *"Turnbull: A Welsh Sporting Legend"* by Andrew Hignell (Tempus, 2001)

☐ Ernest TYLDESLEY

Plaque on 1889 birthplace at Greenleach Lane, Worsley. Stylish middle-order batsman, joining Lancashire towards the end of brother Johnny's career. Scored nearly 39,000 f-c runs, of which 34,222 were highest aggregate scored for the county. In 14 Test appearances was persistently 'on trial', yet notched up 990 runs, average 55. In 1934 became the eighth man to reach 100 hundreds, including 27 in 3 seasons when Lancashire won the championship 1926-28. Winter job travelling for a light bulb company. He died on 5 May 1962 at Rhos-on-Sea, Llandudno, where he had retired with his wife, Nellie, and was buried in Worsley parish churchyard.

St Mark's church, Worsley *Sat Nav* M28 2WH

☐ Johnny TYLDESLEY

Hard-hitting batsman with all the strokes, and dependable defence, too. Hit 152 in his second match for Lancashire 1895 and won permanent place in the team, scoring over thousand runs in each of next 19 seasons. His 2,633 runs in 1901 were the county record for a season. Made 4 centuries in his 31 Tests. Retired from playing in 1923 and became coach at Old Trafford. Died at Monton, Manchester, while getting ready for work, on 27 November 1930 and was buried, like younger brother Ernest, in Worsley parish churchyard.

St Mark's church, Worsley   *Sat Nav*   M28 2WH

Biography : *"J T Tyldesley in first-class cricket"* by H E Holmes (Crompton, 1912)

□ *Dick TYLDESLEY*

A portly leg-spinner, ferocious appealer and very popular cricketer with Lancashire after First World War. Played in 7 Tests, chosen for accuracy if not spin. 1500 wickets in career. After a disagreement with committee, left county staff for league cricket. Landlord of Dog & Pheasant pub (now La Scala) in Wingates. Died at home in Newbrook Road, Over Hulton, nr Bolton, on 17 September 1943 and was buried in the cemetery of St Bartholomew's, the parish church in his birth town, Westhoughton, Lancs. Unrelated to the Tyldesley brothers above. Grave number is NEWCHU/ A /1832.

St Bartholomew's parish church   *Sat Nav*   BL5 2BG

□ *E.F.S. [Sutton] TYLECOTE*

In a school match at Clifton College he made 404*, then highest score ever made, and at Oxford developed as a wicket-keeper. Toured Australia with Ivo Bligh's team which created the Ashes legend. Aged 88 when died at home in Hunstanton, Norfolk, on 15 March 1938. Unusually for pre-War days both his parents and

three brothers also exceeded the age of eighty. Tylecote was buried with his wife in Ringstead churchyard, west Norfolk. in a plot surmounted by a cross, approx. 20 metres west of the church tower.

St Andrew's church, Ringstead   *Sat Nav*   PE36 5JX

□ *Ted TYLER*

Left-arm spinner with slow but dubious action. Taken to South Africa by Hawke 1895-96, and played in one Test. For Somerset his many remarkable bowling analyses assisted county's advance to first-class status. Was landlord of the Fleur-de-Lys Hotel, then proprietor of a sports outfitters. Died at his home, Birch Grove in Taunton, on Sunday 21 (not 25 as in some records) January 1917, being buried in St James's Cemetery, Staplegrove Road, Taunton. Grave is number 141 in Section 5, Div C. Take the path immediately at rear of the cemetery lodge.

St James's Cemetery, Taunton   *Sat Nav*   TA1 1DP

□ *George ULYETT*

Sheffield-born professional with Bradford before playing first match for Yorkshire in 1873. Known as 'Happy Jack', being relaxed and easy going. Became one of Yorkshire's indispensable all-rounders when the county was not very strong. Made five tours of Australia with English sides and played in 25 Test matches. Having retired in 1893, caught a chill watching county match at Bramall Lane and died of pneumonia on 18 June 1898 in Vine Hotel, Pitsmoor (hotel was demolished in 1960). Ulyett's grave is in Burngreave Cemetery, Pitsmoor, whose main entrance is in Burngreave Street. Pass lodge and cabin. Keep left, follow boundary path to section 'X3 consecrated'. Grave number 9 is in front row, low side, nine from the section stone.

Burngreave Cemetery, Pitsmoor   *Sat Nav*   S3 9DN

No biography but a lengthy article at www.chrishobbs.com/sheffield/georgeulyett.htm

☐ *Hedley VERITY*

A left-arm spinner, he was at first turned down at the Yorkshire trials of 1926, but was successor to Rhodes during 1930s decade, taking nearly 2000 wickets at a rate of 5 per match. As deadly as Underwood on a wet wicket, twice took ten wickets in an innings cheaply. He played 40 times for England, capturing 144 Test wickets. In Second World War was Captain in the Green Howards, sustained wounds in battle at Catania, Sicily. Died in a prisoner-of-war hospital camp at Caserta, Italy, on 31 July 1943, and buried in Caserta Town Cemetery, which is 16 miles from Naples. Grave was traced by Yorkshire cricketer Frank Smailes, who asked a local mason to provide a headstone. Later moved to Plot 6, Row E, Grave 15 of Commonwealth War Graves section. M.C.C. holds Verity's Test cap in its collection at Lord's. Yorkshire-Lancashire match at Bradford in August 1945 was set aside as memorial game to Verity. Plaque unveiled by his son at birthplace, 4 Welton Grove, Headingley, on 19 August 2009. The Hedley Verity pub is at 43 Woodhouse Lane, Leeds, Yorkshire

4 Welton Grove, Headingley   *Sat Nav*   LS6 1ES   Hedley Verity pub   *Sat Nav*   LS2 8JT

Biographies : *"Bowling 'em Out"* autobiography (1936); *"Hedley Verity 1930-39"* by E L Roberts (Birmingham, 1945); *"Hedley Verity: Prince with a Piece of Leather"* by Sam Davis (Epworth Press, 1952); *"Hedley Verity"* by B Rickson (ACS, 1998); *"Hedley Verity: Portrait of a Cricketer"* by Alan Hill (Kingswood Press, 1986, and Mainstream Publishing, 2000); *"10 for 10"* by Chris Waters (Wisden, 2014)

☐ *Joe VINE*

An attacking batsman and fastish leg-break bowler with Sussex from 1896. Toured Australia in 1911-12 and played in two Tests but did not get a bowl. Left Sussex after a record sequence of 421 county appearances, to become coach at Brighton College. Died at home in Titian Road, Hove, after a long illness, on 25 April 1946. His funeral was at the Downs Crematorium. A wall tablet in Roman stone, bearing an inscription, was placed on Panel One of the crematorium. His ashes were scattered in the Gardens of Remembrance.

Downs Crematorium   *Sat Nav*   BN2 3PL

☐ *Bill VOCE*

Former miner who became left-arm fast bowler. M.C.C. took him to West Indies as a 20 year-old, and he captured 7-70 in Port of Spain Test. One of four fast bowlers on the 'bodyline' tour, chosen for his accuracy; not, however, selected again for England until making his peace with M.C.C in 1936. Retired 1947 owing to problems with knee, then county coach until 1952.

Died on 6 June 1984 at the Queens Medical Centre, Nottingham, and after cremation his ashes were strewn in the Gardens of Remembrance at Mansfield Crematorium. The Larwood and Voce Stand at Trent Bridge Ground, seating 1000, was officially opened by Reg Simpson in July 1985.

Trent Bridge Ground, West Bridgford *Sat Nav* NG2 6AG

□ Abram 'Abe' WADDINGTON

Tall, left-handed fast bowler came from league cricket to take more than 800 wickets in Yorkshire's championship run of 1920s. Won two England caps in Australia 1920-21. Returned to league cricket in Birmingham League 1927-35, when took over family business in Bradford. Died at retirement home in Scarborough on 28 October 1959. Cremated at Scholemoor Crematorium, Bradford. Ashes placed in niche number 1759 of Gardens of Rest: small, foot-square chamber with stone tablet.

Scholemoor Crematorium *Sat Nav* BD7 2PS

□ Ted WAINWRIGHT

Sheffield bowler who won a regular first-team place with Yorkshire, and became principal all-rounder in Lord Hawke's county team. Following 'double' in 1897, toured Australia with Stoddart and played four Tests. Retired 1902. Died on 28 October 1919 at home in Sycamore Street, Sheffield. Buried in City Road Cemetery. Grave no. 6573 in section D, in front row behind vaults, five from the far side.

City Road Cemetery, Sheffield *Sat Nav* S2 1GD

□ V.E. [Vyell Edward] WALKER

Born at Southgate, Middlesex, one of seven brothers who helped found the Middlesex club. Correct, orthodox batsman, powerful in front of wicket, and, as a bowler, second only to William Clarke with lobs. In 1859 scored 20* and 108, and took 4-17 and 10-74 for England XI v Surrey: possibly the best all-round performance ever, considering time it was done. Died on 3 January 1906 at home, Arnos Grove, and buried in Christ Church, Southgate. Left a huge estate of £1,583,000 from brewing and timber business. Family vault lies in churchyard between site of the east end of former Weld Chapel and present Christ Church, opposite cricket ground.

Christ Church, Southgate *Sat Nav* N14 7EG   Arnos Grove (now Southgate Beaumont Care Community) *Sat Nav* N14 7DJ

Biography : *"The Walkers of Southgate: A Famous Brotherhood of Cricketers"* by W.A. Bettesworth (Methuen & Co, first edition, 1900)

□ Albert WARD

Batsman played for Lancashire from 1889 until 1903, gained success notably on Stoddart's 1894-95 Australian tour. Died at Bolton, Lancashire, on 6 January 1939. Brief service at Ward home followed by burial at Heaton Cemetery. Grave number IB:U:21 in non-consecrated section. Follow path past cenotaph to next broad path on right. Then 2nd path on right, and grave is on left-hand side.

Heaton Cemetery *Sat Nav* BL1 4LH

□ William WARD

Batted for England XI in days of underarm bowling. In 1820 scored first double-century recorded, 278 at Lord's v Norfolk, record unsurpassed until Grace's 344 fifty-six years later. In 1825 purchased lease of Lord's Ground to save it from Thomas Lord selling to building developers. Died at Westminster on 30 June 1849, and buried at St Paul's, Hammersmith, but churchyard has long since been dug up.

□ Johnny WARDLE

Slow left-arm bowler for Yorkshire and England. Took over 1800 f-c wickets in orthodox and unorthodox styles. Dismissed from county club 1958 after writing series of newspaper columns criticising team members and committee. M.C.C. then withdrew place on Australian tour: "..[he] had the misfortune to be a maverick in less tolerant times, when conformity was all…" [Rob Steen]. Proprietor of Ponderosa Country Club in Hatfield. Shortly after appointment as a bowling coach for Yorkshire, underwent operation for brain tumour in April and died at home in Hatfield, nr Doncaster on 23 July 1985, aged only 62. Buried in his wife's family grave in Hatfield Woodhouse cemetery: plot FFF16 in cremation plots next to path, near front wall of cemetery.

Hatfield Woodhouse Cemetery   *Sat Nav*   DN7 6LX

Biography : *"Happy-Go-Johnny"* autobiography (Robert Hale, 1957) ; *"Johnny Wardle, Cricket Conjuror"* by Alan Hill (David & Charles, 1988)

□ [Sir Pelham] 'Plum' WARNER

Born in Port-of-Spain, Trinidad, in 1873. Skilful and determined opening batsman, appointed skipper on first tours M.C.C. made to Australia and South Africa. Appeared in 15 Tests. Last season 1920 when led Middlesex to remarkable championship. Was then founder of *The Cricketer* magazine,

correspondent on the *Morning Post*, long-serving Test selector, M.C.C. committeeman, tour manager in Australia, writer of cricket history and ever-present influence at Lord's. Knighted in 1937 for services to cricket. M.C.C. made him president in 1950-51 and its first life vice-president. Died at home in West Lavington, Sussex, on 30 January 1963 and ashes were scattered at point on Lord's Cricket Ground where, as a Rugby schoolboy, struck his first boundary. In April 1946, in recognition of Warner's service to club and cricket generally, M.C.C. arranged for portrait to be painted and hung in pavilion. Warner Stand at Lord's opened in 1958.

Lord's Cricket Ground   *Sat Nav*   NW8 8QN

Biographies : *"Cricket in Many Climes"* autobiography (Heinemann, 1900); *"Cricket Reminiscences"* autobiography (Grant Richards, 1920); *"My Cricketing Life"* autobiography (Hodder & Stoughton, 1921); *"Long Innings"* autobiography (Harrap, 1951); *"Plum Warner"* by Laurence Meynell (Phoenix House, 1951); *"Plum Warner's Last Season (1920)"* by Ronald Mason (Epworth Press, 1970); *"Plum Warner"* by Gerald Howat (Unwin Hyman, 1987)

□ Cyril WASHBROOK

Assertive opening batsman for Lancashire and England, scorer of six Test centuries. Added 359 in record opening stand with Hutton at Johannesburg in 1948-49. Regarded as best cover fieldsman in the country. England selector 1956: recalled, aged 41, to play against Australia at Headingley and scored 98. Lancashire's first professional captain 1954-59, a stickler for discipline and propriety. Awarded a second benefit in 1959; his first in 1948 had raised a record £14,000. His home was 31 Briony Avenue, Altrincham. CBE awarded 1991. He was commemorated at Old Trafford ground in the Washbrook-Statham Stand. Built in 1993, it was demolished in 2011 and replaced by a new 'players and media centre'. Died in Sale, Cheshire (Greater Manchester), on 27 April 1999. Funeral

Johnny Wardle's grave at Hatfield Woodhouse cemetery

(Below) Memorial to V.E.Walker at Southgate; and to 'Topsy' Wass, at Sutton-in-Ashfield

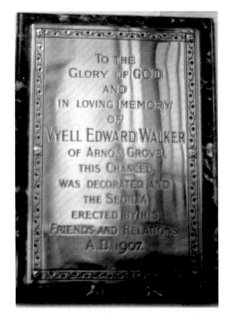

took place two days later at Altrincham Crematorium but no memorial there.

Biography: *"Cricket: The Silver Lining"* autobiography (Sportsguide, 1950); *"Hutton & Washbrook"* by AA Thomson (Epworth, 1963); *"Cyril Washbrook: his record innings-by-innings"* by Malcolm Lorimer and Roy Cavanagh (ACS, 1999)

With the demolition of the Statham-Washbrook Stand went the sole memorial to Cyril Washbrook. It is rather sad. He has no known grave as the ashes were removed by the family after his cremation and what happened to them is unknown. When son Roger died in 2006 and was buried at Bridgnorth Cemetery – in the town where Cyril went to school – there is no indication in the records that Cyril's ashes were put in the same grave.

☐ Tom WASS

'Topsy' was another cricketer of the first rank to be born in Sutton-in-Ashfield, Notts. Fast bowler for Nottinghamshire who was chosen for trial matches but never made the England Test team. Died at his birthplace on 27 October 1953 and buried in grave 7404 in Sutton-in-Ashfield Cemetery.

Sutton-in-Ashfield Cemetery   *Sat Nav*   NG17 2EB

☐ Roy WEBBER

Trained accountant, who made a career as a cricket statistician. Wrote newspaper and magazine articles, BBC TV scorer, secretary of Cricket Book Society. Collapsed in London's Upper Thames Street on 14 November 1962 with a heart attack and dead on arrival at St Bartholomew's Hospital. Cremated at Golders Green Crematorium. Ashes buried in eastern boundary rosebeds but the name plaque, as is customary, was removed after ten years.

☐ 'Ned' [Edward] WENMAN

Best wicket-keeper of his time after Tom Box, he stood up to Alfred Mynn without pads. Also, fine batsman. Manager and captain of Kent. Benefit 1844, but reappeared occasionally for ten more years. Carpenter and wheelwright until his death on 28 December 1879. Was buried in village of his birth in St George's parish churchyard. See also in this graveyard memorial to Richard Mills, which portrays a small bat and ball. On village green a new Benenden village sign (2009) commemorates Wenman and Mills, who also played for Kent.

St George's church, Benenden   *Sat Nav*   TN17 4DL

☐ Jack WHITE

A farmer by occupation and by nickname. Joined Somerset as slow left-arm spin bowler. Career flourished after he took 16 wickets in one day in 1919 v Worcester and then, in 1921, ten in innings for 76. His 15 Test matches, (including five very successfully on 1928-29 Australian tour) were before Verity came on scene. Somerset skipper in 1927-31, led England, too, on four occasions. Test selector. Lost sight of one eye in shooting accident. Died at Yarde Farm, Combe Florey, Somerset, on 2 May 1961 and funeral three days later in parish church followed by cremation at Canford in Bristol and the ashes returned to his family. At Taunton County Ground his memorial was the JCW Gates in St James Road, officially opened by his widow. Gates removed after being struck by a vehicle during ground redevelopment in 2014.

Taunton County Ground   *Sat Nav*   TA1 1XX

Biography: *"A Somerset Hero Who Beat the Aussies"* by Basil Tinkler (Parrs Wood Press, 2000)

[William] 'Dodge' WHYSALL

Opening batsman for Notts between 1910-30. Toured Australia 1924-25 and made 4 Test appearances. Died in Nottingham General Hospital on 11 November 1930. Cause of death was blood poisoning. The week before was dancing The Paul Jones, when music suddenly stopped, he slipped and fell on elbow. Large funeral: buried in Nottingham Road Cemetery, Mansfield, in grave number 1260. Headstone, unveiled by Notts skipper Arthur Carr, is surmounted by Celtic cross in Cornish granite. Records his cricket career and a shield design has bat and wicket on it, with off stump awry.

Nottingham Road Cemetery, Mansfield, *Sat Nav* NG18 5BJ

Rev A.P [Archie] WICKHAM

After being in Marlborough XI and gaining Oxford blue, represented Norfolk while curate in Norwich. Joined Somerset at age of 36 and played 1891-1907 while Vicar of Martock, near Taunton. Once record-holder for no byes in innings - 672 by Hampshire 1899. Somerset president in 1924. While Vicar of East Brent (1911-35) made butterflies and moths collection, given to British Museum. Died at East Brent, Somerset, 13 October 1935. Commemorative stained-glass window inside St Mary's parish church. Buried beneath south wall of St Mary's church, beside the path. In 2005 new gates to church dedicated to him. Nearby road named Wickham Way.

St Mary's church, East Brent *Sat Nav* TA9 4HZ

John WILLES

His memorial stone in parish churchyard of Sutton Valence, near Maidstone, Kent, where he owned land, is worded: "To the memory of John Willes, Esq, of Bellringham in this parish. Born 1777, died 5 August 1852 at Staunton near Gloucester. A patron of all manly sports, and the first to introduce round-arm bowling in cricket." He first applied his method in Gentlemen v Players in 1806 and, in spite of protests, persisted with new bowling style until 1822 when prevented from doing so while playing for Kent v M.C.C. at Lord's.

St Mary's church, Sutton Valence *Sat Nav* ME17 3AW

Edgar WILLSHER

Left-handed bowler for Kent 1850-75. Forced the issue of introducing over-arm bowling by taking his side off the field when no-balled, and next season 1864 it was legalised. Died at his home 18 Lethbridge Road, Lewisham, on 7 October 1885. Cause: liver cancer. A memorial stone funded by subscriptions from many cricketers of the time, over his grave in Ladywell Cemetery, Lewisham, but has now lost its cross.

Ladywell Cemetery *Sat Nav* SE13 7HY

Biography : *"Edgar Willsher: The Lion of Kent"* by Giles Phillips (ACS Lives in Cricket publications, no 24, 2012)

Rockley WILSON

Spin bowling all-rounder, made a century on first-class debut at Cambridge in 1899. In 1903 joined staff of Winchester College to teach French and coach cricket. Plaque placed on pavilion. Unable to devote time to playing for Yorkshire, yet picked to make Australian tour as vice-captain in 1920-21, playing in one Test. Died at home in Winchester on 21 July 1957. Funeral service in College Chapel followed by interment in Magdalen Hill Cemetery, Winchester.

Grave, number P2/35, has a headstone.

Magdalen Hill Cemetery   *Sat Nav* SO21 1HE

Biography : *"Remarkable Cricketer, Singular Man"* by Martin Howe (ACS Lives in Cricket publications, 2008)

•Martin Howe's book provided further information about a plaque in E.R.Wilson's memory on the Winchester College pavilion (strangely known as a 'tent'). It was unveiled by Sir Hubert Ashton in 1966 when the pavilion formally opened.

☐ *John WISDEN*

Despite his size (5' 4"), was successful as fast round-arm bowler with Sussex from 1848 to 1863. 'The Little Wonder' became best since decline of William Lillywhite. Lived in Leamington Spa and, with George Parr, developed cricket ground (now mainly housing), commemorated by plaque on *The Cricketers* public house in Archery Road. In 1850 took ten wickets, all bowled, for North v South. Gave up game when badly injured at racquets, became professional at Harrow School. In 1864 published his first *'Cricketers' Almanack'*, 100 pages long. For 50th edition, Wisden published special portrait of him. The Wisden Trophy for England-West Indies Test series, first presented in 1963, marked 100th edition. He died of cancer on 5 April 1884, collapsing in offices of sports equipment business at Cranbourn Street, London. Buried in West Brompton Cemetery. On hundredth anniversary of death, 5 April 1984, new headstone was unveiled on site of tomb. Archdeacon of Middlesex and Mr Bill Gray, manager of company originating from Wisden's sports shop, performed ceremony watched by David Frith, then editor of *Wisden's Cricket Monthly*, who arranged memorial.

Brompton Cemetery, London *Sat Nav* SW5 9JE   The Cricketers, Leamington   *Sat Nav*   CV31 3PT 21 Cranbourn Street, London *Sat Nav* WC2H 7AB

Biography : *"The Little Wonder - the Remarkable History of Wisden"* by Robert Winder (Bloomsbury, 2013)

• In 1872 Wisden started selling cricket equipment from the shop in Cranbourn Street off Charing Cross Road in London. "Sharp-eyed tourists coming out of Leicester Square station can still see on the rust-coloured antique tile facia in bas-relief... a pair of cricket bats leaning against a set of stumps with the words *J Wisden & Compy* neatly carved around a cricket ball in the centre" (Winder)

☐ *Sammy WOODS*

Born in Australia, 1867. At school fine bowler and batsman, came to Brighton College to complete education, called up by injury-depleted 1888 Australians for Test match. Double blue at Cambridge and England rugby team. First county match with Somerset took 12 wickets for 57. F-c career lasted until 1910, succeeded Hewett as skipper, but naive leader and over-optimistic judge of game. Retired to Bridgwater. Died 30 April 1931 at Melville House nursing home, Taunton, and buried in St Mary's Cemetery, Taunton, in Wellington Road, close to county ground. Grave is number 4131, situated just inside cemetery gates.

St Mary's Cemetery   *Sat Nav* TA1 5AS

Biographies : *"My Reminiscences"* autobiography (Chapman & Hall, 1925); *"Sammy: The Sporting Life of S M J Woods"* by Clifford Jiggens (Sansom & Co, 1997)

☐ *Wilf WOOLLER*

Born Rhos-on-Sea 1912: a QR barcode that can be optically read on mobile phones to provide information is on gate at birthplace. Fast-medium bowler and attacking batsman, achieved 'double' in 1955. Pre-War played rugby for Wales. Posted to Far East in WW2, captured and jailed at Changi under Japanese. Succeeded John Clay as Glamorgan captain and led side to first championship in 1948. Last f-c match 1962, aged 50. Served as county secretary for thirty years and club president for nine. Test

JOHN WISDEN (1826-1884)
Cricketer and Almanack Publisher

A cricket ground was created near this spot in 1849 by John Wisden and his friend and fellow player, George Parr. Many important matches were played here to large crowds. Wisden lived in the town from 1848 to 1852. In 1850 he founded John Wisden & Co. probably selling sporting equipment. They gave up the lease of the ground in 1863. His obituary in his Almanack in the 1885 edition reads:

"...A quiet, unassuming and thoroughly upright man. A fast friend and generous employer. Beloved by his intimates and employees and respected by all in whom he came in contact."

(above) Plaque to John Wisden in Leamington (image © Robin Stott 2013)

(Below) Wilfred Wooller's grave, Cardiff (image © mynwent - both images licensed for re-use under Creative Commons License)

selector 1955-61. His home was in Cyncoed. Died at Llandough Hospital on 10 March 1997. Buried at Thornhill Cemetery, Cardiff, in plot R152. His grey gravestone portrays a Glamorgan daffodil and Prince of Wales feathers. The Wilf Wooller memorial gates officially opened by his widow Enid on 29 June 2001 as part of redevelopment of Sophia Gardens (now SWALEC stadium). New road named Heol Wilf Wooller, in Pontcanna, Cardiff.

Church Road, Rhos-on-Sea (birthplace) *Sat Nav* LL28 4DJ SWALEC stadium, Cardiff *Sat Nav* CF11 9XR Heol Wilf Wooller *Sat Nav* CF11 9JL Thornhill Cemetery *Sat Nav* CF14 9UA

Biography : *"The Skipper : A Biography of Wilfred Wooller"* by Andrew Hignell (Limlow Books, 1995)

☐ *Frank WOOLLEY*

Born 1887. Wall plaque in Tonbridge High Street on birthplace above father's bicycle shop (now a Starbucks) unveiled by his daughter on 25 May 1986. One of greatest English cricketers in history of game. Tall, stylish, commanding left-handed batsman from 1906 (when, despite runs he scored and wickets taken, unable to win regular place in Kent team). Eventual scorer of 58,959 runs, second only to Jack Hobbs. Thousand runs in 28 seasons, equalled only by Grace. 145 hundreds, highest 305* v Tasmania 1911-12, a record for a tourist in Australia for 50 years. Hardly less impressive as left-arm slow bowler, with spin and bounce, took 2,066 wickets, or as fielder in slips where caught most of his record 1018 catches. 64 Test matches for England between 1909 and 1934. Only player to appear in all 5 of 1921 Test series, his two 90s at Lord's being perhaps greatest innings. Retired 1938. Coach at King's School, Canterbury. At age of 84 remarried in Canada. Died Halifax, Nova Scotia, 18 October 1978. Service of Thanksgiving held at Canterbury Cathedral in November. His ashes returned to England and scattered on pitch at St Lawrence Ground, Canterbury, Kent. Commemorative plaque had been placed there 1963 and Frank Woolley Stand opened in 1973. Plaque also inside St Peter & St Paul's church, Tonbridge, above that of Blythe. Another plaque, commemorating Frank Woolley's work as coach, was fixed to Kings School pavilion at Birleys, Canterbury, and another at his former home at 38 Yew Tree Road, Southborough. A road in Tonbridge also named after him.

Church of St Peter & St Paul, Tonbridge *Sat Nav* TN9 1HD Frank Woolley Road, Tonbridge *Sat Nav* TN10 4LE The Spitfire Ground, St Lawrence, Canterbury *Sat Nav* CT1 3NZ

Biographies : *"The King of Games"* autobiography (Stanley Paul, 1936); *"The Cricketing Career of Frank Woolley"* by F H Haigh (Jennings, 1928); *"Frank Woolley"* by Oliver Warner (Phoenix House, 1952); *"Woolley: The Pride of Kent"* by Ian Peebles (Hutchinson, 1969); *"Early Memoirs of Frank Woolley"* as told to Martha Wilson Woolley (The Cricketer, 1976).

☐ *[Sir] Frank WORRELL*

Born on Barbados 1924. Made his name in Caribbean in 1940s before overseas tours and league cricket in England in 1950s established his importance to West Indies as batsman (3860 Test runs and 9 centuries), versatile left-arm bowler and first black man to captain for a Test series. Unifying influence moderated inter-island rivalry and instilled composure and professional approach by West Indian teams. On retirement knighted by Queen (1964). Made West Indies' team manager. Consultant on community development and Warden of university students' hall in Mona (Jamaica). Was appointed to the Jamaican senate. Early in 1967 fell ill with virus of blood, and died of leukemia in University Hospital at Mona on 13 March. State funeral in Barbados with service at St Michael's Cathedral. Body buried on university campus at Cave Hill, Bridgetown. Blue plaque in England at

commemorates

SIR FRANK WORRELL
1924-1967

International Cricketer
Graduate
BA Admin 1959

University of Manchester where studied economics and administration 1957-59.

Plaque: Dover Street Building, Manchester University *Sat Nav* M13 9GB

Biographies: *"Cricket Punch"* autobiography (Stanley Paul, 1959); *"Frank Worrell: The Career of a Great Cricketer"* by Ernest Eytle (Hodder & Stoughton, 1963), *"Sir Frank Worrell"* (Men of Greatness series)" by Undine Giuseppi (Nelson, 1969), *"Frank Worrell: A Biography"* by Ivo Tennant (Lutterworth Press, 1987)

☐ *Stan WORTHINGTON*

Dashing right-hand batsman and fast-medium bowler. Twice chosen for M.C.C. tours and played in 9 Tests. Left Derbyshire 1947 to play minor counties cricket with Northumberland, then Lancashire coach. Electrician at colliery. Died in St James's Hospital, Kings Lynn, while on holiday in Norfolk, 31 August 1973. Funeral service at St Peter's church, Littleover, followed by Markeaton Crematorium. Ashes collected by family.

☐ *Doug WRIGHT*

Fastish leg-spin and googly bowler for Kent (1932-57). Only England leg-spinner

to capture 100 Test wickets. Unplayable on his day, he took a record seven hat-tricks in first-class matches. Retired in mid-season 1957 and in 1959 succeeded Geary as coach at Charterhouse School until 1971. Died in Canterbury on 13 November 1998. Buried in plot XL, grave 119, of Canterbury Cemetery, Westgate Court Avenue. Chosen as one of 12 for Kent's 'Legends Walkway' at Spitfire Ground.

Canterbury Cemetery *Sat Nav* CT2 8JL

Biography: *"Doug Wright: His Record Innings by Innings"* by Ian Phipps (ACS Famous Cricketers Series, 1998)

☐ *[R.E.S.] Bob WYATT*

Born in Surrey but schooldays in Coventry. Resolute and courageous batsman for Warwickshire, scoring 22,000 runs before WW2 when joined Worcestershire. Their most successful skipper until Kenyon. Played for England forty times, 16 as captain. Last man to lead England to win over Australia at Lord's (in 1934) until 75 years later in 2009; and last to beat West Indies at Bridgetown (in 1935) until 59 years later. Made tours with M.C.C. sides throughout the 'thirties. Test selector 1949-53 and chair in 1950. Lived on the southern Cornish coast at Helford. Aged 93, was oldest England player at time of his death in Royal Cornwall Hospital at Truro on 20 April 1995. Funeral at Manaccan parish church on 28 April (Insole, Clark and Stephenson from Lord's, Chris Old who lived at Falmouth, Paul Getty and Tim Rice all attended); then at Penmount Crematorium. The R.E.S.Wyatt Stand at northern (city) end of Edgbaston Cricket Ground opened shortly after his death: a tier of seating beneath two rows of executive boxes, and two restaurants with pitch-view for members.

Birthplace - Milford Heath House (private residence) *Sat Nav* GU8 5BW   Edgbaston Cricket Ground *Sat Nav* B5 7QU   Manaccan parish church *Sat Nav* TR12 6 HN

Biography *"Three Straight Sticks"* autobiography (Stanley Paul, 1951); *"R.E.S. Wyatt: Fighting Cricketer"* by Gerald Pawle (George Allen & Unwin, 1985)

• His ashes were collected by the funeral director who has long since ceased trading, so it is not known where they ended up. As an irregular but frequent pick for Test sides and an England captain and chair of selectors, too, it was essential to include R.E.S. 'Bob' Wyatt in any collection of significant cricket personalities. While, unfortunately, none of my queries led to finding a personal memorial other than the stand at Edgbaston, I am grateful to a number of local people who helped me establish this.

☐ *Edward WYNYARD*

Born Bengal, India, 1861. A career soldier who played much cricket in India. Batsman regarded as good enough to play for Hampshire whenever available 1878 to 1908, and captain for 4 seasons. Toured South Africa twice but also turned down Australian tours. Played in 3 Test matches. All-round sportsman, won FA Cup Medal with Old Carthusians. Briefly on administrative staff at Lord's. Died at home, The Red House, Knotty Green, in Beaconsfield, 30 October 1936, and buried at Penn churchyard, Buckinghamshire.

Holy Trinity church, Penn   *Sat Nav*   HP10 8NY

☐ *Norman YARDLEY*

All-rounder, played for Cambridge University and Yorkshire (1936-55). England captain in 14 Tests. In 2007 his four children attended unveiling of a blue plaque on western wall of his birthplace and former home, The Grove, at Royston, where North Barnsley Partnership, an EU-funded regeneration project, now based. Chairman of Test selectors 1951-52. Worked in wine and spirits trade. Expert summariser on BBC radio's *Test Match Special*. Member of Yorkshire C.C.C. committee and president

in 1984. Then lived in Broomhall Road, Sheffield. Died after a stroke at Lodge Moor Hospital, Sheffield, on 3 October 1989. Funeral at Hutcliffe Wood Crematorium and ashes scattered there with no memorial.

The Grove, Station Rd, Royston   *Sat Nav*   S71 4EU

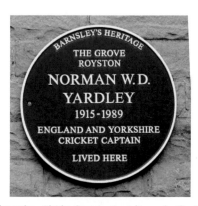

Biography : *"Cricket Campaigns"* autobiography (Stanley Paul, 1950) ; *"Norman Yardley, Yorkshire's Gentleman Player"* by Martin Howe (ACS Lives in Cricket, 2015)

☐ *William YARDLEY*

All-round sports player, batsman at Rugby School and Trinity College. In 1870 scorer of the first hundred in a Varsity match. For Kent 1868-1877, sometimes said to be second-best batsman in country (after Grace). Drifted away from cricket as interest grew in acting and writing for the stage. Died of heart attack at the Sun Hotel, Kingston-on-Thames, on 28 October 1900. Cremated at Brookwood Necropolis on 31 October and subsequently interred there: "buried under a simple marble cross in Actors' Acre, plot 118" [from 'Necropolis News Cricket Special']

Brookwood Cemetery   *Sat Nav* GU24 0BL

Biography : *"William Yardley : "Master of Bat and Burlesque"* by Grenville Simons (Wisteria Books, 1997)

☐ *Dick YOUNG*

Played as amateur with Sussex from 1905 to 1925. As batsman and reserve wicket-keeper on Australian tour of 1907-08, played two Tests. Though wore spectacles, was also talented amateur footballer. Maths master and cricket coach at Eton College for thirty years. Retired 1951. Died in Hastings on 1 July 1968. Funeral at Langney Crematorium, Eastbourne. Cremated remains strewn in Area AR/3 in Gardens of Remembrance: no form of memorial to him there.

Main Sources /Acknowledgements

1   Own research including death notices from newspapers, mainly *The Times* (London); site visits, newspaper reports viewed at local libraries or at the British Newspaper Library, Colindale, London (now closed) and the British Library (St Pancras); county heritage centres of Devon, Somerset, Surrey.

2   Enquiries made to individuals including Chris Airey, Andrea Andrews, Dariel Baldock, John Brady, Robert Brooke, Brian Buss, Stephen Chalke, Ron Challinor, David Eardley, Su Foster, David Frith, Frances Greaney, Guy Curry, Andrew Hignell, Ursula Howard, Martin Howe, Julia Hudson, Tim Jones, Olwyn Kinghorn, John Lacey, William Metcalfe, Patrick Neal, David Orme, Philip Paine, Mick Pope, Rev Mark Roberts, Joan Robinson, Richard Sanderson, Brian Scorer, Mike Small, John Sharp, Nicholas Sharp, Cindy Shaw, Richenda Walford, Rev Lesley Walker, Julia Westgate, the late EW Swanton, late Gubby Allen; funeral directors including Arthur Gresty, G M Luff & partners, H C Patrick, Pendle's (Helston), T H Sanders, E White & Son, and others; schools including Felsted, Barnard Castle, Clifton, Highgate, Marlborough, Malvern, Reading, St Peter's York, Winchester; TTS Rail; Stanmore Tourist Board; Storrington Museum.

3   Cemetery staff, local council bereavement services, Dignity and other companies responsible for the cemeteries and crematoria, who provided most of the guidance about locations; and church offices including Holy Trinity (Minchinhampton), St Mary's (Lutterworth), All Saints (Jo Asplin, Wokingham), St Andrew & Mary's (Fletching), Methodist church (Audley), Claines church, St Michael's (Urchfont), St Leonard's (Aldrington, Hove) and others.

4   First made aware of location of some memorials in *"Innings Complete"* by Philip Paine (Mischief Maker, 2000 onwards), including Cowdrey, Fender, Fielder, Greenwood, Lyttelton, McMaster, Marriott, Penn, Place, Rawlin, Sandham, Wright; also aware through findagrave (Alston, Armitage, Peebles, Wardle, Wooller); some confirmed through ancestry.co.uk findmypast.co.uk, or deceased online.com

5   "Necropolis News: Cricket Special" by Brookwood Cemetery Society (2003); "The Cricket Statistician" (the ACS journal); history.trentbridge.co.uk; amounderness.co.uk website; newsletters of Friends of West Norwood Cemetery, Friends of Nunhead Cemetery, Friends of Kensal Green Cemetery, Friends of Wombwell Cemetery; Gidea Park & Romford Cricket Club (Farnes); Charlie Connolly (Gover); Mike Farley www.goodkinghal. blogspot (Jessop); Southborough Society; Elgin Museum; Somerset and Sussex Cricket Museums; "Walter Robins" by Brian Rendell (ACS); www.gravestone photos.com (Charles Sale); statistics from www.cricinfo, www.cricketarchive, and contemporary newspaper obituaries.

6   Special thanks to Marion Catlin and Chris Overson

In the text biographies are listed after each cricket person's entry as a source of further reading. These were not my original source of information on memorials but have sometimes been useful to confirm it.

Photographic acknowledgements

Several images in the text and front cover from the internet, licensed for reuse under Creative Commons Licence at http://creativecommons.org/licenses with copyright acknowledged to :

Dave Dunford (Bagshaw), Mike Harris (Duckworth), Martin Kirk (Larwood), Roger Pagram (Slindon), Robin Stott (Wisden), John Sutton (Dixon Gates); 'Rich Tea' (Hutton), David Ward (Fartown) - all from www.geograph. org.uk; Brian Cooper (Worrell) from www.flickr.com; londonremembers.com (Grace); craigallan.za (Lohmann); Julia Keld (Hobbs grave) from findagrave.

Thanks also to Gina White (Wooller); Graham Hill (Royle); Ken Goldfinch (King Cole); Frances Greaney (Dollery); Ian Kingholm (Fagg); Judy Middleton (Hobbs plaque), Alex Picker (Clarke), Philip Paine (McDonald, Summers), Somerset Cricket Museum (Ponsonby-Fane), Anthony Eden (Leyland Gates).

The use of these photographs is believed to be free from restrictions and in the public domain. Any incorrect acknowledgement will be put right in a future edition.

England Test cricketers
and, in italics, other cricket people included in the guide, listed by date of death

Charles Lennox	1750	A Shrewsbury	1903	IFW Bligh	1927	FW Tate	1943
R Newland	*1791*	*A Haygarth*	*1903*	*D Hunter*	*1927*	GJ Thompson	1943
Dick Nyren	*1797*	T Emmett	1904	W Attewell	1927	CH Parkin	1943
Lumpy Stevens	*1819*	*Frederick Gale*	*1904*	H Bagshaw	1927	RK Tyldesley	1943
John Small	1826	J T Brown	1904	HR Butt	1928	H Verity	1943
Thomas Lord	*1832*	*R A H Mitchell*	*1905*	R Kilner	1928	W Newham	1944
John Nyren	*1837*	*V E Walker*	*1906*	J Lillywhite jnr	1929	JT Hearne	1944
J Cobbett	*1842*	A Shaw	1907	VPFA Royle	1929	*Sir Julien Cahn*	*1944*
J Broadbridge	*1843*	*Francis Thompson*	*1907*	JM Read	1929	AC MacLaren	1944
William Ward	*1849*	*C W Alcock*	*1907*	JEP McMaster	1929	WM Bradley	1944
F Beauclerk	*1850*	WW Read	1907	*IC I Thornton*	*1929*	MJL Turnbull	1944
John Willes	*1852*	*Albert Craig*	*1909*	AFA Lilley	1929	*P A Perrin*	*1945*
W Lillywhite	*1854*	*Earl of Sheffield*	*1909*	JT Tyldesley	1930	AE Knight	1946
Wm Clarke	*1856*	*A Hill*	*1910*	JWHT Douglas	1930	J Humphries	1946
A Mynn	*1861*	M Sherwin	1910	WW Whysall	1930	J H King	1946
Wm Beldham	*1862*	EM Grace	1911	*G A Faulkner*	*1930*	*F E Lacey*	*1946*
King Cole	*1868*	WL Murdoch	1911	*Frederick Toone*	*1930*	J Vine	1946
G Summers	*1870*	T Richardson	1912	*James Seymour*	*1930*	J Iddon	1946
Fuller Pilch	*1870*	A Lyttelton	1913	CT Studd	1931	FA Mackinnon	1947
Thomas Box	*1876*	W Chatterton	1913	SMJ Woods	1931	FS Jackson	1947
N Felix	*1876*	*A E J Collins*	*1914*	*J A Dixon*	*1931*	J Hardstaff sr	1947
J Caesar	*1878*	AG Steel	1914	Lord Harris	1932	CA Smith	1948
E G Wenman	*1879*	AE Trott	1914	AJ Fothergill	1932	WE Astill	1948
GF Grace	1880	AO Jones	1914	WH Lockwood	1932	S Christopherson	1949
Jemmy Dean	*1881*	RE Foster	1914	*FS Ashley Cooper*	*1932*	*C A Ollivierre*	*1949*
C Pond	*1881*	WG Grace	1915	H Howell	1932	*G Cox sr*	*1949*
R A Fitzgerald	*1881*	*S Ponsonby-Fane*	*1915*	FH Sugg	1933	A Fielder	1949
J Lillywhite sr	*1882*	AE Stoddart	1915	KS Ranjitsinhji	1933	D Denton	1950
F Morley	1884	F Penn	1916	LCH Palairet	1933	SJ Staples	1950
W Mortlock	*1884*	KL Hutchings	1916	MC Bird	1933	*A J Holmes*	*1950*
J Wisden	*1884*	*C E Green*	*1916*	*A W Pullin*	*1934*	WG Quaife	1951
E Willsher	1885	MW Booth	1916	H Philipson	1935	*Hugh de Selincourt*	*1951*
Jack Juniper	*1885*	EJ Tyler	1917	W Brockwell	1935	LH Tennyson	1951
G Bennett	*1886*	C Blythe	1917	F Mitchell	1935	JWH Makepeace	1952
F M Lucas	*1887*	*R Percival*	*1918*	*A P Wickham*	*1935*	*C Kortright*	*1952*
HRJ Charlwood	1888	RG Barlow	1919	CP McGahey	1935	EG Hayes	1953
A Greenwood	1889	G Magregor	1919	NA Knox	1935	*T G Wass*	*1953*
H Jupp	1889	*William Ansell*	*1919*	FSG Calthorpe	1935	*W Findlay*	*1953*
CA Absolom	1889	*W Caffyn*	*1919*	R Abel	1936	GH Hirst	1954
WE Midwinter	1890	E Wainwright	1919	J W Sharpe	1936	H Leveson-Gower	1954
R Pilling	1891	J Shuter	1920	EG Wynyard	1936	CF Root	1954
Geo Parr	*1891*	W Gunn	1921	BJT Bosanquet	1936	GL Jessop	1955
Ted Barratt	*1891*	F Martin	1921	GHT S-Hayward	1936	LC Braund	1955
J Hunter	1891	AW Mold	1921	W Brearley	1937	*R C N Palairet*	*1955*
WH Scotton	1893	S Haigh	1921	*E A McDonald*	*1937*	CB Fry	1956
J Selby	1894	T Armitage	1922	*E G Dennett*	*1937*	MW Tate	1956
G Freeman	*1895*	AP Lucas	1923	CP Buckenham	1937	*M Tompkin*	*1956*
H H Stephenson	*1896*	G Bean	1923	*George Beldam*	*1937*	*Sir Home Gordon*	*1956*
G Ulyett	1898	JH Board	1924	EFS Tylecote	1938	ER Wilson	1957
W Barnes	1899	WS Lees	1924	Lord Hawke	1938	*Frank Chester*	*1957*
W Bates	1900	*E J Diver*	*1924*	Albert Ward	1939	*Bill Ferguson*	*1957*
E Peate	1900	*W Humphrey*	*1924*	*R H Mallett*	*1939*	J R Mason	1958
JJ Ferris	1900	*J Rawlin*	*1924*	*Walter Lawrence*	*1939*	G Gunn	1958
R Daft	*1900*	GB Street	1924	TW Hayward	1939	FR Foster	1958
D Buchanan	*1900*	AN Hornby	1925	GG Macaulay	1940	CP Mead	1958
W Yardley	*1900*	*Sydney Pardon*	*1925*	GB Legge	1940	DR Jardine	1958
FW Milligan	1900	W Flowers	1926	R Peel	1941	A Waddington	1959
GA Lohmann	1901	*D L A Jephson*	*1926*	K Farnes	1941	CWL Parker	1959
J Jackson	*1901*	*F Spofforth*	*1926*	EG Arnold	1942	AS Kennedy	1959
J Briggs	1902	AD Pougher	1926	A Ducat	1942	*Alex Skelding*	*1960*

FL Fane	1960	RA Young	1968	*Dudley Carew*	*1981*
VWC Jupp	1960	R W V Robins	1968	G Geary	1981
RH Spooner	1961	*Denzil Batchelor*	*1969*	WE Hollies	1981
CAG Russell	1961	*J S Buller*	*1970*	KF Barrington	1981
J C White	1961	H Strudwick	1970	A Sandham	1982
APF Chapman	1961	P Holmes	1971	JCW MacBryan	1983
MS Nichols	1961	WH Copson	1971	AH Bakewell	1983
EH Hendren	1962	*L Constantine*	*1971*	W Voce	1984
Roy Webber	*1962*	C Hallows	1972	JT Ikin	1984
GE Tyldesley	1962	*Henry Grierson*	*1972*	PGH Fender	1985
Ted Alletson	*1963*	W Rhodes	1973	JH Wardle	1985
PF Warner	1963	TS Worthington	1973	WJ Edrich	1986
J N Crawford	1963	*Howard Marshall*	*1973*	JC Laker	1986
John Daniell	*1963*	JC Clay	1973	WE Bowes	1987
J B Hobbs	1963	*A Booth*	*1974*	HE Dollery	1987
AW Carr	1963	*Neville Cardus*	*1975*	GOB Allen	1989
G Brown	1964	AER Gilligan	1976	WN Slack	1989
C B Llewellyn	*1964*	*M Falcon*	*1976*	*W H R Andrews*	*1989*
FT Mann	1964	A Mitchell	1976	NWD Yardley	1989
RT Stanyforth	1964	AE Fagg	1977	*C L R James*	*1989*
JW Hearne	1965	FE Woolley	1978	LEG Ames	1990
JW Hitch	1965	H Sutcliffe	1978	J Hardstaff jr	1990
AP Freeman	1965	GAE Paine	1978	L Hutton	1990
H S Altham	*1965*	*G C Grant*	*1978*	C Milburn	1990
WR Hammond	1965	H Gimblett	1978	FR Brown	1991
R C Rob'-Glasgow	*1965*	*W H Ashdown*	*1979*	*John Arlott*	*1991*
NE Haig	1966	E J Smith	1979	*W S Surridge*	*1992*
G Duckworth	1966	E Paynter	1979	*Jim Kilburn*	*1993*
TWJ Goddard	1966	C I J Smith	1979	PBH May	1994
CS Marriott	1966	*Hubert Ashton*	*1979*	*Rex Alston*	*1994*
SF Barnes	1967	IAR Peebles	1980	*Brian Johnston*	*1994*
M Leyland	1967	WW Keeton	1980	H Larwood	1995
F M Worrell	*1967*	JH Parks	1980	RES Wyatt	1995

RO Jenkins	1995
GAR Lock	1995
TB Mitchell	1996
C Cook	1996
JDB Robertson	1996
D Kenyon	1996
D C S Compton	1997
Wilf Wooller	*1997*
Alan Gibson	*1997*
DVP Wright	1998
C Washbrook	1999
TG Evans	1999
M D Marshall	*1999*
J B Statham	2000
M C Cowdrey	2000
J M Hutchinson	*2000*
E W Swanton	2000
AR Gover	2001
FG Mann	2001
W Place	2002
Geoffrey Howard	*2002*
J P Getty	*2003*
JA Flavell	2004
W E Alley	*2004*
Geoffrey Saulez	*2004*
Rev DS Sheppard	2005
CH Palmer	2005
BW Luckhurst	2005
F S Trueman	2006
C D Ingleby-McK	*2006*
Bill Frindall	*2009*
A V Bedser	2010
B L D'Oliveira	2011

Index of locations by postcode.

	Postcode	Location
	CM21 9AH	Great St Mary ch Sawbridgeworth
CR	CR0 2UY	144 St James's Road Croydon
	CR0 5EE	St John's ch Shirley
	CR4 4LD	St Peter and St Paul ch Mitcham
CT	CT1 1QU	St Gregory's (old churchyard)
	CT1 3NZ	St Lawrence Ground Canterbury
	CT2 8JL	Canterbury Cemetery
	CT4 5BP	St Mary's ch Patrixbourne
	CT13 9EH	St Clement's ch Sandwich
CV	CV6 1QT	St Nicholas ch Radford
	CV21 3QT	Clifton Road Cemetery Rugby
	CV31 3PT	The Cricketers Leamington
CW	CW5 8LE	St Mary's ch Acton Nantwich
DA	DA1 1RZ	East Hill Cemetery Dartford
	DA1 4RW	St Paulinus ch Crayford
	DA12 3BZ	St Mary Magdalene ch Cobham
	DA12 3EB	St Peter and St Paul's ch Shorne
DD	DD2 2UJ	Balgay Cemetery Dundee
DE	DE65 6FH	St Wystan's ch Repton
DH	DH3 3QR	Emirates Riverside Stadium
DN	DN7 6LX	Hatfield Woodhouse cemetery
DT	DT1 1LB	St George's ch Fordington
DY	DY1 2DA	New Cemetery Dudley
	DY9 9LQ	St John Baptist Hagley Hall Park
E	E2 0QD	Meath Gardens East London
	E3 3AH	St Mary's ch Bow
	E7 9DG	West Ham Cemetery
	E12 5DQ	City of London Cemetery
EH	EH45 8NU	Stobo Kirk nr Peebles
EN	EN2 0TN	Lavender Hill Cemetery Enfield
EX	EX1 2PX	Higher Cemetery Exeter
	EX8 2RG	St Margaret's ch Littleham
FY	FY3 7BD	Layton Cemetery Blackpool (2)
	FY3 9HD	Rose Lea Woodland Grove
GL	GL4 4PA	Coney Hill Crematorium
	GL8 8DS	St Saviour's ch Tetbury
	GL50 1JP	Cambray Place Cheltenham
	GL52 5JT	Cheltenham Cemetery
	GL54 1JE	St Mary's ch Icomb
GU	GU6 7AE	Cranleigh Cemetery
	GU6 7PX	St Peter & Paul ch, Ewhurst
	GU7 2PG	Nightingale Cemetery Godalming
	GU9 7PW	St Andrew's ch Farnham
	GU21 4AA	Bedser Bridge, Woking
	GU21 4HQ	Horsell Common Woking
	GU21 5SH	All Saints ch Woodham
	GU24 0BL	Brookwood Cemetery (6)
	GU28 0LB	The Cricketers Inn Duncton (2)
	GU32 1LF	St John's ch West Meon
	GU32 3HS	St Peter's ch Petersfield
HA	HA4 7SJ	Breakspear Crematorium
	HA7 4AQ	St John's ch Stanmore
HD	HD2 2QA	Hirst Haigh & Rhodes Memorial
	HD4 7PD	St Paul's ch Armitage Bridge
	HD5 0BH	St John's ch Kirkheaton
	HD5 0EP	Lane Side Cemetery Kirkheaton
HG	HG2 9BP	Harrogate Cricket Club Ground
	HG3 1PZ	Harlow Hill Cemetery
HP	HP8 4JH	St Giles' ch Chalfont St Giles
	HP10 8NY	Holy Trinity ch Penn
HU	HU15 1PS	Welton Cemetery
IV	IV36 1DW	Cluny Hill Cemetery Forres
IP	IP21 4EP	St Andrew's ch, Thelveton
KT	KT12 2QS	St Mary's ch Walton
	KT22 0AG	Leatherhead Crematorium
L	L1 7AZ	Anglican Cathedral Liverpool
	L15 2HD	Toxteth Park Municipal Cemetery
LA	LA23 3HB	Bowness on Windermere Cemetery
LE	LE2 6BB	Welford Road Cemetery (5)
	LE2 8AD	Grace Road County Ground (2)
	LE8 5QP	Foston Road Cemetery
	LE12 5QW	Stanford Hall
	LE15 9TJ	St Peter & St Paul's Uppingham
	LE17 4AN	St Mary's ch Lutterworth
	LE17 4HX	St Mary's ch Cotesbach
LN	LN10 6YE	Woodhall Spa Cemetery
LS	LS2 8JT	Hedley Verity pub Leeds
	LS6 1ES	4 Welton Grove Headingley
	LS6 3BU	Headingley Carnegie Ground (2)
	LS7 3QF	St Matthew's ch Chapel Allerton
	LS16 6AH	Lawnswood Cemetery Leeds (2)
	LS28 7BD	St Lawrence ch Pudsey
	LS28 7SQ	Tofts Road Ground Pudsey
	LS29 6GF	Bill Bowes Court Menston
LU	LU6 1QD	West Street Cemetery Dunstable
M	M13 9GB	Dover Street Manchester
	M16 0PX	Emirates Old Trafford Ground
	M24 5QU	Basil D'Oliveira Court Middleton
	M28 2WH	St Mark's ch Worsley (2)
	M32 8HX	Stretford Cemetery
	M33 7QX	Brooklands cemetery Manchester
ME	ME9 0RX	St Mary & Holy Cross ch Milstead
	ME13 0PJ	St Michael & All Angels ch Throwley
	ME14 3LH	St Mary the Virgin ch Thurnham
	M14 4EJ	Bearsted village sign
	ME17 3AW	St Mary's ch Sutton Valence
N	N2 0RZ	East Finchley Cemetery (2)
	N3 2LE	Wilf Slack Sports Ground
	N6 6PJ	Highgate Cemetery (2)
	N14 7DJ	Arnos Grove House
	N14 7EG	Christ Ch Southgate
NE	NE16 6QL	Milburn Green Burnopfield
	NE34 0JS	Stoddart Street South Shields
NG	NG1 4HT	Church Cemetery (The Rock) (3)
	NG1 6HL	The Bell Inn Angel Row
	NG2 6AG	Trent Bridge Ground (3)
	NG4 4BG	All Hallows ch Gedling (2)
	NG5 8LS	Red Hill Cemetery (2)
	NG7 3ND	Nottingham General Cemetery (3)
	NG10 4LF	West Park Cemetery Long Eaton
	NG11 6HB	Ruddington cemetery
	NG12 2FB	Radcliffe-on-Trent Cemetery (2)
	NG17 2EB	St Mary ch Sutton-in-Ashfield (3)
	NG17 7BQ	Larwood Statue Kirkby in Ashfield
	NG17 7FJ	New Cemetery Kirkby-in-Ashfield
	NG17 9EE	Chapel Street Nuncargate
	NG18 5BJ	Mansfield Cemetery
	NG19 7BB	Mansfield Woodhouse Cemetery
	NG24 1SQ	Newark Cemetery
NN	NN4 9RN	Counties Crematorium
	NN7 1NG	The Elms Cogenhoe
NR	NR10 3AQ	Manor Park Horsford
	NR12 7AU	Horstead House Norfolk
	NR20 5EA	Horningtoft village sign
NW	NW1 6QJ	Lord's 1st ground (Dorset Square)
	NW2 2TP	Moreland Court London

	NW6 1DR	West Hampstead Cemetery (2)
	NW7 3PD	Sunnydale Gardens Mill Hill
	NW8 7RH	Lord's 2nd ground (Park Road)
	NW8 8QN	Lord's Cricket Ground (7)
	NW10 9TE	Willesden Cemetery
	NW11 7NL	Golders Green Crematorium (3)
OL	OL15 8NJ	Dearnley Cemetery
OX	OX9 5TH	St Margaret's ch Lewknor
	OX17 2NR	All Saints ch Middleton Cheyney
PE	PE36 5JX	St Andrew's ch Ringstead
PL	PL28 8ND	St Merryn ch nr Padstow
PO	PO8 0UB	Broadhalfpenny Down (2)
	PO8 0UB	Hambledon Bat & Ball Inn
	PO18 0NT	St Peter's ch Westhampnett
	PO19 1PX	Chichester Cathedral
	PO40 9PE	All Saints ch Freshwater
PR	PR25 3EL	St Andrew's ch Leyland (2)
RG	RG1 5LW	Reading School
	RG8 8QB	Holy Trinity ch Buckhold
	RG20 0BL	St Laurence's ch West Woodhay
	RG20 8HR	St Gregory's ch Welford
	RG21 5TD	Old Cemetery Cottage Basingstoke
	RG27 8DB	St Mary's ch Winchfield
	RG40 1UE	All Saints ch Wokingham
	RG42 6EG	St Michael's ch Warfield
RH	RH2 7RN	St Mary's ch New Reigate
	RH6 9FB	Surridge Court, Horley
	RH8 0SD	St James's ch Titsey
	RH12 3QW	St Margaret's ch Warnham (3)
	RH15 0LG	St Andrew's ch Burgess Hill
	RH17 5JZ	Holy Trinity ch Cuckfield
	RH20 1EG	St Mary the Virgin ch Stopham
RM	RM2 6NP	Gidea Park Sports Ground
S	S2 1GD	City Road Cemetery Sheffield
	S3 9DN	Burngreave Cemetery Pitsmoor
	S32 5QH	St Lawrence ch Eyam
	S40 2NX	Boythorpe Cemetery
	S61 4JH	Greasbrough Cemetery
	S71 4EU	The Grove Royston
	S73 8DY	Roy Kilner Road Wombwell
	S73 8HY	Wombwell Cemetery
	S81 0RS	The Innings Worksop
SA	SA8 3BP	Alltwen chapel
SE	SE7 8DZ	Charlton Cemetery
	SE9 4RT	Fairmount Mottingham
	SE11 5SS	Kia Oval Kennington (5)
	SE13 7HY	Ladywell Cemetery
	SE15 3LP	Nunhead Cemetery (3)
	SE16 2EH	Southwark Park Café Gallery
	SE20 7YA	Grace's Bar & Grill Penge
	SE24 0LU	Railton Road Brixton
	SE26 6DZ	Lawrie Park Road
	SE27 9JU	West Norwood Cemetery (6)
SN	SN8 2QH	Holy Cross ch Ramsbury
	SN10 4RT	Urchfont Cemetery
SO	SO16 6LP	Hollybrook Cemetery
	SO21 1HE	Magdalen Hill Cemetery
	SO23 9LS	Winchester Cathedral

	SO23 9PN	Altham Gate New Field Winchester
	SO24 0NA	St Andrew's ch Tichborne
	SO24 9BU	The Old Sun Alresford
	SO30 3HK	Ageas Bowl Southampton (2)
SR	SR4 7SU	Bishopwearmouth Cemetery
ST	ST7 8QE	Audley Methodist Cemetery
SW	SW1V 1QP	Warwick Way Victoria
	SW5 9JE	West Brompton Cemetery (north)
	SW10 9UG	West Brompton Cemetery (south)
	SW12 9PA	Englewood Road
	SW15 3DZ	Putney Vale Cemetery
	SW18 2HD	East Hill Wandsworth
TA	TA1 1DP	St James's Cemetery Taunton
	TA1 1JT	Taunton County Ground
	TA1 1XX	Somerset Cricket Museum
	TA1 5AS	St Mary's Cemetery Taunton
	TA9 4HZ	St Mary's ch East Brent
TD	TD6 0RQ	Dryburgh Abbey
TN	TN4 0NS	London Road Southborough
	TN4 0UJ	'Maridon' Southborough
	TN5 6AA	St Peter & St Paul's ch Wadhurst
	TN9 1HD	St Peter & St Paul's ch Tonbridge
	TN9 1JX	Tonbridge School
	TN9 2BT	Goldsmid Road Tonbridge
	TN10 4JW	Godfrey Evans Close Tonbridge
	TN10 4LE	Frank Woolley Road Tonbridge
	TN12 9HS	St Michael & All Angels ch Marden
	TN15 0QB	Plaxtol parish ch
	TN17 4DL	St George's ch Benenden
	TN22 3SS	St Andrew & St Mary's ch Fletching
	TN30 7EA	St John's ch Wittersham
	TN34 1PR	Wellington Square Hastings
	TN34 2AE	Hastings Borough Cemetery (2)
	TN39 5HT	Bexhill Cemetery
TS	TS25 5DD	Stranton Cemetery Lodge
TW	TW9 4LL	North Sheen Cemetery
	TW10 6HP	Richmond Cemetery
UB	UB6 9DU	Greenford Park Cemetery
W	W3 8LE	Gunnersbury Cemetery
	W8 6JN	Lexham Gardens Kensington
	W9 3HL	Croxley Road West Kilburn
	W10 4RA	Kensal Green Cemetery
WA	WA3 6AN	George Duckworth Island
WD	WD7 9DW	Shenley Cricket Centre
	WD23 1BD	St James's ch Bushey
WF	WF1 5LF	Wakefield Cemetery
	WF2 8DN	St James with Christ Ch Thornes
WR	WR2 4QQ	New Road Ground Worcester (4)
	WR3 7RN	St John's ch Claines
	WR3 8HA	Astwood Cemetery
	WR9 0ET	Ombersley Cricket Club
	WR14 2AS	Great Malvern Cemetery
YO	YO7 1JG	St Oswald's ch Sowerby
	YO7 1PQ	Kirkgate Thirsk
	YO12 7JH	Dean Road Cemetery Scarborough (2)
	YO22 4PF	St Stephen's ch Fylingdales Thorpe
	YO26 8DL	St John's ch Kirk Hammerton
ZE	ZE1 0YB	Lerwick New Cemetery

Michael Ronayne next to David Sheppard's 'conversation' memorial in Hope Street, Liverpool.